ROUTLEDGE LIBRARY EDITIONS:
SOUTH AFRICA

Volume 14

RACE AND SUICIDE IN
SOUTH AFRICA

RACE AND SUICIDE IN SOUTH AFRICA

FATIMA MEER

R Routledge
Taylor & Francis Group

LONDON AND NEW YORK

First published in 1976 by Routledge & Kegan Paul Ltd.

This edition first published in 2023
by Routledge
4 Park Square, Milton Park, Abingdon, Oxon OX14 4RN

and by Routledge
605 Third Avenue, New York, NY 10158

Routledge is an imprint of the Taylor & Francis Group, an informa business

British Library Cataloguing in Publication Data
A catalogue record for this book is available from the British Library

ISBN: 978-1-032-30347-5 (Set)
ISBN: 978-1-032-32670-2 (Volume 14) (hbk)
ISBN: 978-1-032-32675-7 (Volume 14) (pbk)
ISBN: 978-1-003-31614-5 (Volume 14) (ebk)

DOI: 10.4324/9781003316145

Publisher's Note
The publisher has gone to great lengths to ensure the quality of this reprint but points out that some imperfections in the original copies may be apparent.

Disclaimer
The publisher has made every effort to trace copyright holders and would welcome correspondence from those they have been unable to trace.

This is a reissue of a previously published book. The language is reflective of the time in which this book was published. In reissuing this book, no offence is intended by the Publishers to any reader.

Race and suicide in South Africa

Fatima Meer

Department of Sociology
University of Natal

Routledge & Kegan Paul

London, Henley and Boston

First published in 1976
by Routledge & Kegan Paul Ltd
39 Store Street,
London WC1E 7DD,
Broadway House,
Newtown Road,
Henley-on-Thames,
Oxon RG9 1EN and
9 Park Street,
Boston, Mass. 02108, USA
Manuscript typed by Jacqueline Bayes
Printed and bound in Great Britain by
Redwood Burn Limited
Trowbridge & Esher
A member of the Staples Printing Group

ISBN 0 7100 8228 2

Contents

part one

Suicide incidence

1 Methodological problems in the study of suicide

The sociological interest in suicide is only partly due
to the fact that it is a social problem.   Its interest
is equally due to the idea that it inhibits more general
dimensions of social and personal behaviour.   Thus
Durkheim (1) feels the 'pulse' of his 'collective conscience' through his suicide-genic currents, Jack
Douglas (2) searches for the 'meaning' of social
behaviour through suicidal behaviour and Karl
Menninger (3) probes the human psyche through suicidal
syndromes.   The very extreme nature of the suicidal
response, so extreme as to result in the rejection of
all life responses, stimulates expectations of new
insight outside the perception of those committed to
life.   The problem is how to get at that perception.
The fact that the suicide is inaccessible to the
researcher presents unique methodological problems.
Researchers have been obliged to reach that 'perception'
indirectly through the traces left in official records
and the notebooks of psychiatrists.   The fundamental
problem confronting them has been that of ascertaining
that these are reports about suicide.   To answer
this, they have to (i) identify suicide and (ii)
evaluate the extent to which official and psychiatric
records in fact refer to suicide.

IDENTIFYING SUICIDE

Durkheim points out that although the word suicide
occurs constantly in conversation, its meaning is far
from standard since it is not derived analytically but
is simply a translation of the confused impressions of
the crowd resulting in the combination of very
different sorts of facts under the same heading. (4)

Jack Douglas goes further and states that though the
word suicide and its equivalent non-English terms are
shared in Western culture, its definition is so vague
and so inadequate that its real meaning is known
neither to the suicide himself, nor to those with whom
he becomes involved, nor to the specialist who concerns
himself with the suicide problem. (5)

Practically all students of suicide begin by identifying their subject, but practically all, in the
absence of direct access to the suicide, end by accepting as suicide those defined as such in court records
or psychiatric reports. The question is thus raised -
to what extent have they in fact studied suicide?

Two factors are vital in the definition of suicide:
(a) the intention to die; (b) death at one's own hand.

(a) The intention to die

It is so difficult to elicit intention or motive *after*
death that prominent sociologists have in effect ruled
out this important criterion in determining suicide.
Thus Durkheim, while conceding the importance of intention, asks: (6)

Shall only he be thought truly to slay himself who
has wished to do so, and suicide be intentional
self-homicide? In the first place, this would
define suicide by a characteristic which, whatever
its interest and significance, would at least
suffer from not being easily recognized since it
is not easily observed. How to discover the
agent's motive and whether he desired death itself
when he formed the resolve, or had some other
purpose? Intent is too intimate a thing to be
more than approximately interpreted by another.
It even escapes self-observation. How often we
mistake the true reasons for our acts!

Douglas likewise, while holding intention to be the
kernel of suicide asks: 'How could one construct a
"real rate" of "intention" so necessary in almost all
formal and common-sense definitions of suicide and
problematic in itself?' (7)

Despite advances in psychoanalysis, phenomena of
the mind and motives are at best recognized as only
partially knowable. Such knowledge is even more
restricted when the study is that of the dead man.
Thus Menninger states: 'The analysis of motive is
made difficult not only because of the untrustworthiness
of conscious and obvious motives but specially by

reason of the fact that a successful suicide is beyond
study.' (8)

Court records do not take intention into consideration when determining suicide. They accept as suicide
practically any form of death which is established as
having occurred at the hand of the dead person himself.
Thus Durkheim accepts as suicides the 26,000 subjects
produced by the Bureau of Legal Statistics, even though
he cannot be sure in terms of his own definition that
these were all suicides.

Intention can be probed directly in attempted
suicides; in cases of completed suicides, it can be
abstracted from psychiatric histories or searched out
through interviews with survivors. This implies
studying individual cases, rather than depending on
official records. There is no question that case
studies lead to a gain in depth analysis which court
records rarely even suggest, but the weakness of
psychiatric records lies in their high level of selec-
tivity, and hence their non-representative nature.
Not only are they selected on the basis of psychological disturbance - Durkheim's neurasthenic and psychopathic types, but also on the basis of economic class
and cultural affiliations. In Durban a small proportion of the total number of suicides had sought psychiatric assistance, and these were in the main White
suicides drawn from the relatively more affluent
strata. Members of lower economic strata rarely seek
psychiatric assistance. The consciousness, first,
that something is wrong, and second, that something is
wrong to the extent of requiring specialized treatment
differs substantially from stratum to stratum.
Affluent cultures are more self-centred, far more
sensitive to distress signals, often over-reacting to
these. Those of the lower strata, not having the
material resources for self-pampering, often remain
insensitive to grave distress signals, the relative
insensitivity being in fact nurtured in the family and
by the culture. Thus even those offering 'frontier'
medical services in so-called underdeveloped countries,
often have to search out the patients and point out to
them that they are physically ill.

The researcher who tries to probe intention by
interviewing the associates of the deceased will very
probably find that his returns are in favour of the
lower classes. Members of the lower strata are less
aware of privacy and less sensitive to its infringements. They are also unaware of the idea that they
have a right to keep their secrets and that they could

exercise this right without serious consequences to themselves.   This is particularly so with Black people in South Africa; they are thus from the researcher's point of view more 'exploitable'.   Not only does the troubled person in the higher echelons turn to the private cult of the psychiatrist but even his willingness to admit to an outsider that he is undergoing such treatment would depend on the attitude to such treatment in his society, (9) and since the attitude is usually that of shame, he chooses to insulate himself from inquisitive researchers who trespass on his privacy and threaten his 'humanity' by converting him into a guinea-pig, and succeeds in doing so.

Yet intention is so fundamental a component of suicide that a number of well-known studies have used just this factor in identifying suicide and have studied not those who have killed themselves, since their intention would not be directly accessible, but those who have intended to do so. (10)   Stengel thus defines suicide as the fatal and non-fatal act of self-injury undertaken with conscious self-destructive intent.   Death, he states, is not the only aim of suicide. (11)   He proposes that one who kills himself and one who attempts to do so suffer from the same malady, and by implication the best means of understanding suicide is by studying attempted suicides. (12)

Attempted suicides, however, are not suicides. They may be potential suicides but until the 'intention' to die is converted into death, intention itself remains questionable.   They provide valuable material in advance of becoming cases when the attempt finally succeeds; but when the attempt is foiled and the 'patient' continues to live, it suggests that he, like the living, has in fact chosen life in preference to death.   The sheer fact of failure suggests absence of intention.   Stengel, in his comparison of the 'social dynamics' of attempted and completed suicides expresses the opinion that most attempted suicides are indifferent to life, neither rejecting nor accepting it, but expressing the attitude that they do not care whether they live or die.   He states however that attempted suicides occur in public places and in the presence of others to a far greater extent than completed suicides. (13)   This suggests that such acts may well be neither real nor incipient suicides, but techniques to shock and coerce significant others into submitting to the suicide's will.   Thus in one case, a mother bitterly opposed to her daughter's planned marriage outside their endogamy, takes an overdose of sleeping pills and forces the daughter to choose between the marriage and the mother. The mother has no *intention* of dying but conversely is motivated by a strong desire to live, on her own terms, beyond her own life span into that of her daughter's.

On the other hand, one who seriously attempts to die, has the intention of dying and does not succeed, may subsequently be so overcome by remorse that he may well deny all intentions and gladly conspire against himself to interpret his attempt as accidental.

Of course all persons who have died by their own hands are not suicides either, and hidden among them are many cases of accidents. While it is very difficult to establish intention *post facto*, it is possible from court records to structure a picture of a brewing suicide, or a movement towards suicide. Thus the man who has for years followed a pattern of erratic employment, of neglecting his family, of beating his wife and drinking his earnings, has clearly rejected society and is on the brink of rejecting life. This is a typical suicidal syndrome that emerges from the records.

The search for intention, given the available resources, is so difficult that, had sociologists insisted on establishing it as an essential prerequisite for suicide, they might well have been discouraged from studying the phenomenon altogether and Durkheim's masterpiece might never have been written. Whatever the research problems in locating intention, its importance cannot by that consideration alone be spelled out of a definition of suicide. The problem of observing the behaviour of the suicide directly remains insurmountable, particularly in the case of the 'normal' type, which is by far the more usual type and which generally remains unidentified and takes society by surprise and shock. A posthumous investigation has valuable sociological possibilities with restricted psychological ones. The problem however remains - how to confirm intention? The search for 'motive' is ultimately a search into the psyche, and Menninger states that while (16)

> there are too many instances where the motives cannot be interpreted, and most pertinent of all are not to the slightest degree recognized by the person himself. Psycho-analysis enables us in a particular case to overcome these obstacles because it gives us access to the unconscious motives .

Yet psychoanalysis in itself would not explain suicide; it would throw significant light on the responses of the individual person, to his social

situation, but since his responses are stimulated by
the social situation, the understanding of that situation is imperative. The personality sees its final
disintegration in the social setting, and an assessment of the kind of situations which are interpreted
as constituting a crisis is of vital importance to
sociologists. If we adopt the sociological view that
the individual psyche or personality, that syndrome of
influences which makes a person behave as he does, is
derived from society - his family, his friends, his
church, the clubs to which he may belong, that personality is a product of the impacts of these social
agents on the personal potential for acquiring a personality, then we must look for the meaning, the cause,
and the purpose of suicide in the interactive relations
that existed between the deceased and his 'society'.

(b) Death at one's own hand

Intention does not in itself constitute suicide.
Intention must be fulfilled in self-executed death.
The suicide flings himself before a moving train, pours
paraffin over his body and burns himself, or resorts to
some other mode of self-destruction. The thought of
dying does not appear in a flash, the death action is
not suddenly provoked. The desire to die builds up
over a long period of time, and may have been expressed
in a death-wish such as is contained in the following
statements by suicides - 'I don't want to live any
more'; 'My time has come'; 'Why don't I die?'; 'I
have had enough'; 'I can't take any more'; 'I can't
go on any more'. The desire may have even taken the
form of an unsuccessful attempt. The suicide occurs,
however, when the idea or intention of dying has been
successfully executed. The moment of execution may
follow a great whipping-up of passion, and occur at
the height of a conflict, or it may be a cool, calculated act, executed in lonely calm. A history of self-
destruction or family destruction through alcoholism
or deliberate non-work, even in the absence of active
death statements or attempts, distinguishes the second
kind of execution from an involuntary execution of
blind rage in which anger, not will, is the executioner.

(c) Locating the suicide

The problem of locating the true suicide, one who has
both intended and successfully executed his death is a
problem of effective discrimination at the data-
recording level, both in public institutions, inquest
courts, hospitals and in private psychiatric practices.
Sociologists, dependent as they are on records accumulated by others, are obliged to take as suicides those
defined as such in official sources. Their only
checks at present lie in the use of reliable tests
that may minimize the chances of including non-
suicides, or overlooking suicides classified as homo-
cides and accidents. It is simultaneously a problem
of changed social attitudes to suicide, from one that
dismisses it as an irrational and aberrant act, and
hence of little social concern, to one that sees it
as an act that occurs in the course of normal and routine
relations. It is thus a problem of normal society
as Durkheim in fact saw it. Yet though it is almost
a century since he emphasized it as such, it continues
to be treated as a personal rather than as a social
problem, largely, one assumes, because ultimately its
aggression is self-directed, and society is not
materially hurt by it. If, like the alcoholic and
the habitual criminal, the aggression of the suicide
violated others, official records might begin to be
kept meaningfully.
    This aggression is reflected in the more general
social attitude to suicide, which on the one hand
defines the situation in which it could or should
occur, and on the other, exonerates survivors from all
responsibility for the act by holding that no matter
how provocative the situation, it would never be so
provocative as to drive a person to suicide. Thus
the prescription for suicide is implicit in Western
culture in statements like: 'I died of shame',
implying one *should* die when in shame, and explicit
in the Indian rebuke: 'You should drown yourself.'
At the same time, the suicide is typed as unreasonable,
or mad, as in the following reactions: 'My husband
would not even allow me to go outside my house - so
strict he was. How much trouble *I* had, but I did not
do such a thing' (an Indian mother assessing the
behaviour of her daughter who had burnt herself).
'It was a bad thing to do. What reason was there to
do it?', is the Zulu reproach. 'Her husband gave
her a lot of trouble and was quite impossible. OK
leave him. You have your children. But to take

your life.   My God, that is silly', is the comment of
a young White woman on her friend's suicide.   'True
his wife was a nag but what of that?   Nagging comes
to an end after all.   But to kill oneself!   Why, he
could have gone for a holiday, or moved away from her',
is the comment of a Coloured woman.

An Indian daughter-in-law, commenting on her father-in
law's suicide says:

You can't justify it.   Sure the old lady [her
mother-in-law] was a nag, but what of it - all
women nag.   It was his fault.   He was all burnt
up inside himself.   He never opened his heart,
never cleaned his soul.   What's going to happen to
you if you store up all the dirt?   You are asking
for trouble.   All right she got on his nerves,
well he should have just left her - come and stayed
with us.   He had so many relatives.   We were
there and we all loved him.

Finally, not only is society exonerated, but suicide
is in fact used to elevate it.   The monopoly of the
Supreme Authority over all life is invoked, suicide is
seen as defiance of God's power and God's right to
create and destroy;   the suicide is condemned as
sinner, and by contrast those who survive him are the
virtuous and the good, those who submit to the will
and the law of God.   The Christian, the Muslim and
the Jew see it as defiance of God's power and God's
right to create and destroy.   They move away from the
suicide in shame.   It is a shame shared by the
suicide, who often begs forgiveness for his act:
'Please don't think too badly of me';   'I tried but I
couldn't go on.   Forgive me';   'Try and make the
children understand';   'Bury me in the cheapest box
money can buy.'

THE RELEVANCE OF OFFICIAL STATISTICS AND CASE STUDIES
IN THE STUDY OF SUICIDE

Official statistics and case histories are the two
available sources to which researchers turn in their
study of suicide.   They are by no means mutually
exclusive.   In fact they are complementary.   Court
records contribute to the representative nature of a
suicide study, case studies provide the necessary in-
depth meaning and contribute to the vitally important
psychological dimension.   Researchers however have
tended to use the one or other source exclusively and
have supported their choice with strong methodological
backings.

Thus Durkheim uses official statistics or court records and rejects the use of individual case histories on the ground that these are indirect manifestations of the social cause and not the cause itself, which must be studied directly in the social environment. (17)   Accordingly he studies suicide in its collective or statistical form and his object of study is the social rate.   This is in keeping with his general view that social behaviour is the manifestation of the 'collective conscience', of a force *sui generis,* and it is at the collective level that it projects the uniformities conducive to scientific analysis, its individual manifestations in particular persons and particular events being variable, shifting in relation to each other, and therefore incapable of objective perception. (18)

Douglas by contrast sees social reality in individual social events and rejects the use of official statistics not only because he considers these inconsistent and unreliable, but more importantly because they are confused with the 'reality' from which they are derived; they replace that reality.   To study statistics, he holds, is to study abstractions, and then to attempt to explain the 'real', 'concrete' situation on the basis of such abstractions.

He rejects the idea that suicide can be understood through its presumed statistics and emphasizes that the understanding of meaning is essential.   He proposes the construction of meaning patterns or dimensions of meaning, from an intimate 'inside' investigation of the situation in which suicide occurs. While his dismissal of the value of court records is questionable, his emphasis on the indispensability of concrete experiences of actual suicides to understand the phenomenon 'fully' is unquestionable.

(a)   The problem of the particular and the general

Fundamental to the methodological issues they raise, is the relation between the particular and the general in social phenomena.   Durkheim asserts that progress must be from the whole to the part, (19) since the whole alone is representative of the objective reality; Douglas that the valid procedure is to move upward, from the single entity, since 'meaningful' interpretation can only be made in the concrete individual situation. (20)

The interactive importance of the 'particular' and

'general' is indispensable in scientific research.
The effective aim of the study of any phenomenon is
to arrive at a finding which represents a 'reality'
in both these dimensions.   The efficacy of the
physical sciences is due precisely to this achievement.
Physical science proceeds from the convenient starting
point, the 'part' not because it is more 'meaningful'
or more 'representative' than the whole, but simply
because it alone is accessible for empirical analysis.
The only 'reality' is the single physical event, and
the validity of the 'general' is seen established when
it projects, or realizes that event.   If the general
or theoretical fails to explain or 'construct' the
concrete physical event, a spaceship for instance, then
it is redefined.   General principles thus have no
existence apart from the particular events they define.
Laws are not 'realities' in themselves, but constructs
that interpret 'realities'.
     In Durkheim's analysis, the 'general' assumes a
function that goes beyond that of a system of theoretical principles.   It is not simply a means to 'interpret' or 'construct' the particular, but is converted
into reality in itself, into the force *sui generis*,
and the particular is reduced to its individual manifestation characterized by instability and therefore
not conducive to scientific study.   According to
him, then, to study a particular suicide case is to
study the distinctive stamp that that case gives to
the social cause of suicide. (21)
     Durkheim thus not only separates the general from
the particular, but also dismisses the particular from
scientific analysis on the grounds of its subjectivity.
     A phenomenon is 'objective' or object from the
'subjective' or subject's point of view.   The
observer's, or subject's response to that 'object' or
phenomenon may reflect a range of subjectivity or may
be guided towards objectivity.   Once a social
phenomenon is admitted as object, one cannot then
restrict its 'objectivity' to its general dimension
and exclude it from its particular dimension.   In
fact it is methodologically impossible to arrive at
any 'generality' without a close understanding of the
particular representations, and if the 'particular'
is deemed 'subjective' then there can be *no* objective
dimension, and the view must be taken that that
'phenomenon' has no existence for the observing
subject.
     Durkheim could not have intended this, and that he
did not is indicated by the fact that towards the end

of his discussion of this problem he realizes that however changeable and unstable concrete data may be, they
cannot on that account be assumed unintelligible. He
thus contends its omission to be temporary and explains
the study of the general to be prompted by the fact
that it offers the easiest access to scientific investigation. (22)

Social facts, both in their particular and general
dimensions, are emotional facts and in that context subjective. This subjectivity is not to be confused with
subjectivity that implies faulty or prejudiced observation. Durkheim uses subjectivity in this second sense
and claims that natural science discards those data of
sensation that are too subjective and substitutes for
them 'objective' devices. (23)   There is no emotion
in physical phenomena and the natural scientist is not
involved with emotion. His error is due not to the
fact that his observation is coloured by emotional
prejudice as would occur in the observation of social
phenomena, but to his subjection to inferior and
ineffective techniques. In the absence of a thermo-
meter, a hand may be used to measure temperature. The
large margin of error is not due to the introduction of
emotion, but due to inferior technique. Sensation is
thus subjective not in the sense that it is emotionally
prejudiced but in the sense that it is dependent on a
crude measuring device.

Since social phenomena are emotional phenomena, to
leave emotion out of them is to distort them. Thus
the view that emotional, cultural phenomena can and
should be studied unemotionally is quite invalid. In
fact the greater the 'subjectivity' cum 'emotionality',
the greater the empathy. To arrive at proximate
generalizations of the 'real' social situations, one
would have in the first place to put oneself into the
concrete representations of those situations, and then
emerge out of them, and, 'rising above' them, define
the broad patterns. The fundamental problem is as
Dilthey saw it, and in the context of Mead: (24) how
can the observer be both subject and object simultaneously in order first to 'understand' and then to
interpret social phenomena?

The concrete social event is not as easily accessible to the social scientist, because he himself
constitutes that event. His fundamental difficulty
lies in the fact that he has to become at once both
the researcher and the material of his research, both
the subject and the object. He himself is the part
of the whole he sets out to study. This being so, he

cannot but start from himself, from the concrete
event. Durkheim confused this with subjectivity,
with bias error and hence in conflict with scientific
analysis. (25) Yet Durkheim's study of suicide is in
fact based on concrete individual events, on individual
cases of suicides from which the statistics are
computed.

The dilemma of the social sciences continues to be
one of developing a valid and interactive relation
between the particular and the general, as presently
obtains in the natural sciences. Physical science
moves logically from the concrete to the general, and
then returns to the concrete. The social scientist
often moves to the general on so inadequate a support
from the 'concrete events' or on so vague, semi-
conscious, uncontrolled notions of these, that the
general becomes dissociated from the concrete and
ceases to reflect it. He appears too, to become so
exhilarated by the sheer feat of his trip into the
'abstract' that the trip becomes an end in itself, a
fact *sui generis*. This exercise is then often
followed by an attempt to compel the 'concrete
reality' (single events) within the frame of such
sociological 'laws'. Douglas accordingly accuses
Durkheim of having first conceived his theory and then
forced his data into it. (26) Coming in the wake of
philosophical and theological 'truths', sociological
theory has tended to acquire some of the aura of those
'truths', resulting in the misplaced pride in theory
for the sake of theory, knowledge for the sake of knowledge and the invalid dichotomy between 'pure
sociology' and 'applied sociology'.

The problem then is the problem of attaining an
interactive balance between the general and the particular, the problem of returning to the particular, of
humanizing social phenomena which have become distorted
into unrecognizable abstracts, into physical- or
chemical-like laws or philosophical- or theological-
like treatises, difficult to reconcile with the inter-
play of human passions, which is the social reality.
It is a problem of abstracting general principles and
simultaneously retaining the individual point of view.

Douglas moves towards this end in constructing
significant patterns from the suicides of individual
persons. His demonstration of this method is
weakened, however, by the fact that it is dependent on
a small number, ten in all, of highly selected cases -
seven from the works of other social scientists and
three from newspaper reports. He errs too in dis-

counting the value of official statistics, since their
source, the court records, are a valid avenue through
which the 'representative reality' may be attained.
While case studies inhibit the potential for developing worthwhile theories, they may be, deliberately or
unwittingly, drawn from so selective a source as to
represent only that source and to have no general
sociological relevance.

(b) The nature and value of court records

The search for any 'social reality' must be based on
data which are representative of the defined group.
Such data, in the case of suicide, are found at
present in court records alone, and thus court records
constitute the effective starting point in the study
of suicide. Yet court records have been seriously
criticized. Durkheim, though basing his studies on
court records, considered them to be highly suspect,
both in the evaluating of motives and the establishing
of obvious material facts. (27) Douglas commenting
on the subject almost 100 years later finds nothing to
suggest that the technique or premise of investigation
has so changed as to inspire greater confidence in the
accuracy or suitability of the data for sociological
purposes and points out that the inconsistency in the
use of operational definitions and search procedures,
works against objectivity and uniformity. (28)
     Court records are weakest in recording data of
crucial sociological significance, data of motives.
The standardized'manner, both in terms of language and
form, in which 'the apparent motives of suicides are
recorded by investigating officials in Durban suggests
the influence of the recorder. The court official
however is not exceptional in resorting to such
'doctoring' of data. The psychiatrist uses his own
brand of doctoring and forces his subjects into pre-
existing conceptual schemes. Bias is thus present in
both interpretations and it may be argued that it is
easier to deal with the blatant misconceptions of a
minor official than it is to deal with the obtuse
authoritative pronouncements of specialists. Thus
one readily and easily discounts the prejudices of the
Durban official who states: 'It is an Indian custom
for their women to commit suicide by pouring paraffin
on their clothes and setting themselves on fire when
they are in love and their lover no longer loves them.
The mere data will refute such a statement and expose

it for what it is, an opinion; but an explanation in
terms of a psychological 'doctrine' would be difficult
to check.

While court records are usually brief they contain
on average as much information as sociologists concern
themselves with when using psychiatric records.   The
average length of the cases used by Douglas in constructing his meaning patterns was about 600 words - the
largest being over 2,000 words, and the smallest 40
words.   When a suicide case is formally investigated
in an inquest court, the record of proceedings may run
into thousands of words and, when defence council is
engaged and there is cross-examination of witnesses,
at times into numerous typed pages.   In such cases,
there is considerable information about the character
of the suicide and the nature of his relations with the
'significant others'.   Generally the quality of information is better in the case of Whites and of persons
in higher social strata than of Blacks and persons in
lower strata, not only because the officials tend to
take more care with regard to the former, but also
because they leave more information about themselves.
Despite this bias, court records are more representative of suicides in the general community than any
other records that a researcher may use.   They are
inadequate in themselves, in constructing the *meaning*
of suicide, but they constitute the only representative
group of suicides accessible to the sociologists whose
interest lies in discovering the general features of
suicide in a particular society, rather than a suicide
syndrome in a particular person.   They provide the
invaluable clues to the concrete situation.   But
effective study of suicide cannot be limited to court
records.   The procedure is to move from one order of
the particular - the case histories derived from
official records, to one level of the general - to the
models constructed from the emergent statistical
patterns; and from such 'generalizations' or general
models, to the 'particular' instances which illustrate
those models, that is, to the concrete, real-life
situations in which suicides occur, and from the study
of these to the development of a general theory.   The
first level generalizations are the necessary cluse to
the real life attitude, but they are inadequate in
themselves to provide a valid theory of suicide.   The
support of the personal information is imperative,
also because it animates and humanizes the recurrent
model or statistical abstract.

Accordingly, this study begins with the 'concrete'

cases of suicide recorded in the Durban Inquest Court.
Characteristics general to these cases are abstracted
and classified to construct theoretical models of
suicides by race and sex.   The validity of these
models is then tested by following a few of the Inquest
Court cases to the real-life situation.

2 Sociological and psychological causes of suicide

The controversy relating to the primacy of statistics
and case studies coincides with the controversy over
the fundamental importance of sociological v. psychological factors represented by Durkheim and Menninger
respectively. Durkheim interprets suicide as an
expression of social disintegration, Menninger as an
expression of individual personality disintegration.

Both base their theories on concepts of an authoritarian moral conscience. But whereas Durkheim
locates this conscience externally in society and conceives it as 'collective conscience', born of social
interactions but distinct from and transcending the
individual interacting consciences, Menninger, following Freud, locates it within the individual and views
it as an internal authority derived primarily from the
experience of parental authority.

Durkheim describes a state of conflict between the
'collective' and the 'individual' consciences. (1)
Menninger describes a state of conflict within the
individual between the Ego and the libidinal instincts
of the Id. (2)   For both writers, a state of adjustment implies a compromise in the respective antagonistic states. Durkheim's collective conscience,
under optimum conditions coerces and controls the
individual, thereby adjusting and integrating him
into society. Freud's Ego similarly controls the
demands of the antisocial Id, and thereby integrates
the personality. Failure of the individual to adjust
himself to society is interpreted by Durkheim as due
to the action of the disintegrative forces in the
'collective conscience'. Menninger interprets this
failure as due to the disintegrative forces of the
individual personality.

Durkheim's 'collective conscience' is composed of

three main elements - altruism, egoism, and anomie (3)
and their subsidiary conflicting currents which impinge
on the individual from without and cause him to react
to them in the same way as he would to physical and
chemical forces. He says of these currents: 'so true
are they things *sui generis* and not mere verbal entities
that they may be measured, their relative sizes compared,
as is done with the intensity of electric currents or
luminous foci.' (4)   The 'suicido-genic current' is
released when the factor of melancholia predominates
over that of joy. The current sweeps through society
and takes its toll of victims. A strong anti-suicidal
tendency in an individual helps him only to the extent
that the current is directed towards a less resilient
victim.   But since the current is social, the omission
of an individual from its sweep in no way affects the
group suicide rate which is dependent on the strength
of the current. (5)

Durkheim's analysis of the phenomenon leads to an
aetiological classification of three types of suicide:
altruistic, egoistic and anomic. He defines a
dominantly altruistic society as an over-integrated
society, in which the importance of the group is
exaggerated and the will of the individual minimized.
The individual's identification with the group in its
religious, political and domestic spheres, is so great
that when pressures become too strong he commits
suicide in an attempt to become sublimely integrated
within it, in a great psychic unity. (6)   According
to him preliterate societies, and highly regimented
institutions like the army, have strong altruistic
tendencies. He also classifies the Japanese *hara-kiri*
and the Indian widow's act of *sati* in this category.

A state of egoism exists when society, in terms of
its structure, is underintegrated.   In such a state,
overemphasis on the role of individual members
associated with comparative relaxations of social
bonds, i.e. social norms, produces social alienation.
Individual members are unable to identify themselves
with their society, and society fails to integrate
and support them in its system. Life becomes meaningless and suicide is the final act of alienation. (7)

In the anomic state it is not the structure of
society that is at fault, but rather its functioning
as a moral authority. The 'collective conscience'
breaks down and fails to exercise the controls that
modify individual desires in conflict with society.
Durkheim conceives these desires in much the same way
as Freud conceives the components of the Id.   He

describes them as insatiable, and unless controlled,
driving the individual person to a state of restless
striving in which successive achievements only intensify the craving.   There is never content and
satisfaction.   The disintegration of the 'collective
conscience' and subsequently its 'dysfunctional'
effect on society, occur in situations of rapid change,
and rapid accumulation of power and wealth, as in
industrialization and urbanization.   Society continues
in the lawless state until a new moral force realigns
its members and dispels the nightmare. (8)
     Where Durkheim locates disintegration in the
'collective conscience', Menninger, basing his interpretation on Freud, locates it in the 'individual
conscience'.   It is the result of a state of imbalance
between the natural antagonistic instincts of man
rooted in the Id, between 'Eros' and 'Thanatos', i.e.
between construction and destruction, which, according
to Menninger, constitute the anabolism and katabolism
of the personality, no less than the cells and the
corpuscles. (9)   The state of disintegration in the
individual conscience follows much the same course as
in the collective conscience.   Under optimum conditions the instincts of life and death grow outward and
become neutralized in external objects where they are
expressed in emotions of love and hate and their
ambivalence kept in balance.   This characterizes the
development of an integrated personality.   The 'reso-
lution', however, is never complete and the threat of
disequilibrium between the two is always present.   In
traumatic situations such as bereavements, when an
external object on which emotion has been invested is
lost, the transmissions of love and hate become detached
from their outer moorings.   In the integrated personality these, after a temporary period of maladjustment,
are re-attached to new objects, but in the malinte-
grated personality they rebound to their points of
origin in the Id where they resume their natural
erotic, ambivalent state and the equilibrium between
them is destroyed.   When 'Thanatos' is predominant,
its components, the wishes 'to kill', 'be killed' and
'die' are released, and the act of suicide is seen as
the result of any one, or any combination, of these. (10)
     When the 'wish to kill' leads to suicide, a dis-
placement of aggression occurs, through the restraining
effects of the Ego, and the self is identified with the
external object that becomes introjected into the personality.   In killing the self, there is the symbolic
killing of the true target of aggression.

In the wish 'to be killed', the individual becomes
the victim of an overgrown conscience and develops
strong feelings of guilt which drive him to suicide.
The wish 'to die' is observed in all incipient
suicides, in suicides of a chronic or partial type,
where it becomes active and a passive resistance
against life results. Many cases of accidents, over-
drinking, deliberately ignoring the doctor's orders,
and behaving in a manner that aggravates rather than
improves a physical malady, are defined as falling
within this category by Menninger.

Menninger rejects social maladjustment as the primary
explanation for suicide and states that tendencies for
self-destruction appear long before the act, and long
before the aggravating social situation. Suicide is
determined by 'inherent variation, abnormality or weakness in the individual, or by acceleration or powerful
reinforcements of the destructive tendencies of the
personality during the formative period of life'. (11)
Extraneous factors, including social factors, may com-
plicate the act, but do not determine it.

Durkheim by contrast states that 'for each social
group there is a specific tendency to suicide explained
neither by the organic psychic constitution of individuals nor the nature of the physical environment.
Consequently, by elimination, it must necessarily
depend upon social causes and be in itself a collective
phenomenon - a force *sui generis*'. (12)

His analysis of available European statistics led
him to the conclusion that the suicide rate in a community remains constant as long as the fundamental
conditions of its existence remain unchanged. This
constancy, he maintains, is not due to some sort of
individual transmission from generation to generation,
but 'to the permanent action of some impersonal cause
which transcends all individual causes'. (13)

Though Durkheim and Menninger consider the sociological and psychological factors independently of each
other, in the production of suicide, no doubt remains
that the two are interactive.

3 The Durban records

The data for suicide in Durban have been obtained from
the records of the Durban Inquest Court.   Suicide
forms a category in the classification of unnatural
deaths.   These include accidental deaths, deaths due
to negligence of a medical officer, or cases of homicide (except those in which murder is suspected) and,
generally, all types of deaths for which a 'natural'
explanation is not immediately forthcoming.   All such
cases of death are investigated by the police and the
results of their investigation are submitted to the
prosecutor who may decide to hold a formal inquiry
into the matter, usually when a civil or criminal
inquiry is suggested, or simply to submit the file to
the magistrate for his verdict.   The magistrate determines the nature of the death, suicide, homicide,
murder, etc., and records this on an official standardized form, under the heading 'Stated or likely cause
of death'.   This form is sent to the Registrar of
Births, Deaths and Marriages, and it is from the
statistics recorded in this State Department that
official birth, death, suicide and homicide rates are
estimated for the country.
   The courts of the magisterial areas in which such
deaths occurred keep the records of evidence of individual cases for as long as the court has room for
their storage.   Thereafter, they are removed to the
provincial archives to make room for newer records.
   Information on all categories of unnatural deaths
in South Africa is available in two forms in the
courts.   The first is the index to the inquest
register which classifies the names of all those thus
deceased and defines the nature of death.   The second
is the inquest register, which contains the actual
inquest proceedings, and records such information as

on-the-spot investigations by the investigating
officer, evidence of witnesses and close relatives,
and reports of the medical officer in charge.   It
also includes crucial exhibits such as photographs
and letters and, when of convenient size, the actual
instrument of death.   The information thus available
is of differing value and detail in each case.
Generally, it is possible to construct a picture of
the suicide's marital status, family relationship,
occupational status, social background, housing conditions, time of death and, to a limited extent, presumed
reasons for the suicide.
     The data for this study were collected in two
periods - in 1960 and in 1971.   In 1960, the Durban
Inquest Court had information in the form of the index
to the Inquest Court register from 1924 to 1939 and
the actual records of Inquest Court proceedings from
1940 to 1960.   The records prior to 1940 had already
been removed to the archives in Pietermaritzburg.   The
index to the register listed the name, sex, locality
and means of death of persons who had died 'unnaturally'
In 1971, Inquest Court records were available from 1962
to 1970, and records prior to these years had already
been sent to the archives.   The suicide rates for
Durban are thus calculated from 1924, but the more
pertinent analysis in respect of status variables and
probable reasons is restricted to the periods 1940-60
and 1962-70.   Suicides occurring in 1971 were studied
for the specific purpose of tracing recurring models
to the social situation in which the acts had taken
place.   In all 2,238 cases of suicides were abstracted
and studied.

OFFICIAL CRITERIA FOR IDENTIFYING SUICIDE

There is no correspondence between the motives of the
sociologist and that of the Inquest Court record.   The
Court is purely interested in determining or removing
evidence of foul play and all information recorded is
incidental to this.   Accordingly the investigation is
concentrated on the condition of the body itself and
around the act of death - the events that proceed,
succeed and occur during death.   The quality of the
information is far more accurate on the physical than
on the sociological factors.   Thus it is far more
precise about the suicide's age, height, weight, the
time of death, condition of the body, viscera, womb,
etc., than on the social and psychological conflicts

that motivated the death.   It records information
about the character of the deceased, the situation in
which he interacted with others to the extent that such
information is incidental to determining whether death
was suicidal, homicidal or accidental.   It is from
such incidental information, then, that the sociologist
must construct a picture of the individual suicide.
The information is clearly inadequate in itself, and
any interpretation of meaning with regard to a particular case based on the Inquest Court record alone is
hazardous.

The investigating technique used by officials in
Durban is sufficiently standardized to make available
fairly accurate and recurring information about selected facets of the suicidal act - the age, sex, occupation, time, date and means.   These in themselves
provide valuable information about the status situations
in which suicide occurs.   Information about the
religion, marital status and family size is less uniformly available.   The suicide's relations with those
who constituted his world - his relatives, friends,
employers, employees, his state of mind, and the state
of his conflict or the nature of his stress as reported
by witnesses is available to an even lesser extent -
yet some information of this nature was abstracted
from 73 per cent of the total number of cases.   While
both police and magistrates are guided by common rules
of investigation, it is reasonable to presume that
they in addition respond subjectively in every single
case, and are influenced by the peculiarities of the
case, and by the responses of the witnesses.   Though
these responses are subjective they contribute to the
understanding of the act, to the extent that they cast
some light on its meaning for the suicide, his close
associates, and the larger anonymous society around
him on whose behalf the police and magistrate act.
They provide the invaluable clues to the concrete real
world situation.   These clues may be analysed in themselves and through them an attempt made to recon-
struct the situation of the suicide, and the mood of
the victim it claimed.   Though the information thus
gleaned is of little value in interpreting individual
cases, the recurrent tendencies may be abstracted to
form suicide types and these in turn provide reliable
meaning patterns for the whole new group.   These
meaning patterns or typologies culled from the
totality of the evidence can then be traced to a rep-
resentation of the 'generalization' in the concrete
situation and studied at closer quarters.

INACCURACIES IN OFFICIAL STATISTICS

It may be reliably presumed that suicide statistics
abstracted from court records are usually much lower
than the actual incidence in any country. (1)
Influenced by the Christian attitude that has defined
a suicide as one who has criminally offended God and
the State, (2) South African magistrates tend to give
suicides the benefit of the doubt and unless there is
fairly conclusive evidence that the suicide had in
fact committed suicide he is presumed, following legal
tradition, to be innocent, not having been proved
guilty.

This attitude of the law, associated with the
strong desire of immediate relatives, influenced by
religious and other reasons, to suppress the fact of
suicide, and combined with superficial investigation
techniques, keeps the reported number of cases of
suicide lower than the actual position.

It is reasonable to assume that the Black suicide
data and the African data in particular, suffer more
from ineffective recording machinery than do the
White. The African suicide rate is comparatively
low, and it is highly probable that this low rate is
due to faulty recording rather than to 'preservative'
cultural factors. To arrive at a rate closer to the
actual fact of suicide in Durban every case of suicide
that had occurred during the period under discussion
was studied and the author's judgment was added to
that of the presiding magistrate's to determine
whether a suicide or an accidental death or a death
classified as unnatural death was in fact a suicide.
This has resulted in a larger number of suicides than
actually recorded by the census data. Thus during
the period 1940-60 the Census Department reported 707
suicides for Indians, Whites and Coloureds in Durban.
The author found 830 suicides for these three groups,
a total discrepancy of 123. The greatest discrepancy
occurred among Indians, 90 cases, the smallest among
Coloureds, 6 cases. There was a discrepancy of 27
suicides between the two records for Whites. In one
case the presiding magistrate stated: 'Deaths of
this nature are too common among Indians to be always
accidental.' The magistrate had none the less determined death in that case to have been accidental. It
is suggested that the evaluation of the suicide rate
for Durban in this study is closer to the actual rate
than the official estimate. Taking the period 1940-
50, 177 cases of death by burning of Indian and African

women and 39 cases of deaths of Black persons due to
train accidents are listed in the index register.
From these a total of 45 cases were extracted and
included in the suicide list of this study.   The
proximity of this estimate to the real situation would
have been further increased had all cases of unnatural
deaths due to falling off moving vehicles and auto-
mobile accidents also been investigated.

Contradictions in the evidence of witnesses, apparent
resistance by deceased when offered help, and obvious
statements pointing to self-destruction were the prime
factors determining the reclassification of presumed
accidents into suicides.   The factor of intuition cannot be completely ruled out of this exercise.

The official suicide rate is probably further
affected by the fact that officials do not record
obvious cases of suicide in standardized, unambiguous
terms.   Thus suicide through poisoning may be recorded
as 'lysol poisoning', 'caustic soda suicide', 'overdose
of seconal tablets', 'self-administered poison',
'poison - open verdict', 'poison - no foul play'.   In
this list only three of the six types of entries could
reliably be isolated as suicide.   Yet 'no foul play',
'open verdict' and 'lysol poisoning' could well be
clear cases of suicide, and have in certain cases upon
investigation of the Court records proved to be so.
Among the various forms used for death by drowning,
are 'death through drowning', 'suicidal drowning',
'drowning'.   Falling from heights is entered as, 'fall
from seventh floor' or 'falling from ninth floor -
suicide'.   A suicidal collision may be entered as
'death due to impact with a train', 'struck by train',
'suicide by train', 'threw herself on the railway line
before a moving train' - 'suicide, lay on railway line,
in front of train'.   Suicidal hanging may be entered
as 'consistent with death by hanging', 'consistent
with history of hanging - apparently suicide'.   Death
by shooting as 'death due to shooting', 'gunshot
wound of head self-inflicted'.   Cause of death is
reluctantly categorized as suicide.

To minimize error, all such entries in the index to
the register, were traced to the register and investigated there.   Unless the evidence showed fairly
obvious suicide the 'accident' was given the benefit
of the doubt by the researcher as well.   Since there
can be no burial order without a doctor's certificate
and cases of collusion between doctor and relatives
are rare it can be reliably assumed that practically
all cases of suicide that occur in Durban are in fact

recorded.   They may not be recorded as suicide but
the records are there for the researcher to study and
evaluate.   The incidence of concealing suicide is
probably higher among Whites than Blacks, and probably
higher among the upper, more influential social strata,
than the lower.   This means that the White rate is
probably even higher than actually recorded.

Indian and Coloured suicide records are probably
closest to the actual incidence, African suicides the
furthest because of the essentially migrant nature of
the population, the difficulty in locating relatives
and at times any witnesses, and the many instances of
finding bodies days after the event, making the recognition of the cause of death well nigh impossible.

4 The incidence of suicide

According to available South African statistics approximately 124 suicides occur annually among Indians,
Whites and Coloureds: by contrast there are approximately 80 cases of homicide. (1)
   The occurrence of a high suicide rate in urban
society prompted the belief that suicide was a function
of civilization and non-existent in preliterate
society, a belief since rectified by anthropological
evidence. (2)   Available statistical analysis, however, shows a positive correlation between urbanization
and suicide.   In the USA, the rate of suicide falls
steadily from its highest point in towns with populations of 100,000 to its lowest in rural areas. (3)

PATTERNS OF GROUP AGGRESSION IN SOUTH AFRICA

A wide range of opinion conceives man to be naturally
aggressive.   Christian theology sees man as born in
sin, Freud sees man as primarily libidinal and in
search of selfish gratification; Hobbes decrees human
life to be nasty, brutish and short.   Such models
view society as the cage in which the human animal is
tamed, the taming being the sublimation rather than
the elimination of natural sin or aggression.   However one conceptualizes 'evil', as inherent in man,
inherent in society, or willed by man through his
action as in the Hindu theory of karma, violence,
aggression and conflict are accepted as components of
normal society.   The good society is not one without
conflict, but one that successfully controls conflict,
not by suppressing it, but by transforming it into
acceptable and constructive forms.
   In modern urban society, aggression may be intellec-

tualized into an ideological position taken for or
against a current war, or ritualized through the
symbolic destruction of the enemy, as on celluloid,
when Whites massacre American Indians, or Blacks make
'mincemeat' or a 'bonfire' out of Whites. Sport,
education, recreation and meaningful political and
economic involvement may be assumed to offer the more
'positive' modes of sublimation.

If aggression is accepted as a natural social component, and if group cohesion demands its sublimation,
then South African society is singularly ill equipped
to contend with this demand. Blacks are provided
with minimal opportunities for sublimating aggression -
society attempts to deal with Black aggression by
repressing ir, and thereby aggravating it, rather than
transforming it into forms acceptable to the actors,
and their society. Township and rural life is
virtually unrelieved by outlets for 'cooling' 'libidinal energy' - there are few opportunities for competitive games, members are excluded from the highly
structured hassle for economic and political power
that deflect and consume so much 'natural' energy';
labour laws repress strike action and a list of
security laws undermine protests and demonstrations.

Aggression builds up and its pressures are severe,
but it is contained for the most part within the
Black community and consumed in self-devouring
cannibalism. Thus the powerful appropriate and
manipulate even the 'libidinal' energy of the powerless,
directing it against itself in the age-old strategy of
divide and rule. Consequently, the most repressed
are also the most 'violent', as the volume and pattern
of Black crime in South Africa demonstrates. (4) The
consequent emasculation and demoralization of the
Black and the poor are then cited as their inherent
characteristics, and used to rationalize their control, that is oppression. Thus the poor and the
Black are where they are because of what they are.

A crucial factor in the powerlessness of a people
is the extent to which they are forced to internalize
aggression and defuse it in impotent internal wrangling.
The pattern of group violence in South Africa between
1950 and 1965 suggests that 'self-hate' and 'self-
violence' increase with increase in repression. It
also suggests, that given the slightest opening, self-
violence is quickly transformed into other-directed
violence - hence the 'shocking' and 'brutal' murders
of Whites by Africans that hit the headlines during
this time. The 'self' or one's own group is victimized

only so long as the 'other' remains unavailable.   In
that sense, self-aggression is 'perverted' aggression.
While self-violence, owing to the intensive repressive
climate of the South African system, appears to be the
pattern, it is periodically punctuated by other-
directed violence, both organized and spontaneous.

An American study, (5) evaluating civil strife in
115 countries during 1961-5, rated that of South
Africa forty-third, only slightly lower than that of
the USA.   Between 1950 and 1960, at least twenty-four
incidences of spontaneous group violence and fourteen
of 'other-directed violence' roughly coincided with
each other and intensified at the same time in 1952,
1956-7 and 1960.   They occurred, significantly, during
a time when racial repression hardened, but the government itself had not yet consolidated its new characteristic techniques for containing reaction against it.
While the 'other-directed' acts of group violence of
this period - passive resistance, sabotage, terrorism -
did not succeed in Black liberation they did constitute
their own power systems and within these provided
meaningful outlets for frustrated energy and aggression, and functioned positively for the demonstrators
in that they restituted something of the dignity that
had been lost.   Thus, 'though we may live as dogs, let
us at least die as men.'   This, then, is the inner
logic of action that otherwise appears futile.

In that context spontaneous group violence, triggered
off as it seems by an inconsequential event, out of all
proportion to the volume of destruction it wreaks, may
be found on analysis to be pregnant with deep meaning:
the trivial event may turn out to be a potent symbol,
dramatizing the whole oppressed state of the people at
that particular point in their history and rousing
them, out of their emasculated apathy, to a new state
of being.

Many spontaneous outbursts of group violence in
South Africa have been connected with beer, and
municipal beer-halls have often been the apparently
crazy targets of aggression - crazy, because the beer-
hall provides the only relief in the life of a migrant
worker, (6) castrated socially and sexually on a con-
veyer belt between his single man's compound and his
work place.   The 'official' state of celibacy imposed
on the migrant African workers herded into single
men's compounds is possibly the most blatantly
repressive of all modern situations.   A third of
Durban's African population lives in single quarters in
municipal hostels, compounds and with employers. (7)

Beer, however, is of deep ritual, spiritual and social
significance in traditional African society, and its
provocation in the urban situation may be due to the
fact that it is alienated from these qualities and sold
by the Government to the workers for profit.
Traditionally beer was brewed in the sacredness of
the home by the *makoti* (chief housewife) and served
ceremoniously to her lord and his friends in his home.
Only men who had reached adult status and older women
participated in the ceremony. The beer pot was passed
in hierarchical order, and the beer consumed in the
sacred circle of family and friends in a day-long feast
of praise songs and genealogy tracings, of ego-expanding
and ancestor-importuning. Beer brewed in the home left
the home only on very special occasions, such as
marriages and funerals, and then as gifts. It was
never sold. The state of urban beer is in a sense
similar to that of the migrant worker. Both he and
his beer have become transformed into economic units,
both have been alienated from their traditional 'roles'.
Thus in the alien, alienated work situation, the
'alienated' beer of the beer-hall probably symbolizes
and reflects the worker's own emasculated condition,
and in striking the beer he strikes against that condition in himself. The worker, socially and sexually
castrated, drinks at the behest of his master and he
drinks his master's brew which has lost its nutritive
and sacred content and become an agent of his enslave-
ment. Many Africans even believe that it reduces
sexual potency. At the same time it has a high
alcoholic content and drives the men crazy.
More seriously, beer-hall beer flouts the traditional
status of the woman, drains the family economy, and
destroys the family and community. Beer-hall beer
thus competes with the woman for the spirit and body of
the man and in the violence that erupts women are
often the instigators. The women continue to brew the
sacred brew in the townships and resent the beer-halls,
and their resentment at times charges the men into
realizing their emasculation. The apparently suicidal
riot is thus shot with its own inner logic and meaning.
Though materially destructive, it is psychologically
restorative. Such 'other-directed' group aggression,
though apparently futile, may thus inhibit important
functional consequences for the 'actors'.
By contrast, 'in' or self-directed aggression,
though having the temporary effect of relieving personal or factional frustration, heightens group tension
and is group-destroying. Thus, while the 'outer-

directed' group violence of the beer-hall type consolidates the community and redeems it from its ignominy,
'in' or self-directed aggression splits the community
by turning it upon itself. There is a blurring of
situation and people so that not only is the situation
seen as intolerable, but the people in it are also
conceived as intolerable. The 'oppressors' may so
manipulate this state, as actively to provide mirror
images, 'stooges', to whip up self-hate and churn the
process of self-destruction.

In South Africa, in 1960, the Thembus rejected and
demonstrated against the Bantu authorities Act, but
the government forced it upon them and appointed Thembu
chiefs to implement it. The people were pitted
against the chiefs - 'stooges' - who collaborated with
the government, and a situation of minor violence
erupted which the government exploited by sending in
its police to reinforce the home guards of the chiefs.
At the end of the foray, 39 Thembus died, 14 being
shot dead by the police and 13 being wounded by them.
The government 'with justification', clamped down on
the area and declared a state of emergency, whereby it
banned all meetings, arrested hundreds and placed them
in detention without trial, and sealed off the area
from the rest of the country, strictly controlling all
movement to and from it. In all, 524 persons were
charged with crimes ranging from arson to murder. (8)

While intensive repression may project an atmosphere
of peace, violence is the most potent fact in the
country, and it is reflected in the hundreds of deaths
during mass disturbances, thousands of arrests, prose-
cutions and convictions, bannings, house arrests and
banishments for political and technical offences
imposed, in particular, on Africans. (9)

THE SOCIAL SETTING IN DURBAN

Durban is a city of varied culture-contrasts. Mina-
rets, steeples and domes reach up simultaneously to
the sun and cast their shadows on sidewalks and
adjacent buildings.   It is young even by South African
standards, having been established as a township only
in 1835, 183 years after the landing of the first
White settlers under Jan van Riebeeck at the Cape.
Yet almost a third of its population is composed of
people belonging to one of the most ancient civiliza-
tions of the world, the Hindus.

The growth of the town has been startlingly rapid

since 1932 when it extended its municipal boundaries
and increased its population by 74 per cent, and its
surface area from 8,000 to 44,814 acres. (10)   Industry flourished, particularly after the Second World
War, and attracted a large African population from
the rural areas.   Durban is now both the third
largest city and the third largest industrial centre (11)
in the Republic.
    The racial composition of the city is considered to
be unique in South African cities.   The proportion of
Whites is lower in Durban than in any other city, with
a population of over 15,000. (12)   Although Indians,
Africans, and Whites exist in relatively equal ratios,
the Indian ratio is the highest of the three, the proportions in 1951 being: Indian 33.98 per cent, African
31.68 per cent, White 30.51 per cent and Coloured 3.83
per cent.   By 1960, the White and African ratios had
dropped further to 29.2 and 29.1 per cent respectively,
the Indian and Coloured ratios had risen to 39.2 and
4.5 per cent respectively.   In 1970 the ratios were:
African 28 per cent, White 26.18 per cent, Coloured
5.90 per cent and Indian 39.86 per cent. (13)   Thus
today almost 40 per cent of Durban is Indian. (14)
    The White, Indian and Coloured communities have had
residential, land and trading rights in the city;
Africans have been virtually excluded from it since
Union except in the capacity of migrant workers.   This
has resulted in an African population characterized by
abnormal sex, age and marital structures.   There is a
disproportion of 2.18 men to every African woman
(White 0.95, Coloured 0.88, Indian 1.04).   Able-bodied
adults between 15 and 49 years of age (White 53 per
cent, Coloured 50.15 per cent, Indian 57.52 per cent)
constitute 76.75 per cent of the population, and only
one-sixteenth is over 50 (White 22.22 per cent,
Coloured 8.05 per cent and Indian 6.84 per cent). (15)
Casual unions occur to a strikingly high extent among
Africans. (16)
    The Whites have the highest status.   The disparity
between their position in all its component forms and
that of Blacks is wide.   Among Blacks, Coloureds are
probably the least underprivileged.   Yet the sheer
fact of the overwhelming Indian majority makes it somewhat of an Indian city.
    Apart from sharing a common environmental heritage
in the widest context, each race lives its own group
life in an institutionalized system of social, political, economic and cultural segregation.   Separate
residential areas, educational and recreational

facilities and economic and political opportunities,
reinforce the barriers and limit all interracial contact to a bare minimum, in the main to economic
functions between employer and employee, buyer and
seller.   Contact on any other level is virtually non-
existent.

The study of suicide in Durban is made against a
background of such culture contrasts defined by structured variations and status differences.   To understand its significance the trend must be seen in terms
of each race group.   Just as there are 'no South
Africans', there is no 'South African suicide trend'.
The cultural and status factors that differentiate
the lives of the ethnic groups likewise impress their
marks on suicide.

THE SUICIDE RATE IN DURBAN

The distribution of the 2,238 cases of suicide by race
and sex in Durban during the two periods under review
is observed in Table 5.   The highest number of
suicides by race was that of Indians during both
periods; the highest number by sex, that of White men.
Tables 1 and 2 project the annual suicide rate for
forty-seven years in Durban.

Indians had the highest mean rate until 1960; thereafter the White rate exceeded the Indian.   Table 6
analyses the mean suicide rates for component sections
of the forty-seven years.

The African rate shows a steady increase, but this
is very probably due to improvement in recording
African statistics.   Though the African rate for
1962-70 is closer to that of the other groups, it is
still lower and the reason may still be due to poorer
collection of data than to an actual lower incidence.
This view tends to be strengthened by the fact that
there was no improvement in the quality of information
about individual African suicides recorded by the
Inquest Court.

ANALYSIS OF FLUCTUATIONS IN THE SUICIDE RATE OF DURBAN
BY RACE

(a) The pattern is erratic for all races
(b) Each race exhibits a fairly independent tendency.
The fluctuations in the rate (see Table 1) do not
correspond for the races as a whole.   This indicates

that though sharing a common social structure the races
in terms of suicide respond differently to their external
environment.   This might be expected since each race
is characterized by its own cultural system, economic
status and socio-political rights and privileges.
Frenay, comparing the Coloured and White suicide
rates in the USA for the decennial period 1911-20,
finds that though Coloureds maintain an independent
tendency to suicide, the fluctuations in their curve
correspond to those of the curve for Whites. (17)   This
may be due to the American tendency towards integration
and cultural assimilation of Coloureds and foreign-born.
By contrast, South African society emphasizes 'ethnic'
barriers.   Thus whereas it may be possible to have an
American reaction to conditions that depress or elevate
the country as a whole, it is not possible to have a
'South African' reaction.   The reaction is in terms of
ethnic communities.

Blacks as a whole share common fluctuation patterns
more often among themselves than with Whites - in 65
per cent of the period.   However Africans also share
common fluctuations with Whites in 65 per cent of the
period, Coloureds and Whites in 45 per cent of the
period.   The convergence of the fluctuations when they
do occur may be accidental rather than expressive of
the effects of common social or national currents.
At any rate any interpretation of the meaning of such
fluctuations without calculations of the differences in
the actual gulfs would be relatively meaningless.

COMPARISON OF THE DURBAN SUICIDE RATES WITH SOUTH AFRICAN
AND WORLD RATES

The South African mean annual rate for the period 1948-
58 for Whites, Indians and Coloureds is 8.65 per
100,000;   the Durban mean for the same period for the
three races is 14.66 per 100,000 per annum.   The
Durban rate is higher for all three race groups during
this period - WHITE: Durban 15.50, South African
11.43;   INDIAN: Durban 16.97, South African 9.70;
COLOURED: Durban 11.52, South African 2.39. (18)   The
higher rate for Durban may be partly accounted for by
the fact that the South African rate is inclusive of
the rural areas, but over and above this the estimation
of the South African rate by the Bureau of Census is
almost undoubtedly lower than its actual incidence. (19)
The mean suicide rate for thirty-six countries listed
in the 'United Nations Demographic Year Book' for 1955

was 9.69 per 100,000. (20)   The South African mean was
lower than this world mean, and the Durban mean was
higher.   Hungary had the highest suicide rate in 1965,
a rate of 29.8 for 100,000.   Austria, Denmark, Finland,
Switzerland, Sweden, Czechoslovakia, Germany and Japan
have consistently high rates according to available
reports.   Since 1955 Belgium, France and Australia
have had rates that have ranged between 12 and 20 per
100,000.   The Durban suicide rate falls within the same
group.   Countries with a low suicide rate of less than
5 per 100,000 are Chile, Guatemala, Dominican Republic,
Taiwan, Panama, Costa Rica, Ireland, Mexico, Columbia,
Peru and Egypt - Egypt being the lowest - 1 per
100,000.   These variations, it must be borne in mind,
are affected by differential recording techniques, so
that countries with the more efficient techniques may
well project higher rates.   One may assume, however,
that where large variations occur between two countries,
the significance of this factor falls away.

REACTION OF FLUCTUATIONS IN THE DISTRIBUTION OF SUICIDES
TO EXTERNAL EVENTS

Sociologists have found significant correlations for
suicide, war and economic depression.   Suicide has been
observed to decline during war, and to increase during
economic depressions.   Ruth Cavan (21) found that the
suicide rates of Belgium, Switzerland, France, Italy and
the USA decreased during the First World War.   Dublin
reported similar declines after the Second World
War. (22)   Durkheim explained the low war-time rate as
due to an increase in group solidarity.   The fact of
a common external danger integrates and consolidates
the group, in turn lowering its suicide rate. (23)
But Cavan and Frenay (24) point out that America also
experienced economic prosperity during the war and
since suicide has been noted to decline during economic
booms, the lowered American rate may have been as much
due to the 'integrative force' of war as to the effects
of economic prosperity or due to the combined effects
of both.   Gibbs (25) is sceptical about the beneficial
effects of war on suicide.   Dublin supports Durkheim
and emphasizes that the integrative force of the social
movement leaves little opportunity for introspection,
temporarily moves away attention from personal problems,
and thereby lowers the suicide rate. (26)
     Durkheim contends that the integrative effect is
also present in political crisis, elections, revolutions

and *coups d'état* and during all such events the suicide
rate declines. Economic depressions, on the other
hand, are observed to have an aggravating effect on
suicide. He explains this as due to their disintegrative function on an existing regulative system. (27)
Henry and Short in their exhaustive study of suicide
and economic depressions, confirm a correlation between
suicide and business cycles. (28)   This is also
established in a study of business cycles in
Massachusetts. (29)
     That national and communal events disrupt settled
routine and disturb community life is common sense,
that they affect suicide rates universally has yet to
be established. The Second World War, 1939-45, the
economic depression, 1928-33, and the 1948 elections
were national events that involved Durban and South
Africa as a whole.   In addition, there were the events
which affected specific race groups. The Land Tenure
Acts of 1936, 1946, and 1950, depriving Indians of
their traditional land rights, constituted a 'national'
attack on Indians. The passive resistance campaign
of 1948 was a 'national' response to that attack. It
consolidated group loyalties and inspired leadership,
heroism and martyrdom. The 1952 Defiance of Unjust
Laws Campaign, though more crucial to African solidarity, also affected the Indians who joined it. The
Durban riots of 1949 by contrast split the two peoples
apart and against each other; but the splitting could
also be interpreted as consolidating each in the face
of the other.
     How did these national and communal events affect
the Durban suicide rate?

(a) Economic depressions and wars

Durban, contrary to expectation, shows lower suicide
rates for all races during the depression years (1929-
33) and a rise in rates during the post-depression
period (1934-40).   Likewise, the rates are higher
during the war period (1939-45), than in the pre-war
period (1934-9) though they are lower than in the post-
war period (1946-50).   (See Table 7.)   The general
trend of an increasing suicide rate is so strong during
1929-50   that it remains unresponsive to any counter-
currents.   On the other hand, if war and depressions
did contain independent effects on the suicide rate,
these would have counteracted the general trend.   The
White rate however does decline during the war years

to 12.10 as against 13.59 and 14.18 respectively in
the pre-war and post-war periods. African and
Indian rates by contrast are higher during the war
period than during the periods preceding and following
the war.
   It is clear from the case material that the suicide
of a large number of White men in the post-war period
was directly related to post-war disruptions in personal
relations. Thus a number of White male suicides were
directly related to the disruptive effects of war.
Men returning from service were confronted by such
problems as those of unfaithful wives and the inability
to adjust themselves to family situations which before
had absorbed them. There were several cases of men
who had developed neurotic tendencies, melancholia,
depression, insomnia, and consequently resorted to
excessive drinking. The 1949 race riots likewise had
their effects. The case material indicates that a
number of Indian suicides during this period were
directly attributable to the riots. (30) There are
suicides of Indians of both sexes in all age groups, of
persons shocked by the traumatic experience and suffering hallucinations as a result. It is unlikely that
such events affect the rate as a whole.
   South Africa herself was only indirectly involved
in the war, and though it saw a substantial portion of
its young men on service, it also ushered in a period
of industrial boom. The rise in the Black suicide
rate during this period may have been due to the
initial disintegrative effects of the sudden intensification in urbanization as workers flocked to the
urban areas. (31) Huge shack settlements erupted in
South African cities during the war years, and these
were characterized by all the social and material consequences of overcrowding.
   National integration is not only low, but questionable in South Africa, so that one cannot effectively
speak of national influences. South Africa has no
history of a common heritage that wells up in the
hearts of patriots, making them respond as one when
confronted by external dangers. Gulfs exist not only
between Black and White, but even within these broad
divisions. The South African reaction to the Second
World War thus was one of a confused and dissentient
people. Blacks saw it as a White man's war and moreover felt insulted by the fact that though invited to
enlist they were debarred from carrying arms. Whites
were divided in their support and the sympathies of
the opposition Nationalist party for the enemy was
apparent.

(b) Other national events

During 1948 the suicide rates of all the races
increased, the increase being substantial for Africans
and Coloureds. This was the crucial election year
which put the present Nationalist government into
power. The election results came as a surprise, even
to the Nationalists themselves. For Blacks it por-
tended a deterioration in their condition, which in
fact followed.

The disturbing effects of the new anti-Indian Land
Tenure Act, the 1946 Indian Passive Resistance Campaign, the extension of pass laws to women and such
political demonstrations as the 1952 Defiance Campaign,
the 1956 Treason arrests and the declaration of a state
of emergency in 1960 do not suggest any uniform or conflicting effects in the suicide trends of the races.
The period 1946 to 1948 saw a great political revival
movement among the Indians. These were the years of
the Indian Passive Resistance struggle, the first
important organized opposition to the Government since
the days of Gandhi. It was a period that produced
Indian leaders and inspired nationalism, heroism and
martyrdom in the community. Extending Durkheim's
logic, the period might be conceived as having on
Indian suicides the same prophylactic effect as a war.
The Indian suicide rate, however, shows no marked
decline.

In 1952, Africans and Indians jointly engaged in
Passive Resistance. In accordance with Durkheim's
theory the 'group integrative' effect of this interracial event should have been reflected in a uniform
decline in their suicide rates. This is not indicated.
The Indian rate rises and the African rate falls.
Likewise, the African trend runs counter to the Indian
trend in the 1956 treason arrest year, although both
communities in Durban were affected by it.

The Indian and African rates did rise sumultaneously
during 1960, marked by the state of emergency, but the
simultaneous rise may have been due to factors other
than the disrupting effects of the emergency. Extending the Durkheimian war hypothesis however, this
'attack' on 'Blacks' from the White government ought
to have resulted in strengthening group cohesion and
thereby lowering the suicide rate.

The decade 1962-71 is characterized not only by
increased urbanization of Africans, but also by
massive removals of the Black populations from
relatively developed to undeveloped areas, with few

amenities and long expensive journeys to work.   It is
also characterized by stringent legislations which
suppress protest and the 'example' of large numbers of
detentions without trial, convictions for terrorism
and sabotage as deterrents against overt opposition.
There is an atmosphere of economic growth, and
'observable' consumption of urban material goods by
Blacks - in the form of clothing, furniture, etc.,
easily available on hire purchase schemes.   Wage
increases, however, do not keep pace with increases in
the cost of living and in many cases there is no 'real'
improvement in incomes.   Segregation is intensified
and extended to all levels of education.   The country
exudes an atmosphere of colossal frustration, of
repressed passions on the verge of erupting.   The
conscientization of the Church and the emergence of
political groups within the Black communities begin to
provide outlets and appear to defuse the situation.
The suicide rate is higher during this time than in
the decade preceding it, but it is lower than in the
decade 1941-50.   One cannot reliably draw a correlation
between these events and the suicide rate of the Durban
people.   The most general statement one can make is
that the events of 1962-70 were more provocative with
reference to suicide, than those of 1951-60, but less
so than those of 1941-50.

The analysis suggests that it is futile to attempt
an explanation of the suicide rate in terms of crisis
situations of a national or communal nature.   The
apparent associations are very probably due to a
multiplicity of factors, among which the crisis events
themselves may or may not be crucial.   It is more than
probable that, if a relation exists at all, it is of
an indirect nature and does not, as Durkheim contends,
generate magnetic currents that increase or allay
suicidal tendencies, but these events in individual
cases disrupt individual life patterns.   Thus while
their effects may be seen in individual cases the
evidence in Durban suggests that they do not necessarily affect the general rate.

part two

Suicide and social status

5 The relations between suicide, social integration and social status

The universal correlations observed by social scientists between suicide and other social events, and the principles they have abstracted from these correlations, in the main confirm the very general Durkheimian postulate that 'suicide varies with the degree of integration of the social group of which the individual forms a part'. (1)   Though the psychic root of Durkheim's concept of integration in the 'collective conscience' is dubious, his framework and the aetiology it produces continue with some modification and elaboration to provide the fundamental theoretical orientation to suicide.

Merton, expressing anomy as anomie, defines it as imbalance between socially structured goals and normatively available means, (2) Henry and Short as 'strength of the Relational system', (3) implying that people deeply and intensely involved with others are a low suicide risk, while those isolated from meaningful relationship with their fellow men are high suicide risks, Ruth Cavan (4) simply as 'social disorganization', the Strausses as a 'loosely structured' society, (5) and Martin and Gibbs as integration in occupational status, that is the degree of compatibility obtaining between the systems of status an individual is called upon to occupy simultaneously. (6)

The main criticism of Durkheim is that he discounts the psychological factor in suicide, considering its influence to be restricted to abnormal psychopathic and neurasthenic types that constitute only a fraction of the total suicides in a group, and which do not affect its suicide rate.   Thus he propounds a theory of sociological determinism, and does not propose the interactive effects of the psychological and sociological; yet he calls attention to this, for his

view of integration is two-dimensional and provides the
basis for the current approach which sees anomie as the
general social state, and egoism and altruism as the
personal states or the individual's reaction to the
general state. This is due to his two-dimensional
views of integration: integration of the social structure, failure to achieve which results in anomie; and
integration of the person within that structure,
failure to achieve which results in egoism (under-
integration) or altruism (over-integration). Thus
Merton's typologies of ritualism, as the adaptation of
one who, failing to attain socially structured goals,
becomes obsessed with culturally determined means, of
'innovation' and 'rebellion' as the reactions of
persons who, frustrated in the first instance by the
paucity of legitimately available means and in the
second, by both means and goals, strike out for
change, (7) and Elwin Powell's 'envelopment' as over-
integration of occupational roles, and 'dissociation'
as failure to integrate such roles, (8) are restatements
on the personality level of altruism and egoism respectively.

Despite the elaborations, the concept of disintegration continues to be much too wide to be meaningful in
specific social situations in which suicide occurs.
While all individuals seek to be integrated and the
primary institutions of integration, as outlined by
Durkheim - religion, politics and occupation - are
universal, the problem is one of identifying more
specifically the factors in these institutions in
differing cultures that promote or hinder integration
and expose members to breaking points of interpersonal
tension.

Durkheim himself is quite clear that there is no
standardized tension, or standardized reaction to
tension in man. Accordingly, he classifies three
suicide types, each related to his three fundamental
social forces and in addition identifies sub-types,
which arise from the combination of these forces. The
reduction of millions of suicides in thousands of
societies to this relatively simple classification is
questionable in itself. The focal point of the immediate discussion however is directed to the principles
on which these variations are based, essentially those
of class and the level of civilization, or 'socialization'. It is suggested that these are much too wide
to account for the complex effects of interaction in
different culture and status categories. Hence to
explain suicides of 'upper cultures' and 'upper classes'

as due to egoism (i.e. the failure of the social system
to hold its members to its norms) or anomy (the breakdown of the 'collective conscience' or normative order),
and those of lower classes as due to altruism, or over-
internalization of the normative order, or 'collective
conscience' is much too general, and the generalization
becomes gross oversimplification when suicide is
defined as the response of the *superior* man, and it is
asserted that those of high social status, in terms of
education, wealth, sex, age and occupation, are more
prone to suicide than those of lower social status. (9)
Durkheim's analysis of some 26,000 White suicides
occurring in the last half of the nineteenth century,
revealed practically no suicide among children and low
rates among women, the very old, the illiterate and
members of less complex societies, leading him to
suggest that they lived on a more *organic* and a less
social level, and therefore suffered less when deprived
of society.   After all, he points out, suicide is non-
existent in animals.   He observes its tendency in man
to increase in proportion to the presence of society in
him, or the degree of socialization, since he views
socialization to be positively related to civilization.
'Man is a double, that is because social man superimposes himself upon physical man ... social man is the
essence of civilized man; he is the masterpiece of
existence.' (10)
    He accordingly constructs a status scale based on
the index of socialization in which he places animals
devoid of society at the base, the civilized male as
the most permeated with, and therefore most dependent
on, society at the apex, and women, the aged and the
'primitives' in varying positions in between these.
The adult 'civilized' male, according to Durkheim, is
incapable of existence without society and thus commits
suicide when individuated from it in the process of
egoism.   The other status categories by contrast are
conceived as relatively fulfilled by their material
existence and thus not as dependent on 'society' for
their existence.
    The implication that a high suicide rate demon-
strates some sort of congenital superiority has not
found support in post-Durkheimian writings.   However
American and European studies continue to corroborate
a correlation between high status and suicide.   The
explanation for this is contained, with some modification in Durkheim's other statement: (11)
    Everything that enforces subordination attenuates
    the effects of this state.   At least the horizon of

the lower classes is limited by those above them, and
for this same reason, their desires are more modest.
Those who have empty space above them are almost
mentally lost in it, if no force restrains them.
Henry and Short restate it thus: (12)
    The risk of suicide increases as position in the
    status hierarchy rises.   Since the degree of
    'critical' external restraint over behaviour is
    greater, on the average, for the low status than for
    the high status category, we may suggest that the
    risk of suicide decreases as the degree of 'critical'
    external restraint over behaviour increases.
    Behaviour of the high status person playing many
    superordinate roles - like behaviour of the isolated
    person - is freed from the request that it conforms
    to the demands and expectations of others.
They continue: 'Males, because of their greater involvement in the occupational system, enjoy a status position
somewhat higher than females and the superior status
position of Whites is obvious.' (13)
    This proposition emphasizes a direct link between a
high suicide rate and high social status, low social
control and low social integration.   Durkheim postulates, and his successors confirm, that the greater the
social involvement, and consequently the internalization and dependence on social norms, the higher the
status.   At the same time, the greater the social
involvement, the greater the dependence on social
restraints for existence; and when these break down
the greater the dangers of suicide.
    Durban provides a strategic situation for the exam-
ination of this correlation particularly because of
its multi-ethnic nature.   The city is a multicultural
component of a multicultural society in which the four
'races', Indian, White, Coloured and African constitute
four distinct subsystems in the total matrix, each
characterized by its internal behavioural and struc-
tural differences and its differential access to power
in the total complex.   In terms of status, Whites are
at the top, Blacks at the bottom; and within the
Black 'caste', Africans are on the lowest rung while
the positions of Indians and Coloureds may interchange,
depending on the Province, despite the stronger political position of the latter.   Following the assumption
that a high suicide rate accompanies a high social
status, higher rates would be predicted for Whites by
race, for men by sex, and for persons in higher socio-
economic and occupational positions than for persons in
lower socio-economic and occupational positions in

society.   Also persons in relatively more valued and
useful age categories, young adults, would have lower
rates than aged social incumbents.   The results fail
to establish this and suggest instead:

(a)   that high suicide rates are not necessarily the
function of high status.   They can also occur in low
status categories as is inferred from Merton's postulate that persons deprived of institutionalized means
to pursue socially structured goals are thrust into a
state of anomy; (14)

(b)   that high status is not necessarily associated
with low social restraint.   People in high status may
find that they are subjected to considerable external
critical restraint because they are called upon to act
as leaders, or 'culture' bearers.   This is indicated
by George Homans, (15) when he states that the norms
of a group are most observable in the leader;

(c)   high external social restraint does not in
itself lead to high social integration.   In fact such
restraints may cripple and hence deprive individual
self-expression to the extent where 'dropping out' and
in extreme cases, suicide, offer the only means of
escape.   This condition is not to be confused with
Durkheim's altruism, which is really a condition of
over-integration in which the social member reaches
his goal of psychic amalgamation with the 'collective
conscience' through self-willed death. (16)

6 Race, sex and social integration

The overwhelming weight of available evidence shows that
fewer Negroes commit suicide than Whites and fewer women
than men. (1)   Such evidence does not in itself establish that Negroes and women have greater natural immunity to suicide.   For one thing, the scope of available
statistics is limited and for another the observations
are restricted to European and American data.   The
notion that it has anything to do with race and sex cannot be rejected out of hand, since suicide is a social,
and not a congenital fact.

Moreover, existing cross-cultural comparisons show
that whereas fewer Negroes and women may commit suicide
than Whites and men in the same society, they have
higher suicide than Negroes and women in other cultures.   Thus the Negro suicide rate is lower than the
White rate in Mississippi, but higher than the White
rate in Washington State. (2)   Similarly, while the
female suicide rate is lower than the male rate in
Japan, it is higher than the male rate in thirteen of
twenty-three listed countries. (3)   Instances where
women and Negroes have higher suicide rates than
Whites and males in the same society have also been
observed.   Thus Frenay, analysing the average rates
for the period 1911-20 for American States, found that
the Coloured rate was about equal to the White rate in
Massachusetts and higher than the White rate in Calif-
ornia. (4)   Ruth Cavan reproducing Von Mayer's
figures for India in 1907 shows that the male rate
exceeds the female in two of the ten Provinces. (5)

The average suicide rates by race and sex in Durban
for the two periods 1940-60 and 1962-70, based on the
1951 and 1960 census figures (Table 8), do not
establish a correlation between high social status and
high suicide rate; nor do they establish a correlation
between high integration and a low suicide rate.
48

The African suicide rate is the lowest of all four
groups, and so is his status, but there is strong
reason to believe that the calculation of the African
suicide rate is the least reliable of all, because of
poor recording, and the abnormal sex and age structure
of the predominantly migrant African population.   The
more reliable comparison is thus between Indian and
Coloured, on the one hand, and White, on the other.
The Black rate then, despite the lower status of
Indians and Coloureds, is higher than the White rate,
refuting the correlation of a high rate with a high
status group.

The fact that the highest suicide rate by sex is
that of White men, on the other hand, tends to confirm
the high status, low integration, high suicide rate,
theory since their status is indisputably the highest
of all race and sex groups.   But then White women
have the next highest status, yet they have the lowest
rate of all, and this despite the fact that there is
a greater equality of sexes among Whites than among
Blacks.   The White woman's rate is half that of the
Black woman's, depressed and dominated both by race
and sex.   White women are unique in Durban in that
they have a lower rate than that of their presumed
superior male counterpart.   The difference between the
male and female rate is small among Indians, with
women having a slightly higher rate during the 1940-60
period, and a lower rate during the 1962-71 period.

One would get a very distorted view of the Durban
status scale if one used the suicide rate as its
index.   Clearly there is no standard correlation
between high status, high suicide rate and low social
integration.   Africans apparently have the lowest
suicide rate in Durban, but it would be absurd to
postulate that, living as they do, precariously between
two cultures and deprived of normal family life and so
obviously exposed to all the conditions of urban
instability, they are more integrated in South African
society than its architects, the White men.   It would
be equally absurd to suggest that White men, having
perfected a social system which assures them prestige
and power and having imposed it on Blacks, find that
they themselves cannot be integrated within it.   The
more plausible explanation is that the high White male
rate is due to Whites' anxiety and insecurity about
their position of power, and to the intense tension
discharged in their strivings to retain that power.

Durkheim and Henry and Short propose that people in
high status have high suicide rates because of low

social restraint.   The presumption of low social
restraint in superordinate positions is artificial.
Those in institutionalized power, leadership and control, are continuously straining themselves to justify
and secure their privileged positions.   The universal
hazards of superordinate roles are aggravated in South
Africa by the fact that the legitimacy of White domination is under constant ideological attack and constantly
threatened by indigenous Blacks and surrounding African
states.   As leaders of the South African superstruc-
ture they must adhere to its normative prescriptions
in an exemplary manner.   They must preserve the
social structure, defend its national ethos, resolve
its observable moral, religious and rational inconsis-
tencies and, they must do so from a position of
dominance, which is legitimized neither by popular
consensus nor by a universally accepted ideology.
This forces them into a state where they must depend
on their high material standards to maintain their
dominance, and since the whole structure of South
African society is designed to perpetuate the social
distance between them and Blacks, they have no alterna-
tive but to see all accruing failures as due to their
own personal shortcomings.   The high suicide rate of
White men in Durban is thus not due to their freedom
from social restraint but to the conflict between their
privileged positions and the demands inherent in maintaining those positions.

By contrast, Black men have neither arrogated to
themselves nor have had thrust upon them the responsibilities of preserving the social structure.   Their
cultures are in a state of flux and change and they
are not expected to uphold them as models to others.
From that point of view, they are in relaxed positions,
but if they are freed from strain in this context,
there are other sources of strain that enter their
lives.   The point to emphasize here is that the
apparently lower suicide rate of Black men is not due
to their lower status and thereby higher integration
into South African society.   In fact their positive
rejection of that society is overtly demonstrated in
many ways.

Integration proceeds from personality integration
and is interactive with integration into society.
Personality integration and social integration are
thus intrinsically related to each other.   More precisely, it involves the integration of social roles
in social institutions.   While a person may occupy a
large number of roles in his society, they are not

equally meaningful to him - some are more crucial to his
material and emotional existence than others.   He will
be far more affected by disturbances in his more meaningful role relations than by disturbances in his less
meaningful roles.

Blacks are obliged to live in two social systems -
Black and White.   Their roles in the White system are
almost completely 'contractual', in the Black conspic-
uously primary and consequently more meaningful.   It
is the return to this Black system, to its assuaging,
comforting and redeeming effects, that makes the White
system tolerable at all.   The Black's suicide, one
assumes, occurs because of disturbances in his more
meaningful roles in the Black system.   The White system
affects his roles in the Black system powerfully, but
indirectly.   Thus he may be prevented from effectively
performing his role as husband, father and provider
because of poor income or an unhappy work situation.

The African male suicide not only suggests low
integration in the White system, but also a recoiling
from its impersonal definition of his role.   It at
the same time suggests the absence of an integrated
Black system to which he can withdraw and from which he
can draw consolation.   There is no 'home' to which the
migrant worker may return each evening.

The suicides of Indian and Coloured men and of Black
women generally could be interpreted through the Henry
and Short framework: 'Suicide varies negatively and
homicide positively, with the strength of external
restraint over behaviour.' (6)

Henry and Short state: 'Suicide varies negatively
and homicide positively, with the strength of external
restraint over behaviour.'   External restraint here
implies the extent to which norms or social regulations
have been voluntarily internalized into the personality
structure.   In this sense, external restraint is
really internal restraint.   It is the regulative
force of the superego, constraining antisocial behaviour
and developing strong guilt complexes so that agression
is more likely to be self-directed than other-directed.
It suggests Durkheim's 'altruism', or overintegration
of social norms.   Indians compared to Africans and
Coloureds are more introverted, more restrained;   thus
perhaps their higher suicide rate.   Their technique
of aggression has most usually been *satyagraha*, which
Gandhi defined as 'soul force', (7) in effect the use
of self-aggression, or self-imposed suffering to shame
the enemy into realizing his humanity and changing his
aggression into positive feelings of sympathy.

Satyagraha, shorn of its idealism, is a self-directed
technique of aggression for purposes of revenge through
the exposure of the inhumanity of the oppressor.
Suicidal acts often indicate desire for revenge,
punishment and blame. If one cannot attack the direct
cause of one's affliction, one may attack a substitute,
and the substitute may be oneself.

Coloured and African men are more prone to externa-
lizing aggression than to internalizing it. The
Coloured homicide rate for the Republic is about three
times as high as the Coloured suicide rate. This is
in contrast to the commonly observed trend for suicide
to exceed homicide. The South African suicide and
homicide rates per 100,000 for Coloureds are 1.44 and
8.69 respectively: for Indians 9.26 and 3.9; for
Whites 10.3 and 2.9. (8)

The combined strains of social deprivation and high
external critical restraints are obvious in the
suicide rates of Black women, particularly Indian
women among whom the highest rates occurred in the most
deprived age categories, those of youth and extreme old
age, the average suicide rates being 57.6 per 100,000
in the 15-19 year age category and of 63.8 per 100,000
in the 70+ age category in the twenty-one year period
1940-60.

Durkheim's assertion that fewer women than men kill
themselves because of lesser involvement and consequently lesser dependence on social life finds no
support in the Durban experience. Their lesser participation in 'collective life' is in itself a result
of social restraint. Women by exclusion, and not by
choice, are less involved in social activities. They
resent this exclusion. Their lesser participation in
'collective life' (one assumes that Durkheim means
thereby, public affairs) has not made them less dependent on society and thus more immune to suicide. If
anything their greater state of subordination and
their lesser freedom of self-expression makes them
all the more dependent on society for the definition of
their roles and their self-image. The positive
elements of that image are expressed in the rewards
that accrue to them - in the esteem with which they
are held in society. When that esteem is not
apparent, when the pressures of restrictions exceed
those of prescriptions they obtain negative images of
themselves. Their state of helplessness and despair
can be measured in terms of the degree of imbalance
that develop between their obligations to society and
the rewards which they may expect from it.

Women by tradition are expected to internalize more restraints to be acceptable in society. Their responsibility for practising and preserving rituals and traditions is customarily greater than for men. Among South African Indians, until the last two decades women, largely confined to the home and excluded from political and economic life, were almost wholly responsible for preserving cultural norms. Their socialization process tends to be more prohibitive than permissive.

The rewards that Black women may expect are lower than those expected by any 'race' or sex groups in Durban. There are few institutionalized outlets through which they may expend their energy, while sporting activities exist as a matter of fact for Black men and they may seek conviviality in beer-halls, or get drunk, such 'vices' reduce the status of women. The fact that African women have constituted the hub of African political activity in the past, and today tend to be the more active in religious groups, is partly due to the fact that such activities provide the only outlets available to them and thus act as recreational substitutes.

The life of the average Indian woman with its many restrictions is probably the most impoverished. Barred from smoking and drinking and prevented from leaving the house unaccompanied except on closely defined business, her life is often confined to the stifling atmosphere of the large family in a small dwelling. There are diversions, such as weddings and pujas (prayer rituals), but these are few and far between, and the daily round, unless relieved by warm and friendly chatter, is hard and dull, and if beset with other irritations can easily result in a traumatic weakening in the hold on life. A young girl sets herself alight because she is not allowed a few yards of material to make herself a new dress; another takes rat poison because her mother will not allow her to visit a relative. These are the superficial symptoms of the emptiness that generally characterizes their life. The good Indian woman is defined in terms translatable into such English adjectives as submissive, subdued and passive. She subdues her will and desires in the service of kith and kin. The mythological Hindu model, Sita (9) who remains faithful despite the outrages of the heroic Rama, still hovers in the minds of elders.

The suffering of the African women is due in particular to their peculiar unemancipated position in the

eyes of the law.   Their lives in the urban complex,
characterized by the high proportion of loose unions
and illegitimate births, are fraught with problems of
both emotional and physical insecurity.   The case
material indicates that the largest number of suicides
occurred among women living with men without the
security of marriage.   This was also characteristic
of Coloured women, among whom this condition was often
aggravated by the fact that they were living with non-
Coloureds, either African or Indian, in which case the
pressures of conflicting values were added to those of
insecurity.   Compromises and adjustments, relatively
happily made within the secure setting of marriage,
are fraught with extreme tensions in the suspended
situation where rejection by the group of birth fails
to be supplemented by acceptance in the group of
adoption.

All societies tend to have an intuitive awareness of
the psychological knowledge that aggression is a
natural component of the human personality, and provide
institutionalized facilities for the expression of
aggressive energy.   Group dancing, the organization
of youth into sex and age groups, each with its own
delimited range of power, are the more obvious traditional African modes of solving this problem.

Traditional Zulu life weaves together the recreational needs of men and women.   The life cycle of an
individual is punctuated by institutionalized events
which provide satisfactory recreational facilities
mostly within the close companionship of the age
group.   Thus there is the *Ukuthatha Impahla,* which
secures the young girl's association with the man of
her choice under the surveillance of her companions,
and the prolonged relationship that ensues until
marriage provides all the scope for 'pattern maintenance and tension release'.   There is similarly the
ceremony of cultivating the field for *Inkosazana,
Unom Khululwana* who in turn bestows gifts of beauty and
good manners;   the taking of the *Umbondo,* gifts to
prospective in-laws;   the *Ukuchhambisa,* the girl's
puberty party;   the *Umemulo,* her coming-of-age party;
and associated with most is the dancing that follows,
for girls *Ushaya isi gekle.*   In traditional society,
even the daily routine - gathering firewood, fetching
water, making beadwork, weaving mats - occurs in enjoy-
able associations of peer groups and is marked by its
relaxing rhythm.   Not only does the security of the
familiar and the secure disappear in the city, and
not only is the girl forced to adjust herself to the

55 Chapter 6

alien and the new, but she finds herself without any tension-relieving outlets that may help her to adjust to the strains suddenly imposed on her. (10)

7 Religion and language as indices of social status among Indians and their relation to the suicide rate

In multicultural societies, religion, language, economic and social status often coincide.

Kuper (1) found a correlation between religion and language on the one hand and socio-economic status on the other in Durban in 1951. The Inquest Court does not record systematically religion, language and incomes of suicides. These have to be inferred from names, occupations, residential areas and available evidence of living conditions. Indian names are closely corre-lated with religion and language and it was thus possible to examine the relation of suicide to religion and language in their cases.

South African Indians generally fall into six ling-uistic categories (Tamil, Telugu, Hindustani, Urdu, Gujerati and English) and into three religious cate-gories (Hindu, Muslim and Christian). The distribution of suicides by religious affiliation in the 495 cases of Indian suicides during 1940-60 is observed in Table 9. The highest economic status by language is that of Gujeratis and by religion that of Muslims. The highest suicide rate is found in the lowest economic status group - among Hindus, as is observed in Table 10. That the correlation is between income and suicide and not religion and suicide is indicated when religion is held constant. Thus Gujerati Hindus, predominantly merchant class and with the highest incomes among Hindus, have a much lower suicide rate than Tamil Hindus with the lowest incomes, as is observed in Table 11.

8 Residential areas, status and integration

In *laissez-faire* societies, families sharing common
social standards congregate in common neighbourhoods.
Thus the residential ecology is characterized by distinct socio-economic units.   If the hypothesis, high
status, high suicide rate, had universal application,
then prestige residential areas would be characterized
by higher suicide rates than poor residential areas
and suicide would decline with a decline in the quality
of housing.   Such findings as, suicide increases with
an increase in persons of independent means, (1) that
the privileged groups have higher rates than the down-
tordden, that commissioned officers are more prone to
suicide than enlisted men, (2) corroborate this
expectation.

In Durban, the suicide rate is in fact higher in
the poorer, low-income, low-education, Black residential areas, characterized by slum dwellings or council
housing.

Suicide rates have also been observed to be positively
related to density, rising with a rise in density
towards the centre of the city and falling towards the
periphery, reaching their lowest point in the rural
hinterland.   Thus Cavan, studying Chicago of the
1919-21 period, located the suicide belt in the loop,
and its contiguous districts of cheap hotels and
rooming and lodging houses dominated by unattached
males. (3)   In Durban the reverse trend prevails: the
rate *increases* as one moves towards the periphery of
the city, and is highest in the mammoth Indian township
of Chatsworth beyond its boundary.   This is the effect
of segregation, which, intensified by the policy of
apartheid, has controlled the spatial distribution of
races in South African cities, so that Whites occupy
valuable lands towards city centres or in swiftly

linked suburbs, while Blacks are pushed away to the
furthest borders and beyond.   In Durban the Black
areas sprawl across the semi-developed, poorly serviced,
broken country, off the coast and beyond the ridge
that forms a natural boundary between the greatly
valued beach and beach-facing lands and the less valued
hilly interior.   Consequently, high suicide rate
areas are located away from the centre of the city and
in comparatively low density areas.

Up to about 1960, over two-thirds of the White population lived in the Old Borough, while four-fifths of
the Indian population and two-thirds of the Coloured
population lived in the New Borough, or added areas.
The number of Africans in the Old Borough was comparatively high, mainly because of African domestic servants
and African workers accommodated in industrial and
municipal barracks.   The percentage distribution of
population by race according to the 1951 census in the
Old and New Boroughs was as in Table 12.

Kuper (4) analysed the ecological distribution of
the population of Durban in 1951 into six sociographic
zones, each characterized by its distinctive racial,
linguistic, religious and socio-economic affiliations.
The ecological pattern defined for 1951 remained relatively consistent during the twenty-one year period
1940-60, population growth intensifying rather than
changing the pattern.   The forced uprooting of settled
Black communities since then from the valued central
zones and their resettlement beyond the city boundary,
have converted some of these into exclusive White
areas, and reduced the proportions of Blacks in others.
Had this not happened, the Black suicide rate for
1962-70 would in fact have been higher, for a number
of neighbourhoods which had high suicide rates during
1940-60 have disappeared and their populations have
been placed under the jurisdiction of adjacent magisterial areas.   An analysis of the ecological distribution of suicide in Durban for the last nine years
thus does not have the same meaning as the analysis
for the preceding twenty-one years and therefore the
relation of suicide to residential area in Durban has
been restricted to 1940-60.

SUICIDE RATE AND SOCIOGRAPHIC ZONES

The six sociographic zones identified by Kuper in 1951
were: Alluvial Flats, Peripheral, Inland Transitional,
Seaward Transitional, Seafront, and the Central Berea

Ridge.   The simplest index of the socio-economic
status of a zone in Durban is the proportion of its
White population; the higher that proportion, the
greater the prestige and the wealth of the area.
Thus the Central Berea Ridge with its high elevation,
scenic views and proximity to the central business area
was largely White in 1951 (88.59 per cent)   It also had
the highest income, and was the most desirable sociographic zone.   The Seafront zone (67.43 per cent
White) was next in the order of desirability, and the
Seaward Transitional zone (65.91 per cent White) third.
The three remaining zones were predominantly Black
during 1940-60.   The Inland Transitional zone (23.08
per cent White) was rated fourth, the Peripheral zone
(12.48 per cent White) fifth, and the Alluvial Flats
(4.69 per cent White) sixth.   The major portions of
these zones, because of their relative proximity to
the city, have since been declared White by law, and
their Black populations have been expelled beyond the
city's boundaries.   These zones once characterized by
high density have been converted into fields of demolished houses and empty shops and are sparsely populated
today by transitional populations of Blacks and Whites.
The Whites await better housing, the Blacks, housing in
the peripheral areas to which they will be removed.
The suicide rates in the six sociographic zones is
projected in Table 13.   The rate is comparatively low
in the three predominantly White zones, the average
rate being under 6.90 per 100,000 per annum for the
twenty-one year period.   There is a general pattern of
lower suicide rates in the more affluent, prestigious
White zones, and higher rates in the poorer and less
prestigious Black zones.

SUICIDE RATES, INCOMES AND HOUSING

The relation between high suicide rates and poor residential areas is generally corroborated for Whites and
Coloureds when the rates are compared with the per
capita incomes of these areas.   Low rates occur in
the high-income areas and high rates in the low-income
areas.   The pattern is not so clear for Indians among
whom low rates are also reflected in two low-income
areas and a high rate in the three highest income areas.
The high-income areas, were also racially mixed areas
and this condition may in itself have contributed to
the high rate, as is discussed a little later in this
chapter (see also Table 14).

The study reveals a correlation between poor housing and high suicide rates as is observed in Table 15. During 1940-60 45.5 per cent of the African suicides and 61.38 per cent of Indian suicides lived in shack-like slums.

By 1962, practically all African, and a substantial proportion of Indian, slums had been removed from Durban and its immediate environs and the larger proportion of their populations had been settled in municipal or industrial housing. The highest African and Indian suicide rates thus shifted to subsidised municipal housing and single person compounds which accounted for 61.5 per cent of the total African suicides (including almost 23 per cent about whose housing conditions no information was available). Improved housing units in themselves thus did not relieve suicides. Shack families, shifted to council housing, in fact found themselves in greatly impoverished circumstances, emotionally, because of the forced uprooting, and materially because of higher rentals and transport costs, and deterioration in public amenities. The suicide rate of the new Indian area of Chatsworth, during 1962-70 was higher than that of Riverside (largely shack), the Indian area with the highest suicide rate during 1940-60.

The highest percentage of Coloureds lived in slums during both periods, the percentage being higher during 1940-60 (51 per cent), when there were less municipal houses available, than during 1962-70 (47 per cent). Whites very rarely live in such conditions. Thus a negligible proportion of White suicides were recorded as living in slums and shacks. White slum suicides declined from 3.2 per cent during 1940-60, to 0.6 per cent during 1962-70. The largest proportion of White suicides lived in adequate private houses. The proportion of White suicides living in hotels and boarding houses is very high. This is due to the large number of aged White - often widowed - a large proportion of whom lived alone in the central business area of Durban. During 1940-60, 69 or 83.1 per cent of the total number of White suicides were committed in that area (tract 17). Tract 17 also returned the lowest mean and *per capita* incomes for Whites - £488 and £321 respectively. The small gap between the two incomes suggests a low dependency rate and a lower proportion of married White persons than in other areas. Residentially, it is an area of flats, boarding houses and cheaper hotels. During 1940-60 58 of the 69 suicides lived in such accommodation - 29 in flats, 24 in boarding houses, 5 in hotels.

SUICIDE RATES IN RACIALLY MIXED AREAS

A few mixed residential areas existed in Durban in 1951
and these revealed high rates for the relatively low-
income White groups that occupied these and low rates
for the relatively high-income Black groups.   Blacks
living in mixed areas had in fact 'penetrated' traditional White areas through economic achievement.   The
Whites who remained in the mixed areas did so because
they could not afford to move out into the exclusive
White areas.   Table 16 analyses the relation between
Black and White incomes and suicide rates in mixed
areas.

SUICIDE RATE AND DENSITY

Though density is not related to social status, the
expectation of a high suicide rate in high density
areas was not borne out in Durban, as is revealed in
Table 17.   A number of studies have demonstrated a
correlation between high density and a high suicide
rate.   The highest rate is usually recorded in the
central business district characterized by high density
and a high proportion of non-family, transitional residential population, living in boarding houses and cheap
hotels.
     The central business area has the highest density
in Durban and in census tract 17, closely corresponding
with it in the 1951 census, enumeration showed one of
the highest suicide rates during 1940-60.   The residential population is predominantly White in that area.
During 1940-60, almost 80 per cent of the population in
census tract 17 was White (0.7 per cent Indian, 0.13
per cent Coloured and 17.82 per cent African - the
African being in the main migrant males, housed
singly).   Generally however, as Table 17 indicates,
the expectation of a high suicide rate following high
density is not corroborated in Durban.   This is
because Blacks, who have high suicide rates are
excluded from the central business area.   Even the
12,000 Indians who are presently living in the central
Indian business complex will have to move in terms of
the new proclamation which has restricted the area to
Indian commerce.   The only large concentration of
Blacks tolerated near the centre of the city is the
dock workers engaged on a temporary basis and housed in
single men's compounds.   During 1940-60, the largest
proportion of suicides committed by Africans living
alone in Durban, occurred in this compound.

Since suicide in Durban is concentrated among Blacks, the rate is higher in the relatively sparsely populated Black areas on the periphery of the city.   In fact as the Black population is pushed further and further away from the boundaries of the city, the city's suicide rate declines and that of its satellites grows.   The Indian area of Chatsworth thus has a higher suicide rate today than the municipal area of Durban.
During 1940-60, the average population for the thirty-six census tracts was 11,176.   The average population in each of the Black, comparatively high suicide areas was below that average.   Only one census tract, no. 21 had a population of 10,158, the populations of the others ranging from 2,705 to 6,252.   The area with the highest suicide rate (tract 5) had the lowest population.   Similarly the four census tracts with the highest suicide rates had low densities in 1946, the highest being 6-12 persons per square mile in 1946.
On the other hand, six of the thirteen low suicide rate census tracts had a density of over twenty-five persons per square mile.
Low density suggests an easing of urban tensions and hence a decline in suicide rates.   It does not, however, necessarily suggest a decline in status.   In fact, the suicides in the central business area have low incomes, and low status by White standards.   In American and European cities, it is the upper income, middle classes that retreat into the suburbs.   Lower suburban rates in these countries, thus in fact, correlate with higher status, with the integrated family life of the middle classes and high rates occur in the central areas with their high proportion of disintegrated living patterns.   In Durban, poverty, slums, disintegration are pushed to the peripheries of the city into the Black townships with their high rates of violence.   Thus the suicide rate is higher on the outskirts of the city.   Though density of Black townships is lower than that of the central business area, it is inordinately higher today than that of the White residential areas.   Thus the ruling plot size in Chatsworth (population 160,000) is 25 × 90 sq. ft, that of Kwa Mashu (population 110,000) is 40 × 70 sq. ft, that of Umlazi (population 120,000) is 50 × 70 sq. ft.

9 Suicide, age, status and integration

In proposing that vulnerability to suicide increases
with the progressive action of social life, (1) Durkheim
in effect proposes that the higher the status of an age
category, the higher the suicide rate, for in his mind,
the greater the presence of society in a person the
greater his state of 'civilization' and social efficacy.
The process, however, does not go on endlessly and
Durkheim contends that society begins to recede from
the person with age as he withdraws from it, is less
involved in it and consequently less dependent upon it.
Henry and Short in a similar vein state that the suicide
of persons aged between 15 and 65 is more sensitive to
fluctuations in economic conditions than of persons
aged between 65 and 74, because of their subordinate
status. (2)   This theory has found some confirmation
in subsequent European and American studies. (3)

THE INCIDENCE OF SUICIDE IN RELATION TO AGE IN DURBAN

No common pattern defines the relation of suicide to
age in Durban; and more important, the suicide rate
does not increase with an increase in age and thereby,
increased participation in and control of social life.
This is shown in Tables 18 and 19.   The emergent
patterns are summarized in Tables 20 and 21 in terms of
broader age categories.   The Durkheimian pattern is
observed in only two of the eight projections - in the
cases of Indian and White men.   In the remaining six
projections, the patterns are erratic, Blacks generally
reflecting a tendency for higher rates in the relatively youthful (in whom society's presence according
to Durkheim, must be deemed to be lower), than in the
maturer, and more powerful age categories.   Thus

during 1940-60, young Indian girls between 15 and 19
years of age had a suicide rate of 57.6 per 100,000;
the rates of Coloured and African girls were also high
in this category.

The variation in the patterns by race and sex,
suggest the futility of pronouncing a single uniform
relation between age and suicide rate.   The evaluation
of component age categories is not the same in all cultures.   In simple self-subsistent agricultural
societies, characterized by low literacy and high
dependence on an oral tradition, the status of the aged
is high and their power and authority effective well
after the decline of their physical proficiency.
Their practical wisdom, their control over family
property, and often the belief that being on the threshold of death they are close to the supernatural and
will shortly become part of it, gives them significant
power and status.   In modern industrial society by
contrast, the aged are a liability, and far from being
a repository of knowledge, they are often out of touch
with the new and incapable of adjusting to it.   Consequently they are rejected, or tolerated for their
quaintness.   The economic status of the young adult,
particularly among the working classes, may even be
higher than that of the mature adults.   Among Durban
Blacks, the teenager, entering the market with some
skill, may begin on a higher notch than that reached
by his father after years of unskilled service.

Thus, if the aged in preliterate societies have low
suicide rates this may be due more to their prestigious
status in those societies than to the decline of
society in them.   Likewise, young adults are not
necessarily less involved, or less permeated with
society than mature adults – in fact the modern concern
of youth for social problems is often higher than that
of mature adults, as is demonstrated on University
campuses.

In Durban, the aged (70+) in fact had high suicide
rates in all age groups.   The reason for this is
probably simply due to the terrible experience of
social rejection they suffered.   That the old are
less active does not imply that they are less dependent
on the emotional support of society.   Their need for
love and companionship remains as acute.   It is too
simplistic to suggest that the greater the social
involvement, the greater the social responsibility and
the greater the vulnerability to suicide.   Suicide, also
according to Durkheim, occurs in that situation when
the responsibility is suddenly withdrawn, and thereby

the involvement suddenly ended.   In other words,
suicide is not so much dependent on the state of
social involvement, as in the condition of social
rejection.

Fundamentally, status is a complex of responsibilities
and privileges or rewards.   The absence of suicide
among children is not due to the lesser presence of
society in them, but due to their generally indulged
lives, and their relative freedom from responsibilities.
The old, by contrast, are worn out with responsibilities,
and at the same time sensitive to the cessation of
rewards in a society dominated by able-bodied adults.
Their high rate is not due to the fact that society is
receding from them, but due to their continuing need
for society, social security, and the withdrawal of
factors satisfying these needs.   The high suicide rate
of the aged in Durban is thus due to the less gratifying
and less fulfilling nature of their social roles.

The relatively high suicide rate of young Blacks is
probably due to the premature imposition of adult responsibilities upon them.   Faced with poverty and
deprived of free and compulsory education, they are
dirven by economic pressures to seek gainful employment,
yet they are not accepted as social adults.   Their
position is probably aggravated when their assumption
of adult roles is not compensated with adult prestige.

10 Occupation, status and integration

Elwin Powell (1) analyses the central sociological thesis of suicide to be that its nature and incidence varies with social status, and concludes that by implication this means occupational status, since occupation is the most important single factor in social status. The primary fact of occupation in the evaluation of status is implicit in practically every sociological study.

Ruth Cavan states that there is no magic in any profession which causes or prohibits suicide but that 'the factor of social disorganization is more prevalent in some occupations than in others'. (2)   Jack P. Gibbs and Walter T. Martin emphasize that the suicide rate is related to the degree of status integration, thereby implying the degree to which the systems of status an individual is called upon to occupy simultaneously are compatible with one another. (3)

Powell emphasizes the prime function of occupation in status and says that occupation both by selection and by the nature of the role itself, tends to create either a *dissociated* or an *enveloped* 'selfless' personality.   He sees the status of the adult White male in America as primarily dependent on occupation, and states that it is through work that most men relate themselves to the world.   Though work does not provide immunity to suicide, he demonstrates that occupations have specific suicide potentials, which produce varying degrees of anomie.

While the modern concept of anomie is essentially derived from Durkheim, it differs subtly in implications.   Durkheim saw anomie as a life pattern, which becomes meaningless in the absence of social controls directing it to meaningful goals.   He conceived it as a condition particularly characteristic of high

status positions, the poor and the subordinated positions
being limited in their goals and means by those in
authority over them. (4)   Thus, by implication,
Durkheim restricted anomie to the wealthy and upper
classes.

Merton, extending the concept to a general theory of
deviant behaviour, sees anomie as a condition that
characterizes the whole fabric of competitive indus-
trialized society and interprets it as an imbalance
between socially structured goals and normatively
available means. (5)   He, however, theorizes that it
is the poorer classes who are more frequently exposed
to the frustrations of this discrepancy and postulates
an intensification of anomie among lower and poorer
status groups.

The difference in the two interpretations may be
explained as due to the fact that whereas Durkheim
considers an unequal society, Merton postulates a
democracy in which goals are shared in common - although
the means to their achievement are not equally available.

Powell (6) defines anomie specifically in terms of
integration of the self.   His theory is a more direct
restatement on a personality level of Durkheim's very
general postulate that suicide varies with the degree
of integration of social groups. (7)   Powell seems to
conceive of integration entirely as integration in
occupational status, deeming this aspect of status to
be the most meaningful in the process of male self-
realization.

While Durkheim does not directly refer to integration
through occupation, he clearly implies this when he conceives anomie or social disintegration as the breaking
down of the occupational regimen 'which fixes with
relative precision the maximum degree of ease of
living to which each social class may legitimately
aspire.' (8)   Thus, though Durkheim does not elaborate
his concept of 'integration' he sees it ultimately in
terms of a particular role configuration.   His view
of integration is two-dimensional: integration of the
social structure, failure to achieve which results in
anomie; and integration of the individual within that
structure, failure to achieve which results in egoism
and altruism.

Anomie is now commonly viewed as a general state of
social disorganization in which members of society do
not sufficiently share a common system of norms.
Altruism and egoism are conceived as personal states
of anomie. (9)   Thus Powell conceives 'dissociation'
(egoism) and envelopment (altruism) as polar types of

anomie.   Both refer to personal states of malintegra-
tion due to the failure of the self.   Basing his interpretation on George H. Mead, (10), he views the self
as a dualism of the 'I' and the 'me', 'I' being the
equivalent of Id, and 'me' the equivalent of Ego, which
it calls into being in specific social roles.   Powell
thus defines anomie specifically as failure in the
integration of social roles, either through rejection
or faulty internalization of such roles, that is 'dissociation', or through over-internalization of such
roles, that is, 'envelopment'.   In the first case,
the 'I' fails to call into being the 'me' or social
self.   In the second, the emergence of the 'me' in the
process of socialization is so strong as to suppress
the 'I'.   The personality in both cases is defective.

This is essentially a Freudian concept of social
man, the dualism of which is also present in Durkheim,
who says that social man superimposes himself upon
physical man in response to the demands of the social
environment which arouses sentiments of sympathy and
solidarity and fashions him in its own image. (11)
Powell sees the image reflected in social roles.

This leads to his assertion that each role (i.e.
occupational state) is characterized by its own anomie-
producing potential, the intensity of which is determined by the degree to which the individual integrates
the success ideology dominating the entire occupational
structure.

Powell's theory supports the construction of five
occupational typologies, each of which is differently
related to the anomie continuum, which, in turn, determines its suicide rate.   In Tulsa County of Oklahoma,
the relation of suicide to occupation during the
period 1937-46 was as in Table 22.   Powell finds that
sales and clerical and skilled occupations are characterized by high status integration, and thus relatively
low suicide rates, whereas the professional, managerial
and unskilled at the poles have low status integration,
and thus high suicide rates.

Durkheim and a significant number of researchers
have found high social status to be correlated with
low social integration and consequently high suicide
rates.   Commerce, industry and the liberal professions
have been observed to have higher rates than agricultural occupations; workers have been observed to have
lower rates than employers and persons with independent
means.   Durkheim states: 'The possessors of most
comfort suffer most.   Everything that empowers subordination, attenuates the effects of this state'. (12)

Louis Dublin, agreeing with him, states that the relatively low suicide rate among workers confirms that
self-destruction is more prevalent among intellectuals
and the wealthy. (13)   Henry and Short maintain that
susceptibility to suicide rises with status position,
that suicide is more common among the downtrodden, and
that data from life insurance companies show that it
is concentrated among the well-to-do. (14)   Austin L.
Porterfield and Jack P. Gibbs establish that upper-
class fathers produce more than their proportion of
suicidal sons and that the suicide rate is significantly
higher among persons of higher prestige. (15)

Merton, in contrast to these findings and in accordance with his concept of anomie, predicts high
suicide rates in low occupational rungs where members
are frustrated by the absence of institutionalized
means to pursue socially structured goals. (16)

Elwin Powell finds high rates at the occupational
poles, that is highest and lowest occupational categories.   This finding is corroborated by Doric M. Jean
in his study of suicide in France. (17)

SUICIDE BY OCCUPATIONAL STATUS IN DURBAN

Any investigation into the occupational status of
suicides in Durban is hazardous, since such knowledge
is gained by implication rather than by direct evidence.
This is due to the fact that the coroner's evidence
very rarely lists occupation as a formally noted
fact. (18)

In this study, evidence of witnesses and the suicide's
residential area have been used as indications of occupational position, where no more specific information
was available.   Whereas information on the occupational
status of Whites is reasonably accurate, that on
Blacks is subject to some error, particularly when a
distinction is made between skilled and semi-skilled
occupations of Indians and Africans.   Nevertheless,
the results are a fair indication of the distribution
of suicide in each listed occupational category.
This distribution is observed in Tables 23 and 24.

SUICIDES OF MEN BY OCCUPATIONAL STATUS

The occupational categories listed in South African
census reports were classified into six occupational
classes and analysed with reference to their relation

to male suicides by race in Durban.   The results can
be seen in Table 25. (19)   The only broad generalization that can be abstracted from this table is that
while among Whites there is a tendency for high rates
to occur in high-status occupations, among Blacks the
reverse trend generally holds.   This tendency becomes
more marked when the numerous occupations are combined
and classified into two broad dimensions of manual and
non-manual as observed in Table 26.

SUICIDE OF UNEMPLOYED AND RETIRED MEN AND WOMEN

If the postulate that occupation constitutes the basic
index of status integration for men in an industrial
economy is accepted, (20) then the logical conclusion
follows that absence or deprivation of occupation
results in loss of status integration or, more simply,
loss of status.   Accordingly the unemployed (21) and
the retired may be viewed as living in conditions of
anomie.   Elwin Powell reports the suicide rate of
retired men in Tulsa County between 1936 and 1956 to
be five times higher than that of the entire male population and twice that of all men of the same age
group. (22)
    Comparative suicide rates for retired, unemployed
and employed men and women are as in Table 27.   The
validity of the estimates is entirely dependent on
the accuracy of the census figures, which are particu-
largly questionable with regard to employment. (23)
The migrant labour condition of the African implies
that these are incomplete in this respect, since the
old retire in the 'homelands' and the unemployed are
endorsed out.
    With the exception of Coloured men, the suicide
rates of the retired and unemployed are generally
higher than that of the employed, the rates in these
categories being particularly high for Indian and
White men.   It is however difficult to attribute the
high rates to the conditions of unemployment and retire-
ment in themselves, since the retired are also the
aged, and the aged have a high suicide rate.   The
unemployment are often also alcoholics and emotionally
disturbed persons.

SUICIDE AND OCCUPATIONAL STATUS OF WOMEN

In South African society gainful employment is not the
essential source of social well-being for women as it
is for men. Women constituted 24.1 per cent of the
economically active population in 1970, and they were
concentrated in the main in the lowest categories of
employment, being in most cases pushed into these by
sheer economic necessity. Of the total economically
active population in each race group, African women
constituted 22.8 per cent, White 27.6 per cent,
Coloured 34 per cent and Indian 11 per cent. White
women alone may be said to be favourably related to
the work situation, work being light and in pleasant
surroundings with relatively good salaries even in
semi-skilled and unskilled positions. 'Fulfilment'
through gainful employment for women is probably
restricted to the professional and semi-professional
employment and, to a lesser extent, to upper admini-
strative and managerial positions. Even in these the
traditional attitude that the home, family, children
and domesticity in general are her 'natural' pursuits
conspires against gainful employment providing a fundamental source of fulfilment. The career woman is
often oppressed by pangs of conscience for deserting
her 'natural' role. This is particularly marked among
Indian and African women in Durban who rarely succeed
in seeing themselves in roles other than those of
mothers and wives and who consequently find difficulties
in integrating roles of gainful employment. Their
problems are aggravated by the fact that in both these
communities, women lose status through gainful employment, unless they are employed in prestigious professional, semi-professional or executive posts.
     One would thus assume that, for women, the status
of a housewife would carry a high potential for status
integration, whereas gainful employment would expose
them to anomie. In Durban this is confirmed among
Indian women alone, among whom the gainfully employed
have a higher suicide rate than housewives. This
corroborates the dim view Indian society continues to
take in respect of the gainful employment of women
and accounts for their vey low involvement in gainful
employment. The girl who goes out to work is looked
upon with suspicion. Her need to seek employment is
not observed as a desire for self-fulfilment, but is
seen as failure on the part of the family to integrate
her into her traditional role. While it may be
accepted as the last resort of a family to solve its

economic problem, it exposes the woman to loss of
prestige, since material considerations have clearly
taken precedence over valued traditional ones. In a
society where marriage continues to be considered the
safeguard of feminine virtue, and the legitimate
means through which she earns material comforts, the
employed woman finds herself an outcast, whom respectable suitors in marriage are advised to avoid, and
prospective mothers-in-law exclude. The comparative
mean suicide rates for housewives and gainfully occupied women are observed in Table 28.

Occupation is the most important single factor
determining social status because it is the most
acceptable form of self-expression and the most valued
channel of interpersonal relations. The very concept
of rights and obligations, of reciprocal relations,
implies an exchange of labour or the rewards of labour.
An Indian proverb declares: 'It is not you who are
loved, it is your work that is loved.' Marx sees
alienation of the self intrinsically as alienation of
one's work from one's self. Homans traces the whole
constellation of social relations to economic 'interaction', or interaction in the 'external system' as
he defines it. It is through work that man projects
himself and it is through the value of his work to
others that he is accepted, integrated and loved by
his fellow men in society. The relationship between
a married couple finally breaks down when the expected
work contribution of either falters. Sex is not
sufficient in itself to sustain marriage, and marriage
will often persist despite sexual infidelity because
of the reciprocal work relation.

But while work is the essence of interpersonal
relations and consequently status, there is no universal relation between a particular occupation and a
particular suicidal tendency. The suicide potential
of a common occupation will differ for different
cultures and with time, in the same culture. This is
due, first, to the fact that the evaluation of occupations is neither universal nor constant. Thus
commerce, considered evil and parasitic in mediaeval
Christian civilization gained high status in the sixteenth century and paved the way for modern capitalism.
Second, individuals in all social systems occupy a
multiplicity of social roles, each in turn valued for
their social usefulness. The stress that a person
suffers is hence not so much a function of a particular
occupational role, but, as Martin and Gibbs postulate,
the state of compatibility obtaining within a constella-

tion of roles an individual is required to occupy
simultaneously in a specific social structure. (24)
Thus proclivity to suicide will be high if there is
conflict between roles within a constellation, regardless of whether the person occupies a high occupational
position or low one. The conflict in turn is derived
from the conflicting demands or controls that each
role exercises on the status. Hence the suicide or
anomie rate is not so much dependent on the degree of
restraint to which a person is subjected in a particular role as to the conflict in the opposing restraints
of his multiple roles. While occupational status
possesses the vital capacity to restrict or expand the
scope of social relations it does not in itself determine role conflict. Upper class persons may be
freer to relate themselves to others on their own
terms and having greater choice of interaction, may
be more protected from role conflict. On the other
hand their network of interaction may become severely
restricted through fear of competition from both those
who are in the same class as themselves and those below
them. They have too much and must constantly guard
what they have. Also while they may have greater
power to avoid situations of conflict, they probably
have lower resistance to its disintegrative force when
faced with a sudden confrontation. The lower classes
are possibly more inured to such upheavals and thus it
is that Henry and Short find in Chicago that 'persons
subjected to the deprivations of low economic status
indexed by low rentals, are better protected from
suicide accompanying cycles of business, than those who
have risen to high economic positions'. (25)
    Durkheim's postulate that the upper classes are more
prone to anomie and egoism because they are less restrained by social regulations is questionable. It is
highly probable that the élite are in effect required
to integrate social controls to a greater extent, being
the 'culture bearers' and hence the leaders and repos-
itories of social traditions. George Homans contends
that leaders are leaders by virtue of the fact that
they uphold more precisely group norms. (26) Thus,
by implication, they are more prone to role conflict.
The intellectual may have abandoned traditional
beliefs, and the industrialist may have abandoned
regulations that restrict his economic expansion, but
this does not in itself imply that they are without
regulations or that the regulations are not in conflict.
The upper classes possess the prerogative of invention
and if they are found to be more prone to disregarding

old regulations, it is only because they find those
regulations no longer functional and they have new ones
to replace them with.   Durkheim himself states that
'knowledge is not sought as a means to destroy accepted
opinions, but because their destruction has already
commenced'. (27)   It is invariably the élite who ring
out the old, but the old is rung out with some appre-
ciation of the incoming new.   Hence the upper class
is less likely to pass through an interim of no regula-
tion.   By contrast, the lower classes are more vulnerable to loss of norms since they are less familiar
with the new, and less well equipped to make the
necessary adjustment.

The position of the upper classes is thus probably
not so frustrating as Durkheim defines it to be.
'Envelopment', (28) 'egoism' and 'anomie' (29) are
conditions to which they may be exposed, but it seems
unlikely that as a result they have a greater proclivity for social alienation and suicide.   They are the
free people, free in the sense that they exercise a
greater freedom of choice both in social means and
goals.   In fact, it is more likely that it is the
subordinate classes who are more exposed to anomie,
trapped as they are in the mesh of social regulations
from which there is no escape.

Durkheim conceives egoism and anomie as inherent in
this very freedom of choice available to the upper
classes.   'Those who have empty space above them are
almost inevitably lost in it, for no force restores
them.' (30)   The space, however, is not necessarily
empty.   Science has expanded the vista of man's
concrete achievements to such an extent that his
goals are well nigh limitless.   The problem is one of
a more equitable distribution of opportunities, so
that they may filter through to the lower ranks, more
perceptibly.

The point to emphasize is that while frustration is
common to all classes and persons, its source differs
for different social and cultural categories.   In
South Africa the opportunities by tradition and law
for filling the different occupational rungs are not
equally distributed throughout the four race groups
and hence they have not developed equal attitudes to
them.   It is reasonable to assume that the prestige
rating of a particular class or occupation is in the
first place influenced by the extent to which that
category or class of occupation is observably present
within the hierarchical system of that society.   The
managerial occupational class cannot have the same

significance for Africans among whom it is barely
existent as it would among Whites and Indians in Durban.
Its vague existence implies in effect that it only
exists as an economic status and has not consolidated
itself as a 'social class' in which the various
statuses, which the individual occupies simultaneously
have taken on a functionally related and differentiated
meaning.   Socially, the professional remains a part
of the working class society differentiated from it
only by material externals.   His is an aggravated
marginal situation, that is, a situation of role conflict, for he can identify neither with traditional
standards, or the standards of the economically
deprived.   He aspires towards the affluent models
that he can afford to purchase, but does not have the
opportunities to do so; so that there is little he can
do apart from buying a car, or extending his house, to
project his affluence.   He is excluded from the ego-
expanding resources of parallel Indians, Coloureds and
Whites.   His intellectual and cultural aspirations
depend on the good graces of Indians who take him into
consideration when organizing social events, and who
have segregated him in their cinemas, at times voluntarily in the past and by law in the present.   While
White theatrical companies apply for and often receive
permission to play before Coloured and Indian audiences,
the African is ignored, and he is excluded from the
Durban City Hall as a rule.   Unless he becomes a
leader of the African proletariat and thereby secures
an integrated élite status within the hurly-burly of
African society, life for the upper-class African is
so dismal that it all too easily drives him to the
bottle.   African lawyers and doctors in particular
suffer high rates of alcoholism.   The fact that the
Durban study shows no suicide rates for Africans in
the two upper occupational categories should not be
construed to imply a uniformly happy state of affairs
in these.
    Since suicide is believed to decline with increase
in integration, one might have expected that gainfully
employed Blacks, constituting a large and fairly
undifferentiated labour force would benefit from the
integrative qualities of that experience alone.
Durkheim considered the occupational group, endowed
with political status, to be particularly cohesive,
holding that its capacity for cohesion, in some respects superseded even that of religion, family and the
state, when empowered with political status since it
permeated the whole of life and thereby constituted

the richest channel for a common life. (31)   Implicit
in this observation is of course the positive role of
large numbers in generating social solidarity.   Marx
saw the condition for a massive unity in the shared
work experiences of the lower classes.   Yet the Black
rate by occupation is higher in the manual occupational
rung which involves the mass of Black workers.   Perhaps Weber is correct when he states that the great
mass of workers are as much motivated by factors or
urban achievement and competition as any other status
group, and rather than integration within a deprived
working class, they seek liberation from it and entry
into higher social strata.   However this does not
exclude the validity of the Marxist expectation, that
depressed workers will combine to lift themselves out
of their depression through joint action.

Neither does it negate the importance of numbers in
the process of social integration.   It is clear from
Durkheim's analysis that integration is not implicit
in numbers, but that numbers provide a potential for
integration provided other conditions are present, the
most crucial being intensity and duration of interaction.

The word 'anomie' in the modern context implies a
loose social structure which is incapable of integrating its members.   On the individual level, integration proceeds from the harmony obtaining between an
individual's image of himself, and the image the group
has of him.   The relatively high suicide rate of
Blacks in subordinate occupational status may well be
due to the inherent disparity between these images.
On the one hand, there is the Black's 'dream image'
of himself as a free personality.   On the other, he
is continually reminded of his subservient position
emphasized by White superordinate authority.   In
Durban it may well be that the hitherto successful
power of White domination has prevented the Black from
developing a self-sufficient integrated image of himself as a Black.   The acceptance of Black inferiority,
hard to escape in the face of constant material and
psychological suggestions, has counteracted the force
of internal group cohesion.   African nationalism and
the present Black consciousness movement by contrast
have the potential for liberating confidence and pride
in the internal Black system, providing a strong
integrative force and promoting a new image of the
African personality, which no longer hankers after
unattainable White goals but pursues real Black ones.

CONCLUSIONS

The variations in the patterns of suicide by race or
culture in Durban suggest that each society, by social
prescription, determines its areas of conflict and
the modes whereby such conflicts may be resolved.   It
simultaneously determines the occasions for suicide
and the frequency with which it may be resorted to.
Component members, responding to social suggestion,
generally express their aggressions in directions and
manners prescribed by the group.   While on the one
hand there is pressure to adjust, there is, on the
other, the recognition that friction can become irre-
concilable, and there is an alement of condonation of
the deviant acts which may ensue, such acts being in
effect socially suggested, and extenuated by the
common remark, 'What could you expect under the
circumstances?'

The observed suicide patterns in Durban in relation
to race, sex, age, religion, residential areas, income
and occupation, do not corroborate the association of
a high suicide rate with high status and consequently
low integration and low social control as proposed by
Durkheim and supported by a number of sociologists
since.   It at the same time emphasizes the futility
of drawing universal generalizations from monocultural
data.

The key factor in suicide as in all social relations
is 'integration', or the prevailing state of accord
between the needs, aspirations, attitudes and values
of the person and that of his group.   The greater the
community of interests between these two interacting
parties, the greater the state of integration.   Common
sense suggests that the suicide rate is related to
status, since integration, social and personal, can
only take place through role playing, or more simply,
relating one's self to other selves.   Roles in turn
are structured and thereby differentially and unequally
rated.   The integration capacity of a role and consequently status, is neither universal nor constant in
a particular society.   High status may well be less
integrative in some social situations than low status,
and produce greater stress and greater suicide, but
the reverse is also true as is demonstrated by the
Durban data.

The theory that there is a positive correlation
between external critical restraint, high integration
and low suicide is dubious.   Although social restraint,
that is discipline and control, facilitates integration

of social norms, restraint and integration are in fact
contradictory.   Whereas integration in the context of
accord between self and society is self-operative,
restraint is external and imposed and there is resistance and resentment against it which, if blocked
expression, builds up great internal tension and
threatens explosion.   Restraint or repression is
never internalized.   What is internalized is the
rationalization, often religious, which helps the victim
to cope with restraint/repression and the rationalization is integrated only because it transforms restraint.
Restraint/repression, unrelieved by such transformation,
would thus aggravate suicide, integration inhibit it.

part three

Suicide and other social factors

11 Marital status, family and suicide

Bertillon (1) and Morselli (2) writing in the nineteenth century found that marriage and the family restrained suicide. Researchers writing since, including Durkheim have confirmed this. Durkheim agreed with Morselli, that it is not marriage in itself 'conjugal society', as he called it, that provides immunity against suicide but the integrative force exerted on its members by the family. Thus, he observed that childlessness actually aggravated suicide among married women. He found that childless married women in the French Departments and Prussian provinces had higher suicide rates than spinsters. He also observed that the suicide rate declined in widowhood when there were children. He accordingly postulated: 'Suicide varies inversely with the degree of integration of domestic society', (3) and elaborated:

(a) Married persons from the age of 20 years onwards enjoy a co-efficient of preservation against suicide. (4)

(b) Parenthood increases the co-efficient of preservation, the proclivity increasing with the density of the family. (5)

(c) Widowhood diminishes the co-efficient of preservation, but rarely eliminates it. (6)

(d) Divorce aggravates the tendency to suicide. (7)

(e) The preservative effect of marriage on suicide is greater for men than for women.

He interpreted the high suicide rate of the never-married to be due to the dual effects of egoism and anomie. (8) Marriage, he proposed, regulated human sexual energy, which otherwise would be dissipated in a limitless and thus helpless pursuit of unattainable gratifications.   The unmarried adults, he suggested, were also more prone to egoism since they were not subjected to the social regulations structuring intensive interaction. (9)   The early researchers observed the widowed and divorced to have even higher suicide rates than the single. (10)

Durkheim summarized his findings on marital states and family thus:

(a)   Widowed persons commit more suicide than married persons but generally less than unmarried persons. (11)

(b)   Men find widowhood and divorce more distressing than women. (12)

(c)   Divorce is the most distressing of all marital conditions. (13)

(d)   Widowed and divorced persons with children commit less suicide than those without children.   He found in his investigations that widows with children committed less suicide than the married without children. (14)

Subsequent studies have tested postulates (a) and (b).   The first aspect of (a), viz. that the widowed have a higher suicide rate than the married, is generally confirmed.   The second, that the married have a lower rate than the single is however, not commonly confirmed.   An exception is found in Gibbs's analysis of American statistics for the year 1949-50, where he finds that from the thirty-fifth year, the widowed have lower rates than the single. (15)   Postulates (b) and (c) are generally confirmed. (16)

If one interprets the relation between marital status and suicide as a function of anomie, then one must expect increase in suicide with increase in sexual anomie.   Thus the greater the freedom in sex, the greater the tendency to suicide.   The least restrained are unmarried men of mature sexual development. Their suicide rate should thus be higher than that of the divorced or widowed.   However, even in terms of Durkheim's own observations, divorced men have a higher suicide rate than the single.   There is no reason to explain why the salutary effects of marriage, which according to Durkheim, persist in widowhood, should not likewise do so in divorce.

Henry and Short also interpret suicide in these two marital statuses as due to different causes.   However, their purpose in doing so is primarily to explain the higher rate for divorced persons.   They explain the high suicide rate in widowhood as due to weakening of the relational system constituted by marriage.   In divorce, this factor is combined with an additional psychological condition. Suicide, they maintain, is the response of a highly developed superego incapable of resorting to 'other-directed' aggression when aroused, because of its strong internalization of external restraints. A highly developed superego associated with strong guilt feelings is the product of love-orientated techniques of discipline. Aggression is inhibited and preferably self-directed, because experience has proved that its 'other-direction' frustrates the flow of love. In divorce, they explain, an act of aggression is enacted against the source of love which as a result dries up. The victim thus becomes forewarned. The act of aggression in divorce does not necessarily imply loss of emotional satisfaction, that is, love; that loss has already occurred in marriage itself, when at least one partner, the one who initiates the act of aggression finds that the relationship is not emotionally satisfying. Divorce is an attempt to escape this sterile situation and seek satisfaction elsewhere. Henry and Short's identification of the relation of mutual support between husband and wife with that of parents and children is ill-conceived. Whereas there can be no substitute for the socially internalized idea of biological parenthood, marriage partners who are not bound by consanguinity may be relatively easily replaced.

Scholars, analysing European and American statistics, have confirmed that the divorced have higher suicide rates than the widowed. (17) The reason may well be due to the social attitudes to divorce and widowhood. In the case of widowhood, an intensive collective attempt is made to give sympathy and support. Thus the shock of the private breach is partially alleviated by the group, which adopts the attitude that, in effect, no breach has occurred; the indivudal has submitted to an Act of God. Associates and friends abstract the approved attributes of the dead one and present these to the remaining spouse in an immortalized form, so that he may live with pleasant memories. Although temporary in nature, the effect of public goodwill and positive sanction provides relatively permanent moral support. The widowed and orphaned, are subjects of public concern and sympathy. By contrast, in divorce a private breach is exposed to public condemnation. This not only magnifies the breach and its attendant insecurities, but similarly exposes the parties to self-recrimination. There is a shattering of the self image, and stimulation of feelings of

shame and moral guilt.   Public opinion deplores it,
and even sociology defines it as deviant behaviour.

MARITAL STATUS OF THE DURBAN SUICIDES

Data from the Durban Inquest Court proceedings confirm
the tremendous limitations of official documents for
purposes of sociological interpretation.   Never the
less, while it is not possible to apply empirical
tests, derived from the Durban data, to all of
Durkheim's postulates, it is possible to assess the
relationship between suicide and the more common
marital categories - as the married, never-married,
widowed and divorced - distinguishing this by race and
by sex and also combining the variables of marital
status and age.   It is not possible to examine con-
clusively the effects of family size or density on
suicide since the available information is far too inadequate.   The data permit of a limited examination of
the effects of early marriage on suicide and of
Durkheim's interesting postulate that men gain more
from marriage than do women.
    The Durban Inquest Court does not specifically
seek information on the marital status and family conditions of suicides.   Consequently, no uniform and
direct information is available on this factor.   However, sufficient inferential knowledge emerges from
the detailed reading of the records to construct a
fairly accurate picture of this relationship.   The
data are analysed in greater detail for the period
1940-60 than for the subsequent nine years.
    Census reports use four basic categories to define
marital status - married, never-married, widowed, and
divorced.   The 1951 Census report includes the additional category of 'living together' for Coloureds and
Africans.   These classifications are inadequate and
thus remarried, separated and deserted have been added
to this list.   In 1940-60, the categories of 'no
relatives at time of death', 'alone in urban situation',
and 'living under celibate conditions' are additional
categories.   The first of these latter three refers
to suicides whose records make no references to any
close relatives and who, at the time of death, appeared
to have been without any kin.   The second refers
specifically to Africans about whom no information is
available other than that they lived alone in their
workplaces.   They may well have had families in the
reserves.   The third category includes those suicides

who at the time of death were institutionalized - in hospitals as chronic patients, or in prisons, or living in single men's quarters, or in military service. The precise nature of their marital conditions is not known, but it is clear that they were not living a normal family life. If these additional categories are not used, a fairly large number of male suicides is lost in the category of 'unknown'.

The fact that a man is married is not important in itself. The fact that he is married and involved in family interaction is of prime importance. Sociologically, the migrant labourer without any family bonds in his immediate setting, the soldier on long service, the prisoner and the chronic patient, are all persons for whom their family status has limited meaning.

Information on marital status was available for 89.2 per cent of the total number of suicides, during 1940-60 and approximately 93 per cent of the cases during 1962-70.

Since comparative census figures of marital status of the total South African population are available in respect of only the four categories of married, never-married, widowed or divorced, the calculation of the suicide rate is restricted to these categories. Never the less, an examination of the distribution of suicide in the 1,194 cases in terms of the eleven categories is useful.

THE SUICIDE RATE OF THE MARRIED, NEVER-MARRIED, WIDOWED AND DIVORCED IN DURBAN

The general assumption is that married persons of 20 years and over have lower suicide rates than the never-married of 20 years and over. At the same time, teenage marriages have been observed to aggravate suicide. (See Tables 29 and 30.)

Table 31 projects the suicide rate by marital status during 1940-60 and 1962-70 for the married, never-married, widowed and divorced. Contrary to predictions, the married over the age of 20 do not always have a lower suicide rate than the never-married. Thus married White women, African men and women and Coloured women have higher rates than the never-married. Neither do the divorced always have the highest rates. In fact no suicides of divorced Indian women, Coloured men and African men and women were recorded during 1940-60. Coloured women alone had the highest rate in the divorced category, but then White women had the

lowest rate in that category.   Among Indian and White
men the widowed and not the divorced had the highest
suicide rate; among African women the never-married
had the highest rate.

The data do not establish any firm pattern by sex
either.   According to the Durkheim postulate, the
suicide rate of the 'never-married' men over the age
of 20, and of divorcees and widowers ought to have
been higher than that of the women in these categories.
Among Whites and Indians, men had higher rates than
the women in all four categories; among Africans,
women had higher rates than Coloured men in all but
the never-married category.   Thus the data refute
the notion that men are more dependent on marriage
than women.

Suicide, marital status and sex

The fact that in Durban in the 'living together' category, women commit suicide more than twice as often as
men suggests that women, as was originally proposed by
Bertillon, have greater need for institutionalized
marriage.   This refutes Durkheim's contention that
marriage was designed for the benefit of men, which
women enter with sacrifice to themselves.   Marriage
provides the necessary control over male sexuality,
which otherwise would run into excess and therefore
anomie.   He considered women's sexuality to be less
intellectual and more instinctive than men's and conclude from this that they therefore need   less control than men.   One has the impression from Durkheim
that women derive no benefit from marriage and that
marriage is opposed to their well-being.   Thus, whereas
men find refuge in marriage, women are shackled by
it. (18)

One may agree with Durkheim that the institution of
marriage is a social invention that operates in favour
of men, but one can hardly accept his explanation that
it does so because it restrains their sex life.   Polygamy is fairly common in human societies, and in its
absence extramarital sex for men is widely tolerated,
as Durkheim himself observed. (19)   Marriage is very
probably a male invention, but its purpose could hardly
have been to save him from sexual anomie, but more
plausibly, to entrench his paternity and with it the
attendant prestige, power and emotional well-being.
Without it the male could not have devised the power
of the patriarch, king and God.   The fact of the

situation is that today, in practically all cultures,
the woman and not the man is more dependent on marriage,
both emotionally and materially, society having con-
spired thus against her and having defined all
sanctioned female aspirations within its frame.
Spinsterhood is consequently dreaded, while bachelor-
hood may be enjoyed with prestige and without sexual
repression to the threshold of old age.   While the
modern woman may indulge in extramarital relations to
the same extent as the man, she does not yet succeed
in doing so without some measure of social censure.

Conclusions

If the relation of suicide to marital status is distinctive for the sexes, the reasons will have to be sought
elsewhere than in their different needs for marriage.
Likewise, if it is confirmed that the divorced have the
highest suicide incidence of all marital status, explanations in terms of 'anomie' or greater inner direction
of aggression are not adequate.
     The data in Durban thus do not establish the fairly
common generalizations that marriage restrains suicide,
and that the divorced have higher rates than the
widowed.   Though married Indian men and women and
married Coloured and White men have lower suicide rates
than the never-married, over the age of 20, married
Africans, both men and women, and married White and
Coloured women over 20 have higher suicide rates than
the never-married.   The data, while eluding any
reliable generalizations on the incidence of suicide
among the divorced and widowed, do not confirm that the
divorced state is most vulnerable to suicide.

SUICIDE - MARITAL STATUS AND AGE

(a) Observed patterns

Durkheim made three postulates on the relation of
suicide to age in marital status.   First he maintained
that 'too early marriages have an aggravating influence
on suicide especially on young men'. (20)   Thus he
postulated that the preservative effect of marriage
begins after the twentieth year.   His second postulate
is that the preservative effect of marriage is not the
same in all age categories.   He found it to be
strongest between the ages of 25 and 30 years in France

and between 30 and 40 years in Oldenburg, and noted that
its preservative effect declined thereafter in both
cases though a slight rise occurred in the final period
of life. (21)   Durkheim thus traced a trend in which
younger married persons between the ages of 25 and 30
years, or 30 and 40 years had a high rate, followed by
a drop and then a rise.   Third, he postulated that
married persons of both sexes over the age of 20 commit
suicide less often than the single.   His analysis of
French statistics for the period 1889-91 confirmed this
trend for men and women of 20 years and over in each age
category. (22)
    Henry and Short also confirm this trend in their
analysis of American suicide statistics for 1940. (23)
In addition Gibbs indicates that the differences between
the rates of the married and single also increases with
age.   Thus whereas in the 25-34 age category, the
single committed approximately one-fifth more suicide
than the married, in the 65-69 age category, they committed twice as much suicide as the married of the same
age.

SUICIDE, MARITAL STATUS AND AGE IN DURBAN

(a)   Early marriage

Generally, early marriage does not have an aggravating
influence on suicide in Durban.   This is particularly
evident in the case of young married men (15-19 age
group), among whom there were no suicides.   Married
Indian women were the only exception, those between
15-19 having a suicide rate of almost 40 per 100,000,
but the single Indian women in this age range had even
a higher rate, 43 per 100,000.   Durkheim's postulate
on the aggravations of early marriage thus does not
find confirmation in Durban.

(b)   Suicide rate by marital status and age

No discernable pattern is observed in the relation of
suicide to each age category - the rates fluctuate in
all cases.   The suicide patterns of married persons
by age fail to corroborate the postulates of Durkheim
and Gibson.   The White pattern comes closest to the
trend observed by Gibson in America.   There is a
general tendency among both sexes for suicide to
increase with age, this being more pronounced for men
than for women.   During 1940-60, 75.8 per cent of

suicides of White married men were committed between
the ages of 35 and 69.   The highest suicide rates,
however, occurred between the age groups of 45 and 70
years and over.   Likewise, whereas 76.7 per cent of
the suicides of married White women occurred between
35 and 59 years of age, the highest rates occurred
between 45-49 and 60 years and over.

Black married women had higher rates in the relatively youthful periods of life (see Tables 32 and 33).
The six married Coloured women suicides were all
between 25 and 44 years old.   Of the suicides of
married women 76.6 per cent Indian and 87 per cent
African fell in the 15-19 and 70+ age categories, and
of married African women in the 15-24 age category.

The suicide rate of Black married men appears to be
erratic, higher rates occurring in extreme old age.'
Indian men had high rates in addition in the 20-29 and
40-49 age categories.   In no age category do the
married have lower rates than the never-married, as is
observed by Durkheim and others.   Married Africans
and Coloureds have higher rates than the never-married
in the earlier age categories - Indian between 15 to
29 years, African between 15 and 34 years;   married
Whites have higher suicide rates than the never-
married from 34-70 age categories.   Never-married
Coloured men have higher suicide rates than the married;
married Coloured women have higher rates than the
never-married.

(c)   Suicide of the widowed and divorced by age in
Durban

While Gibbs's (24) data indicate a fairly even distribution of suicides throughout the age categories for
the widowed, they indicate an increase in suicide with
increase in age.   The data also indicate that,
whereas the widowed tend to commit more suicide than
the single in early marriage between 20 and 34 years,
they commit less suicide than the never-married in
later years of marriage.   This tends to confirm
Durkheim's hypothesis of the beneficial effects of
marriage and family life which extend into widowhood.
Gibbs also confirms the Durkheim finding that the
divorced commit more suicide than any of the other
marital categories in all age groups.

The number of divorced persons who committed suicide
in Durban according to available information is so
small, that it would be pretentious to try to establish
any generalizations about their age distribution.

In the study there were only fourteen suicides of
divorced men (12 White, 2 Indian) and four of divorced
women (2 White, 2 Coloured).   From these limited
data, the only valid comparison of suicide rates of
divorced and widowed would be for White men (20 widowed,
12 divorced).   The relation of suicide to age does
not corroborate either the findings of Durkheim or the
two American studies.   The suicide rate of the widowed
was not evenly distributed throughout the age categories, but fluctuated sharply in the six out of ten
age categories where it occurred.   The suicide of the
divorced did not increase with age.   The highest
rates occurred in the 30-49 age categories.   They
declined thereafter and disappeared in the 70+ age
range.   The widowed did not have lower rates than the
never-married (in fact their rates are higher than
that of the never-married after the thirty-fourth
year).   Finally, the widowed White men, and not the
divorced, had the highest suicide rate in all age
categories.   There was a general tendency in Durban
for widowers to have a higher incidence of suicide in
the relatively youthful period of life.   Thus the
highest White incidence fell in the 25-29 age group,
and all cases of suicides of African widowers were
restricted to this age category.   By contrast,
Indian and White widows committed more suicide in
later years.   Thus the highest Indian rate fell in the
60-69 year age category and the highest White rate in
the 35-39 year age category.   The suicides of African
widows fell in the 50-59 year age category.   Among
Coloureds, however, it was the young widow, between 25
and 29 years of age, who had the highest suicide rate.
There were no suicides of Coloured widowers.

FAMILY STRUCTURE AND SUICIDE

Durkheim's final conclusion is that not only does the
family provide immunity against suicide, but that the
immunity increases with family size and density.
Apparently refuting Malthus's association of general
well-being with restriction in family size, he contends:
'Far from dense families being a sort of unnecessary
luxury appropriate only to the rich, they are actually
an indispensable staff of daily life.' (25)
He sees the large family as conducive to the growth
of the collective conscience and to the stimulation of
intensive interpersonal relations that draw members
together into firm and meaningful unions.   'Just as

the family is a powerful safeguard against suicide, so
the more strongly it is constituted, the greater its
protection.' (26)

Durkheim conceives family density to be constituted
by those persons who live together and who actively
form the family.   Thus a large family with absent
children is in fact a small or low-density family.   On
the other hand, a family enlarged by relatives is
'dense'.   Thus his definition of a 'dense' family
includes an extended family.   The preservative effect
of numbers in a family is derived from the more general
preservative effect of group life.   It is due to the
close interaction of its members.   'In a family of
small numbers, common sentiments and memories cannot be
very intense; for there are not enough consciences in
which they can be represented and reinforced by sharing
them.' (27)

THE RELATION OF SUICIDE TO FAMILY STRUCTURE IN DURBAN

Unfortunately, inquest records provide far from adequate
data for such investigations and this, along with the
absence of comparable data on family size in the total
population, makes it virtually impossible to draw any
reliable conclusions about the effects of family size
on suicide.   Durkheim himself was obliged to postulate
without the benefit of empirical evidence.   The Durban
data, however, permit tentative observations and accordingly tentative generalizations are offered, these
being deduced from the 1,194 cases of suicide.

Three factors were considered to determine family
size of suicides: parental status, (28) the nature of
the family (whether nuclear, extended, joint or fragmentary) and the numbers of persons living together in
one household.   These three factors, taken together
cover all the components of family density in Durkheim's
use of the word.   The Inquest Court records however,
do not return adequate information on these factors
(see Table 34).

Adequate information on parental status is restricted
to Indians, on family type to Indians and Whites.
Information on family density is much too thin for any
sort of conjecture, and information on all these
factors is much too scanty for Coloureds and Africans
to risk any worthwhile guess.

Tables 35 and 36 detail the distribution of suicide
by family type as far as is possible.   The data
indicate that, where family type was deducible in the

1,194 cases, more suicides were committed in all races and both sexes by persons living in families than by persons living alone; and by persons living in nuclear families than persons living in extended and joint families.   Coloured women, with a high proportion of suicides in joint families, were exceptional in this respect.

These trends, however, do not prove that persons living alone have lower suicide rates than persons living in families, or that joint and extended families provide greater immunity against suicide than nuclear families. - The proportion of persons living alone constitutes a very small fraction of the total population, and it may well be that if the total number of suicides in this category is calculated as a rate of the total population living alone, it may be very much higher than the rate for those living in a family. Likewise, the extended and joint families are less common than nuclear families.   Even among Indians, more prone to extended family living, the nuclear family is common, its incidence being estimated to be between 57 and 75 per cent by various studies undertaken between 1946 and 1969. (29)

It may thus well be that the incidence of suicide among Africans, Coloureds, Whites and Indians in the joint and extended family situations is, in fact, higher than the comparative distribution of such families in the total population.

This appears to be confirmed for Coloureds, among whom the highest number of suicides of women occurred in the extended family, though there is no tradition of the extended family among the Africans and Indians, and its incidence in the general population is assumed to be low.   'Density' cannot in itself fuse social consciences and stimulate meaningful solidarity. People do get on each other's nerves.   Sharing of joint facilities has to be learnt and unless the extended family is deeply traditionalized, it is more likely to provoke hostility than inspire unity. Even Indian mothers-in-law have been heard to say on occasions that separation of related nuclear units increases love among them.   The members of an Indian joint family, because of its institutionalization over generations, are probably better equipped to contend with its inevitable conflicts, and have internalized the necessary techniques to resist and to accommodate in these.

In the absence of comparable data for the total population in Durban the only conclusions that may be drawn are:

(a) The incidence of suicide appears to be high for persons living alone.

(b) Indians of both sexes, and Coloured women commit more suicide in extended and joint family situations than members of other races.

(c) The Durban data do not support the theory that large families reduce the incidence of suicide.

The distribution of suicide by family density or size and parental status is observed in Tables 37, 38 and 39.

While Indian women may be better equipped to cope with the irritations of the extended family, the evidence in Durban does not prove that high density restrains suicide even among them. Family size is the more pertinent indicator of the relation of suicide to density. Of Indian women suicides during 1940-60, 83.4 per cent lived in families of 5-10 persons (Table 37). Dr Hilda Kuper found that 76 per cent of Tamil families (Tamils contribute the highest proportion in Indian suicides) lived in families of 5-10 members during the suicide period. (30)   This suggests that the proportion of suicide among Indian women in large families is probably higher than the proportion of large families in the total population. The pressures of the large family appears to be further confirmed by the fact that only 2.5 per cent of Indian women suicides were living alone compared with 23.2 per cent of White, 10.7 per cent of Coloured and 8 per cent of African women.

(a) Suicide, family size and parental status

When the situation of 'living alone' is excluded Durban projects the following similarities in the relation between suicide and family size, and suicide and parental status.

(i) The frequency of suicide is generally high when there are two to three children in the family. Among Whites and urban Africans accustomed to nuclear families it is high in a family of three to four persons. Among Indians with larger families, it is high when there are five to seven persons, or two to five children. Among Coloureds it is also high when there are five to seven persons, but the link seems to be primarily with family type rather than number of children, since the largest number of Coloured women suicides lived in joint or extended family situations. Considering that the average family sizes are probably about 3.9 for Whites and Africans, 4.7 for

Coloureds, (31) and between 6.2 and 9.3 (32) for
Indians, the greater frequency of suicide in these
categories is in keeping with their proportionate
distribution in the total population and not really
indicative of a comparatively high suicide rate.

(ii) Women with no children, and women living in
conjugal units of two persons, have a relatively high
incidence of suicide among Whites, Africans and
Coloureds. Childlessness may be an aggravating
factor in these cases, since over 50 per cent of White
and Coloured married women who committed suicide in
the total number of cases were over 40 years of age.

(iii) White and African men show the highest
incidence of suicide when living alone. The incidence
of suicide of White women is only slightly lower among
those living alone than among those living in conjugal
units.
The second highest incidence of suicide occurs among
Coloured women living in large families of five to
seven persons. The Indian frequency appears to be
lower among those living alone, but this is probably
misleading and the proportion committing suicide in
this category is probably high in comparison with the
actual incidence of the total Indian population living
alone.

(iv) Suicide occurs less frequently in large
families - families of ten or more, among Indians and
Coloureds, and five or more among Africans and Whites.
However, this relation may disappear when the rate is
calculated with reference to the incidence of large
families in the total population and prove to be
simply due to the rarity of large families in the component group.

(b) Childlessness and suicide

The Durban data suggest that childless married women
have a high suicide rate. The crucial relation thus
may not be between suicide and family size or family
density as Durkheim holds, but between suicide and
childlessness. In Durban suicide is most frequent
among childless White, African and Coloured women.
Indian women have the second highest suicide frequency
in that situation. The fact that African and White
women living in conjugal units of two commit more
suicide than those in larger families, very probably
indicates the despair of childlessness, rather than
the irritations of 'low density'. In this respect,

the Durban data corroborate Durkheim's postulate that
the immunity of women to suicide in marriage is derived
from the state of motherhood, or domestic society,
rather than the state of wifehood or conjugal society.
Frequency of suicide is lower among childless husbands
than in the total number of suicide cases.

While collective sentiments have a positive effect
in social and personal integration, they may also be
too strong; they may obliterate rather than support
the individual. If excessive individuation leads to
suicide, states Durkheim, insufficient individuation
has the same effect. He sees this state existing in
situations where the group is highly integrated and
the individual is completely absorbed in it, having no
distinct personality of his own. (33)

> Everyone leads the same life; everything is common
> to all, ideas, feelings, occupations ... collective
> supervision is constant, extending to everything,
> and thus more readily prevents divergence. The
> individual thus has no way to set up an environment
> of his own in the shelter of which he may develop
> his own nature and form a physiognomy that is his
> exclusively ... he is only an inseparable part of
> the whole without personal value.

Indian and African women are relatively more enveloped by the social restraints of large 'interfering'
families. Once exposed to a situation of censure,
they are generally defenceless against group sanctions
and, failing to regain their lost prestige, they seek
it in death.

12 Temporal factors

Early suicide studies contended that suicide rates were
related to climatic factors. It was suggested that
the human nervous system, while succeeding in bearing
up to serious difficulties under normal conditions,
tended to disintegrate under the strains of certain
extrinsic agencies, weather being one of these. The
Italian school, represented by Morselli, Ferri,
Lombroso and Gorre, (1) compared meteorological maps
of Europe with the distribution of suicides and weather
conditions. Extreme weather conditions were presumed
to aggravate suicide; moderate climates to inhibit it.
Lombroso and Ferri modified this view when they stated
that it was not absolute temperature that aggravated
suicide but sudden temperature changes.

The correlation between weather and suicide implied
in effect a correlation between temperature changes
and suicide. Differences in temperature on all
levels, regional, seasonal and daily, were used to
explain differences in suicide rates. Despite
Durkheim's classical refutation of any direct connec-
tion between weather and suicide, the view that suicide
was at least partially affected by weather conditions
continued to be held until Miner's statistical investigation of suicide in 174 American cities firmly
established that there was no correlation, or only an
insignificant one, between suicide and climate. (2)

Whereas a meteorological relation in suicide is
generally rejected, Durkheim's contention of a correlation between the suicide rate and cyclic changes in
social activity finds considerable support. Henry and
Short stress that the cyclical fluctuations in suicide
are a response, in particular, to economic activity
and establish that troughs of suicide cycles precede
peaks of business cycles. (3)

96

Durban's sub-tropical climate is characterized by
such slight seasonal changes that, if there was a
correlation between suicide and climate, we would get
an even suicide rate throughout the year with perhaps
a variation at the peak of summer when the days get
hot and humid.   However, time as a sociological
phenomenon, marking the rhythm of culturally organized
life, laying down the pattern of social action, and
predicting behaviour from hour to hour, day to day,
week to week and month to month, is related to suicide.
Suicide occurs within the orbit of sociological time
and is a response to an accumulated complex of irritations occurring in time.   The act is sparked off at
a particular moment.   That moment is of importance in
terms of the social activity associated with it.   If
any relation exists between suicide and time, then it
will more probably be in this context rather than in
any other.

Information on temporal factors was available in
98.1 per cent of the total number of cases, the information relating to women being better than that for
men.

Durkheim, analysing the data assembled by Pierre de
Boismont for Paris, and Guerry for France, in the nineteenth century, contended that since suicide was a
function of social activity, its incidence would be
highest during those periods of the day when activity
is at its peak and concomitant tensions high.   Basing
his conclusions on the social situations of his day, (4)
he maintained that 6 a.m. to 11 a.m. and midday to
4 p.m. were the most critical times for suicide. (5)

Romilly Fedden, (6) supporting Durkheim, describes
a suicide cycle for the day and contends that troughs
and peaks in the daily incidence correspond with rest
and activity respectively.   Thus suicide is rare at
dawn, it rises towards breakfast, reaches its peak in
the late morning, drops sharply during lunch and begins
to rise again until the resumption of work in the
afternoon.   It drops again with the cessation of
work in the evening.

Similarly the suicide rate is high during the days
of the week and the months of the year when there is
much activity.   Durkheim found high rates on Mondays
and Tuesdays which he considered in his time to be the
days of greatest economic activity in the week. (7)
Fedden (8) maintains that whereas the law of 'maximum
activity, maximum suicide' holds for the time of day,
it does not hold for days of the week, since a week,
unlike a day or a season, is an artificial division.

None the less, he agrees with Durkheim that with a
return to labour on Monday, suicide rises, the rise
being continued up to and including Thursday.   On
Friday, as labour begins to relax, a perceptible
decline occurs.   Saturday, with its expectations of
wages and weekend relaxation, reduces the rate to its
lowest point.   The rate rises on Sunday.   Durkheim
contends, and Fedden confirms, that women maintain an
even rate throughout the week, with a marked tendency
for an increase in suicide on Sunday.

In accordance with the theory of 'maximum activity,
maximum suicide' a high incidence of suicide should
precede all pre-holiday periods.   In terms of the
week, a high incidence should occur during Friday and
Saturday, since this is clearly the time of greatest
economic activity, particularly in respect of shopping.

Table 40 indicates the distribution of suicide by
the time of day (for the races and sexes), Table 41 by
day of week, Table 42 by week of month and Table 43 by
month of year, for the races and sexes.   Though
periods of activity and rest operate fairly uniformly
for all race groups in South African cities, they do
not share the same suicide peaks and troughs during the
day, week, month and year.   The only features common
to the races is that the women have their highest rate
in the last week of the month.   Indian, White and
Coloured men have their highest rate in the second week.

(a)   Time of day

The most general conclusion that one may draw with
reference to time of day is that suicide is lowest from
10 p.m. to 4 a.m. or, that is, during hours of sleep,
and that it occurs during the active, wakeful period of
life.   The evidence does not show a high incidence of
suicide during hours of intensified activity.   The
high suicide rate of Africans between 4 a.m. and 7 a.m.
is due to the fact that, with long distances to travel
to work, their hive of activity and concomitant flow
of tensions begins earlier.   (It does not establish
that 4 a.m. to 7 a.m. is fraught with particular irritations and a higher suicide potential for Africans.)
Similarly, the somewhat higher frequency of suicides by
White men between 10 p.m. and 1 a.m. is probably indicative of a relatively affluent social pattern, which
runs late into the night in pursuit of 'pleasure'.
The comparatively higher incidence of Coloured male and
African female suicides between 7 p.m. and 10 p.m. may
be due to supper and after-supper tensions.

The absence of a uniform suicide response to time of day demonstrates not only that there is no intrinsic relation between time and suicide, but there is no direct relation between tempo of social activity and suicide either.   Second, the fact that there are as many variations as similarities in these fluctuations for the races and sexes finally confutes the view that there is any significant relation between the incidence of suicide and the time of day.

(b)   Day of week

The relation of suicide to day of week shows the greatest similarity between Whites and Indians on the one hand and Africans and Coloureds on the other.
    The Indian and White suicides fluctuate fairly evenly through the week, though their troughs and peaks differ.   The male rate declines on Sunday, the female rate shows no variations.   The Indian male incidence is lowest on Sunday and highest on Saturday.   The White male incidence is lowest on Saturday and highest on Wednesday, the high rate continuing until Friday. The highest Indian female rate occurs on Fridays.   It may be influenced by the generally held Indian idea that Friday is a good day and blessed for any major activity, including death, particularly in view of the fact that Indian women are more ritualistic than Indian men.   On the other hand the 'ritual' link may be purely incidental.   White women commit suicide slightly more often on Thursday.   There is a slight drop in the suicide of both Indian and White women during Sunday and Monday, the drop being more marked in the case of the latter.
    Africans and Coloureds reach their suicide peaks over the weekend, the female incidence exceeding the male.   The suicide of African women begins to rise earlier in the week on Thursday, rapidly reaching its peak on Sunday.   It drops on Monday.   Suicides of Coloured women rise steeply from their Friday ebb of 3.6 per cent to the Sunday peak of 28.5 per cent.   The incidence continues to be high on Monday when 21.4 per cent of the suicides occur.
    There is also a weekend rise in the suicide of Coloured and African men, but the rise in their cases is more gradual than that of the women.   The suicides of Coloured men are fairly evenly distributed throughout the week.   The peak occurs on Sunday when 20.2 per cent of the suicides are committed.   Though the pro-

portions of suicides committed by African males are
high during Saturday and Sunday, they reach their peak
on Monday.   The lowest number of African male
suicides occurred on Thursday.

Black suicide rates are generally higher on weekends
and Mondays, White rates high on Wednesdays to Fridays.
Africans, Indians and Coloureds, men and women, have
more suicide incidences on Saturdays and Sundays.

This high Black weekend suicide rate may be due to
the virtual absence of organized recreational facilities for Blacks in South African cities.   Drinking
appears to be the main outlet in the townships, drunkenness reaching its excesses during weekends.   The
fact that Blacks 'know' what Whites are doing, or have
had exaggerated accounts of their weekend life projected to them through the massive advertising media,
makes their lot the more unbearable.   The weekend
brings for them the problems of free time, nowhere to
go, nothing to do.   Cramped living conditions stifle
individual expression, and family members twang on
each other's nerves.   Predominantly a community of
semi-skilled and unskilled workers, Blacks are the
least equipped materially and intellectually to meet
the challenge of free time.   Yet they are the worst
provided for in terms of organized amusement.   Private
enterprise ignores them, since they do not provide a
lucrative market, and the Municipality, the Durban
Publicity Association, and other voluntary bodies
organize events generally with 'Whites only' tags.
The cinemas are the only Saturday night outlet, and
invariably, regardless of the offered fare, these are
filled to bursting point.   The more privileged -
usually Coloureds and Indians - may dance at night at
one of the dozen 'Black' hotels.   On Sunday they may
attend a ball game, (9) and this, more or less, is the
sum total of available recreational outlets for those
who can get in.

The problem is further aggravated in the case of
the migrant African with his rural background unaccul-
turated to urban recreational facilities.   Whereas
the week integrates him as a worker, the weekend
finds him statusless, a cipher in the shacks. (10)
The woman in the situation is often a kept woman knowing neither the security nor pride of wife or
mother. (11)   The weekend bleakly focuses attention
on a half-lived life, a suspended existence between
the reserve and the city, between *kipita* (12) and
traditionally legitimized family.   It is common knowledge that the outpatients department and the casualty

wards of the local hospitals grimly await their weekend rise of patients.

Indians and Whites have the lowest weekend suicide incidence and the explanation may well lie in the buffering effects of a relatively entrenched family life.

(c)   Week of month

Available suicide studies do not investigate and comment on the relationship between the incidence of suicide and the week of the month. (13)   However, in Durban this is the only temporal factor in which a clear pattern emerges among all groups.

Men generally have a higher suicide incidence in the second week of the month, and a lower incidence in the third week (Table 42).   This is the male pattern in the total number of suicides and with slight variations in each race group.   The highest male African incidence occurs in the fourth week, and the lowest male African and Coloured incidence occurs in the second and first weeks respectively.

The highest proportions of suicide of women - all races - occur in the fourth week of the month.   The lowest proportions of suicide of both Indian and White women occur during the third week of the month, of Coloured women during the first week, and of African women during the second week.

(d)   Month of year

The division of time into months of year is most closely linked with the original interest in the relationship of suicide with cosmic factors.   The sub-tropical climate of Durban is not characterized by the extreme weather changes of a cold or temperate climate, necessitating a reorganization in the tempo and type of activity.   Thus, the postulate that the rate of suicide changes with seasons cannot be expected to be substantiated in Durban.   If the contentions of Lombroso and Ferri that suicide rates are high in extreme temperatures were valid, then a rise in suicide should occur in Durban in the fairly hot summer, when the population of Durban wilts with the complaint, 'It is the humidity, not the heat.'   The analysis in Table 43, however, fails to establish any distinguishable pattern between the incidence of

suicide in the hotter months of November to about
April, and the cooler months that follow.

The distribution does not suggest any relation to
the tempo of social activity either.   The times of
greatest economic and associated activities occur
during the tourist season in the cooler months of June
and July, and during the pre-holiday period around
December, when there is a rush to complete orders and
attend to the thronging shoppers.   Coloured women
alone show a rise in June and July.   Other than this,
both periods are actually flanked by a decline in
suicide for the races and sexes, the decline being
more apparent when the total suicide cases are analysed
by sex.   There is a rise in the suicide incidence of
Indian men in November, when *diwali* occurs, but so is
there a rise in that month for White men.   Indian
women show an apparent decline in the incidence during
November.

If the year is divided into three periods of four
months each (Table 44), the incidence is highest for
both sexes taken together in the first four months,
and lowest in the middle four months.   The trend for
women suggests a progressive decline from the first to
the last four months.   The male rate is highest in the
last four months.

When this pattern is considered by race, it is
found that the general trend observed for the total
number of men is repeated in the masculine trend in
each race.   It is highest towards the end of the year,
and lowest during the mid-year cooler months.   The
pattern for women by race, however, shows no uniformity.

COMMENTS

These investigations clearly demonstrate that there is
generally no correlation between the nature and tempo
of social activity that characterizes a particular
time and the incidence of suicide.   While some times
of the day, week and month, may be busier than others,
and consequently more anxious, this does not necessarily suggest that they are more provocative of
suicide.   In fact, their very demands may allay
suicide.   Durkheim's hypothesis of a rise in suicide
with a rise in the tempo of social activity, is in
conflict with his general hypothesis that suicide is a
function of social integration.

Periods of peak activity may well involve, absorb
and integrate persons into social action, thereby

allaying the dangers of isolation, self-pity and self-recriminations.   Suicide rates should, in terms of that theory, be lower, not higher, during such periods.

13 Methods adopted in committing suicide

The sociological approach to the choice of suicide
means is a commonsense one. Psychologists tend to
see a relation between the choice of means and the
suicide's deep-rooted, hidden motives. Durkheim dismisses such a relation and contends that the choice
of means of suicide like the cause of suicide, is
determined by social factors. But though he considers
both cause and means to be socially determined, he
does not consider them to be related to each other.
Thus the three basic suicide types which he identifies -
anomic, altruistic and egoistic - are not expressed in
related means.
    Durkheim proposes that the choice of a particular
method in suicide is primarily determined by availability of means and current cultural conditions. (1)
Thus hanging, gross and violent, is more common in
the country than the city, and more common in smaller
cities than larger ones, the 'cultivated' classes
being more repelled by it. By implication he
suggests that the means of suicide projects both the
technological development of the society of the
suicide, and his status within that society. The
implications of this interpretation of the choice of
means of suicide has continued to be substantiated in
successive investigations. (2) The methods used in
different societies appear to have remained constant
over generations, new means being added to these with
technological changes and urban expansions. (3) The
implication of this theory is that the less technologically advanced a community, the poorer its
resources; and the lower the status of a member in a
society, the more restricted and simple the technique
for self-destruction. Thus hanging and stabbing, and
to a lesser extent, burning and crushing by train, are

the only means of suicide reported among East African
tribes. (4)   Women, leading more confined lives, have
access to fewer means than men.

Romilly Fedden, (5) agreeing with Durkheim that
availability and cultural experience determine choice
of method in suicide, observes that carbolic acid is
peculiarly Egyptian, coal gas asphyxiation French,
trains Belgian and Italian, and coal gas and lysol
English means of suicide.

THE CHOICE OF MEANS IN DURBAN

The choice of suicide means exercised in Durban by
race and sex are classified in Tables 45 and 46.   The
tables confirm the fundamental Durkheimian proposition
that availability and familiarity, dependent in turn
on culture and status, are the fundamental factors in
choice of means.   Hanging is thus the predominant
suicide means of Black men drawn from the poorest
section of the Durban society.   It is the most common
suicide means universally.   Frenay found it to be the
most prevalent suicide mode in Europe and Great
Britain, the second most common means in the USA. (6)
Of cases of suicide studied by Bohannan in East Africa
218 out of 299 were due to hanging. (7)   It is the
most usual suicide means used in hospitals and asylums
where care is taken to remove all lethal weapons.

White men in Durban usually shoot themselves.
Shooting is a relatively upper-crust form of self-
killing.   The gun in Western society in particular, is
a symbol of masculine power and strength.   It is the
instrument of colonialism and imperialism, the vital
instrument in the subjugation and continued suppression
of Black peoples.   It is very much a White 'thing',
the companion of the cowboy, the White policeman, the
White soldier - the gun against the assegai, the gun
against the tomahawk.   Frenay finds firearms to be
the most common means of self-destruction in the
American army. (8)   The gun not only emphasizes
technological superiority, but also a technological
efficiency in the elimination of life, often confused
with greater 'humanity'.   Thus the traditional or
folk approach to death is 'ritualistic', and long-
drawn-out.   The Japanese Samurai reaches poetic
height when he disembowels himself.   The Buddhist monk
burns himself, as do Black women in Durban.   To the
White, and the technologically advanced, these are
horrifying, macabre, messy means of dying.   The English

Robert Clive retains historical respectability by
neatly pointing a gun against his temples.

Poisoning and drowning are recognized as character-
istically female means of self-destruction.   In Durban
they are used most often by White women, but their
incidence is also high among White, Indian and Coloured
men.   There is a difference in the kinds of poisons
used by Whites and Blacks.   Whites use the more
sophisticated, gentler poisons, in the form of sleeping
tablets;   Blacks the more corrosive household varieties.
Indians invariably use wintergreen, a cheap embrocation
usually kept in homes to massage painful limbs.

Electrocution and gassing are very rarely used by
Blacks.   Gas is not the usual form of fuel in Durban,
so that when used it implies gassing oneself in a car.
Those who electrocute themselves have some technical
understanding of electricity.

Death by throwing oneself before moving vehicles,
often trains (usually described as death due to crushing in official   records), is more prevalent among
men.   It is probably used more often as a suicide means
than is recorded, since it has a greater tendency to be
confused with accident. (9)   Whites rarely kill themselves by this means.   Suicides who have resorted to
this means have usually had regular contact with the
railway as passengers, workers or residents.   Self-
destruction by laceration is very rarely used by Blacks
and is almost entirely restricted to White men.   It is
the one method that defies explanation purely in terms
of availability and familiarity.   Lacerating weapons,
knives and razors are used constantly by men and women
of all races.   Blacks resort to such methods readily
in acts of homicide; but rarely in suicide.   In East
Africa, though laceration is a common mode of homicide,
it is rarely used in suicide. (10)

Over 70 per cent of African women suicides burnt
themselves during both periods.   The incidence of
burning rose from 67.9 per cent among Coloured women
during 1940-60 to 77 per cent during the last nine
years.   Among Indian women, the incidence declined
from 69.7 per cent to 47 per cent in that time.   The
explanation of its high prevalence among these culturally differentiated and physically separated women
can only be explained in terms of the easy accessibi-
lity of this death means.   Paraffin and matches are
common domestic commodities, and the primus stove the
usual means of household cooking.   Yet setting oneself
alight is not commonly listed in suicide studies, and
if employed at all, is included in the category of

'other means'.   It does not appear in South African
census reports.   Bohannan found only three instances
of such suicides and they were all of physically unfit
women, two being lepers who burnt themselves together
with their huts, and one an epileptic.   Hanging,
which occurred seventy-nine times in the eighty-three
cases, was the common suicide means of East African
women. (11)

SYMBOLISM OF MEANS

Though familiarity and availability are fundamental
factors in the explanation of the choice of suicide
means the influence of cultural and psychological
factors cannot be dismissed.   Thus while the common
use of 'burning' by Black women suicides may in the
final analysis be due to its immediate presence,
paraffin and primus being the most commonly used
cooking mode, its use among Hindu women may also be
influenced by the traditional Hindu attitude to fire,
and the historical practice of Sati, or the burning of
the widow on the funeral pyre of her husband.   Fire
is of central religious significance in Hindu life.
In the sacred ritual of *havan*, (12) it paves the way,
through the smoke it raises, to holy communion.   It
represents at once creation - being one of the three
forces in the creation of the cosmos - and destruction
or dissolution.   It is at the same time a means of
expiation, purification and appeasement.   Thus it is
through the ritual fire that the Divine is propitiated,
and the fury of a god is allayed, that the sins of men
are expiated, and their souls purified.   The original
Sati in Hindu lore offered herself to perform the sublime act of expiation and purification so that her
deceased Lord would be saved.   Her ritual burning was
tapas, an act of self-purification in which her outer,
physical, transient shell was burnt out to liberate
her inner, eternal essence.   It was at the same time
an infinitely more meaningful communication with God,
since the offering of the *havan* took the form of one's
own body, and the 'channel' to God was through one's
own smoke.   Sati, or the public offer of the widow of
herself as a sacrifice on her husband's funeral pyre,
was an intensely dramatic and traumatic God-appeasing
means of expiating guilt.   It was at the same time an
act of making peace with society.   In that context,
Sati was not suicide.   It was the public atonement of
the widow who in some mysterious way had offended God,

her being widowed being proof of it, and who had as a
result become potentially dangerous to her society. (13)
     Though the custom of Sati has fallen away, its idea
continues to be revered in many minds, and a Hindu
woman who burns herself may see herself as involved in
a sublime, rather than a pathological, act of release
from intolerable bondage rather than as a tragedy; as
an act that saves her society or her immediate family
from the taints they may suffer from her tainting.
But how then does one explain the emotional significance of burning among African and Coloured women who
use it just as often as a suicide means?
     Menninger holds that the suicide means symbolizes
the psychological state of the suicide.   Thus he
interprets the act of the suicide who embraces a red
hot stove as symbolizing his ultimate conquest of cold
loneliness.   'At last my heart is warm.'   Following
his thesis that suicide is the function of the triple
unconscious psychological needs, to kill, to be killed
and to die, which on the conscious level are expressed
as conscious hate, conscious guilt and conscious hopelessness, he proposes that the chosen means indicates
which of these three conditions predominate in the
suicide.   Applying his thesis to Durban, one would
have to conclude that Black women - African, Indian
and Coloured - despite their significant cultural
differences, are all motivated by the same psychological factor - all suffer from conscious guilt.
     Menninger classifies suicide means into active/
aggressive and passive/receptive.   Since suicide is
an overtly accomplished act, it is active, and it is
aggressive.   In this context, Menninger's classification strikes a strange note.   Therefore the classification of some suicide means as 'active' and others as
aggressive cannot but be subjective.   Menninger classifies shooting as active/aggressive one assumes,
because in shooting the actor is shooting himself,
acts upon himself, whereas in drowning and poisoning
he submits himself to the action of other agents -
poison and water.   Significant, or insignificant, as
the difference may be, extending the same line of
argument, hanging, burning, shooting, electricity,
lacerating, jumping from heights and throwing oneself
before moving vehicles may be classified as active/
aggressive means.   In each of these death is expected
to follow almost instantly upon the action, and the
action itself is of a violent nature.   Poisoning,
drowning and gassing, on the other hand, may be recognized as passive/receptive.   The situation shown in

Table 47 emerges in Durban when the suicide means are
divided into the two proposed classes.

Table 47 shows that men resort more often than
women to the use of passive/receptive means even
though hanging, shooting and laceration are predominantly male suicide means.   On the other hand, no
women were found to resort to the passive/receptive
means of gassing.   Women resort more frequently to
active/aggressive means than do men.   Within each
race group, Indian, African and Coloured, women show
a high preference for active/aggressive means.   The
White women alone differ in this respect in their pro-
portionately greater use of passive/receptive means.
Among males, except for Indians, there is likewise a
marked preference for the use of active/aggressive
means.

The role of the Indian women in Indian culture is
observably more passive/receptive than that of White
or Coloured women in their respective cultures.   Yet
the Indian woman resorts more frequently to the use of
active/aggressive means.   In contrast, the dominant
White woman resorts more often to passive/receptive
means.

The characteristics of passivity and aggressiveness
may be presumed to differ not only in terms of sex
but also in terms of subordinate and superordinate
position.   How else does one account for White male
domination generally?   Yet the African male resorts
more to active/aggressive means and less to passive/
receptive means than does the White male.

It is thus clear that there is no relationship
between the choice of means and aggressive or passive
social roles.   On the other hand, the dominated often
conceal a reservoir of repressed aggressions, which in
psychopathic conditions come to the fore in various
forms of violence.   Suicide is an act of violence.
It may well be that the greater the obligation to
observe passive roles, the greater the outer expression
of active aggression in psychopathic conditions.

The 'active/aggressive' means used by Black
suicides in Durban were also the most easily available
means.   This tends to support the view that availability is the most important factor in the choice of
means.

But availability and familiarity do not offer a
complete explanation, except where the suicide is
wholly spontaneous, and charged by a sudden passion,
in which case suicide itself is questionable.   The
'true' suicide is one who kills himself after having

given due consideration to his intended act.   Why
then do people resort to unpleasant, aggressive means
of self-destruction even where relatively less painful means are available?   Why do White women in
Durban, for instance, not resort to passive/receptive
means to a significantly higher extent?   And why do
African and Coloured women in Durban burn themselves?
If they have learnt to do so from the Indians, then
what is it that has made them so amenable to this type
of acculturation, when apart from the adoption of
certain food habits, they have remained generally
immune to other forms of Indianization?   Why do
Blacks resist the use of lacerating weapons in suicide,
though they use them freely in homicide, and why do
Indian males use passive/receptive means almost as
often as they use active/aggressive means in a society
where a general and overwhelming tendency for aggressive self-destruction exists?

These are problems for psychological consideration.
Sociologically the study confirms Durkheim's view
that availability and familiarity with means of destruction determine their use by the person committing
suicide.   The variation in the adopted methods of
suicide is largely related to the cultural and
material factors operating on the lives of men and
women of the different races.

part four

Humanizing statistics

14 The probable factors precipitating suicide

INTRODUCTION

It is generally believed that the fundamental natural human instinct is for life and survival. Consequently, suicide is abnormal. Yet Sigmund Freud theorizes that the human personality is a component of both life and death instincts and that the world is shaped by the dual forces of construction and destruction. (1)

This makes the desire to die as normal as the desire to live and in the largest number of cases, the suicides had in fact been accepted by their associates as normal persons.

As a very broad generalization, one may state that suicide occurs because life has become intolerable. But then the definition of an intolerable life situation is always subjective and as dependent on the objective condition as on the internal psychic equipment of the responding person. Thus on the one hand, the disposition of two persons may so differ, that A will crumble where B may thrive and on the other, though two persons may have the same disposition in relation to suicide, the one may never be exposed to a stress situation or his personality may have been specially reinforced against a suicidal tendency in the process of socialization.

While the psychological aspect is crucial to the total understanding of the suicidal phenomena, it is the most inaccessible: access to it in fact lies through the sociological. If suicide is the result of personality disintegration, then that disintegration occurs in society. A study thus of the social situations in which suicide occurs, the apparent motives given by suicides in statements and notes, and the apparent motives gleaned by those who survive them are

of utmost importance in indicating the situations in
which suicide occurs.

Durkheim rejected the study of motives, considering
their recording by officials to be too faulty for
scientific consideration, but Bohannan asserts: (2)

The word 'motive' has two meanings: it means the
psychic reason the suicide was committed; it also
means the cause which is assigned to it by survivors.   Now, we must agree with them that the first
sort of motive, that is, what was in the mind of
the person who committed suicide - is of little
scientific use, because it is not knowable.   However, the second sort of motive ¬ the cause assigned
by survivors, is of ethnographic interest.
Durkheim, or at least some of his followers, should
have recognized that these motives were important
not as causes, but as popular ideas about what is
worth living for and what is worth dying for.   As
such, these statements of 'incidence' made in
suicide notes by surviving kinsmen, by police
officers and coroners, or by anyone else, are
important.

CLUES TO SUICIDE

Though the act of suicide is a personal act, it is the
result of interpersonal relations and so it is that it
shocks and plunges into depths of despair, guilt and
shame those who have been personally and closely
associated with the deceased.   Its meaning lies locked
in the community of relations that held the actors of
the tragedy together and it is the nature of these
relations that the sociologist attempts to prise open.

The Inquest Court records provide the most peripheral clues to that meaning.   They record available
and, in practically every case, limited reports of the
physical and emotional state of the suicide during the
act, his attempts to draw attention or call for help,
the statements he made and letters he wrote and the
conflicts and problems he faced prior to the act.
The Inquest Court through cross-examination of
witnesses, may attempt to gain some insight into
evidence of previous suicidal attempts or threats.

Some information on the probable reason and conditions under which suicide occurred was available in
approximately 73 per cent of the 2,084 cases abstracted
from the Durban Inquest Court between 1940 and 1970.
Most information was available for Whites and least
for Africans (see Table 48).

PROBABLE REASONS ASSOCIATED WITH SUICIDE

The probable reasons were investigated in terms of
physical incapacity, psychological stress, family
disruption and breakdown of intimate relations, financial problems, loss of employment and shame or fear
arising from involvement or accusation of involvement
in some deviant act.   The emergent patterns indicate
greater similarity in the probable reasons, probable
social situations and probable personality syndromes
between component Black groups than between Black and
White.   The differences were more marked between the
sexes in each race than they were between the races.
    Whereas the listed factors are common to all the
suicide groups, some factors predominate among men,
some among women and some are more characteristic of
one race group than another.   Unemployment and
anxiety over business matters are rarely associated
with the suicide of women.   Fear of arrest or discovery of a shameful act are likewise more prevalent
among men, particularly African men.   Family disorganization and breakdown in valued relations is the
most common single factor among Black women.   Physical
ailment followed by emotional stress predominated
among White women, while emotional stress, followed by
physical illness predominated among men generally (see
Table 49).

THE PSYCHOLOGICAL AND EMOTIONAL STATE OF THE SUICIDE
DURING THE ACT

The statements of witnesses, in the main to the police,
give some information about the behaviour of the
suicides just prior to or during the act, and from
these something of their emotional state can be
deduced.   The choice of death weapon, the search for
privacy, resistance against 'interference' from
others, evidence of alcoholism, depression, violence,
and previous threats and attempts at suicide are some
external indications of internal emotional states.
The analysis revealed important differences both by
race and sex.
    The suicides of Blacks tend to be impulsive, that
of Whites meditated.   Most of the suicide notes in
the court records have been written by Whites (Tables
50 and 56), and while this may in part be due to the
greater letter-writing habit among Whites, it is also
a reflection of the greater thought given to the

planning and implications of the act.   White suicides
reveal a greater search for privacy and a greater
resistance against interference from others.   A
violent quarrel, a passionate explosion of anger,
verbal abuse, physical assault, drunkenness and, after
the act, regret are the more usual features of Black
suicides; depression, insomnia, physical illness,
self-blame, relief, and a plea for forgiveness, of
White suicides (Tables 51, 52, 53 and 54).   The
differences in the emotional states of Black and White
are probably as much due to the age factor as to
differences in life styles, social attitudes and economic conditions.   Eighty per cent of the Black women
and 60 per cent of the Black men were under 40:   66 and
63 per cent respectively of the White men and women
were over 40.

In both suicides, a traumatic break in a valued
relationship is the most common precipitating factor:
among White men and Black women it is most usually a
break in the marital, or love relationship, among Black
men and White women the breach is not so markedly related to a single person.

15 The psychological and emotional states of suicides

Suicides are most generally persons who appear 'normal' to their associates, (1) yet among them are a proportion who would be deemed neurotic or psychotic. Apparently 20 per cent of the suicides in Durban were classifiable into this category (see Table 57). The proportion of Whites so classifiable was higher than that of Blacks, and while among Africans and Coloureds the proportion of men was higher than that of women, among Whites and Indians the proportion of women was slightly higher.

The common symptoms were depression, insomnia, nervous tension, withdrawal, and repeated threats or attempts at suicide. In a large number of cases the 'patients' had been driven to drinking and drug-taking in search of refuge. The usual pattern was for a patient to struggle along with such 'incapacities' until a sudden change in an economic or personal relation eliminated all available supports and drove him to suicide.

The higher incidence of psychoneurotic syndromes found among White suicides in Durban, may in part be due to the recognition, awareness and acceptance of such syndromes in White culture. Africans and Indians are far more inclined to impute such personality disturbances to supernatural factors than to the more sophisticated concept of psychoneurosis. To them, people are 'mad' or behave strangely because of possession by supernatural spirits, and since such beliefs belong to subordinate cultures, there is some embarrassment in admitting them to European officials for fear of ridicule. Whereas Indians generally attempt to conceal psychoneurotic conditions and talk of them in whispers, the psychoneurotic states of Whites, encouraged by the academic support of psychiatry and psychology, are discussed relatively freely, often by the patients themselves.

It is probable that Blacks have a much higher incidence of psychoneurosis than reported; their ignorance
of such maladies creating a false impression.   On the
other hand, it may well be that they actually have a
lower rate of psychoneurosis.   It is evident that
cultural indoctrination plays an important part in
inducing psychological ailments - a people's vulnerability to both folk spirits and psychopathic states
is dependent on the extent to which such ideas are
present in their social system.   Blacks in Durban are
in a marginal situation.   On the one hand, the whole
process that weans them away from their traditional
cultures and attracts them to the modern urban form
undermines their belief and consequently their vulnerability to 'folk spirits'.   On the other hand, they
have not sufficiently integrated modern psychological
concepts to be exposed to the maladies they define.
They may thus in fact be less susceptible to such
maladies.

WHITE SUICIDES

During 1962-71, White women suicides revealed greater
symptoms of deeply rooted emotional disturbance than
White men - in 40 per cent of the female cases compared
with 15 per cent of the male.   Only three of the
cases were certified as insane, one woman and two men.
One of the men suffered from epilepsy, and the disturbed emotional state of another was closely linked
with an inherited cleft lip.   Most of the emotionally
disturbed cases had sought expert attention and in
many cases the records included reports from consul-
tant psychiatrists.   The men were on average younger
than the women, two-thirds of the men and a third of
the women being under 30.   More of the women were
married and living with their spouses than were the
men - 62 and 54 per cent respectively.   At the same
time, more women lived alone than men.   The unmarried
men were usually in their twenties - over a third of
the total, and living with their parents.
    The young woman suicide in this age range, whether
single, widowed or divorced, invariably lived on her
own though she had close access to and a ready response
from her immediate family.   In a number of cases she
had migrated to Durban to escape family 'interference'
or to spare her family the burden of her afflictions.
Often her struggle against depression had pushed her
into drinking and drug-taking and her primary struggle

had become complicated by the attendant one with drugs
and drink.   In some of the cases, she had drifted
through a number of sexual unions to dispel some of
the loneliness, to find some root and some meaning.
In one case, this had resulted in two pregnancies, one
abortion, and a child given out for adoption.

The single women, eight in all, and five in their
twenties, had longer histories of depression.   In four
cases, the death of the father in early childhood
appeared to have been an important event in disorganiz-
ing the socially accepted orientation.   The depressions
of the married, widowed and divorced were of more recent
history, usually less than three years old and appeared
to have been provoked, or at least aggravated by the
change in marital status.

BLACK SUICIDES

There is very little direct evidence of psychoneurotic
tendencies in the reports of Black suicides, recorded
in the Inquest Court.   Indications of such tendencies
have in most cases to be deduced from statements that
describe the suicide's behaviour as 'queer', 'irres-
ponsible', 'funny'.   There is rarely any evidence
submitted by a psychiatrist or medical practitioner
and when there is, it relates to a professional or
middle-class Indian.   In most cases, where a suicide
who had acted 'queerly' had received attention it had
taken the form of hospitalization for nerve trouble.
A larger number of men than women had been so treated.

With the exception of African men, it was the older
Black suicide (40 years and over) who appeared to
suffer from psychoneurotic symptoms.   Depression,
crying, worrying about other members of the family or
accusing them of evil intention, were common.   Indian
and Coloured men had in addition become vagrants.
Alcoholism and drug addiction were rarely attendant
symptoms.

During 1962-70, 60 per cent of the African suicides
suspected of psychoneurotic tendencies were in their
early twenties.   All but three were unmarried and all
but three were unemployed - the rest being employed as
domestics or labourers.   The usual syndromes were
severe headaches, talking to oneself, threatening and
leaving home for short spells and threatening suicide.
In the employer's view, the symptoms appeared suddenly
and the suicide followed shortly thereafter.   Nimrod,
20 years old, general labourer, suddenly falls ill at

his place of work.   His father fetches him to consult
an *inyanga* (Zulu medicine man) but he runs away.   He
is discovered a little later in a canefield talking to
himself.   Later still he is found hanging.   Mandlen-
kosi, 24 years old, becomes violent.   His father
takes him to an *inyanga*, but he breaks loose and is
found later hanging in a near-by bush.

Examples of suicides with symptoms of emotional
disturbance

Age	Occupation	Method	Symptoms
WHITE MEN			
41	-	Hanging	Excessive drinking, patient in a mental hospital, several attempts at suicide, gave child money to buy wreath of red roses for him.
52	-	Poison	Had attempted suicide six years before with caustic soda, damaged throat as a result and fed himself with tube. Stuffed blades and glass in tube on various occasions prior to suicide. He and his wife were without a house for three weeks prior to the suicide.
38	-	Shooting	In the habit of sleeping with rifle. Drank heavily - trouble with wife over this, had threatened suicide before and on one occasion had sent false message of his death to wife.
32	Engineer	Shooting	Single. Treated by psychiatrist for nerves.
33	Greaser on ship	Jumping from height	Described as of unbalanced mind.
30	Salesman	Jumping from height	Hospitalized for psychiatric treatment - became afraid of people on discharge. Readmitted for treatment. Became very quiet and withdrawn on second discharge. Threw himself from thirteenth floor.

Age	Occupation	Method	Symptoms
37	Machine operator	Shooting	Suffered depression and insomnia - feared psychiatrist would suggest hospitalization.
39	Café assistant	Jumping from height	Treated for mental illness for five years. Jumped from tenth floor
50	Machinist	Drowning	Depressed since discharge from hospital after an operation. Repeatedly stated he wished to die.
55	Proof reader	Poison	Suffered from inferiority complex - complained of depression.
54	Area manager	Gassing	Depressed when demoted by firm.
61	Mechanic	Shooting	Very depressed.
55	Pharmacist	Poison	Suspended from post of chief pharmacist in hospital on allegation of theft of a bottle of tincture of opium. Hospitalized thereafter for depression. Depression continued on discharge and deteriorated into a complete loss of interest in life.
52	Army officer	Shooting	Perfectionist who prided himself on his efficiency. Became anxious and depressed when his work performance began to lag.

WHITE WOMEN

Age	Occupation	Method	Symptoms
23	Unemployed	Burning	Described as mentally deranged.
17	Salesgirl	Poison	Hospitalized for nervous disorder. Complained of boredom after discharge, took a job at chemist where she poisoned herself.
64	Retired spinster	Jumping from height	Immigrant from Scotland. Nervous, in bad state - had made several attempts at suicide.
58	Widowed housewife	Poison	Suffered from depression and insomnia, often stated she had no desire to live.

Age	Occupation	Method	Symptoms
26	Nurse	Jumping from height	Lost father at 8, lost fiancé in accident at 20 and attempted suicide. Became pregnant thereafter. Deserted by lover. Attempted suicide again. Gave baby away for adoption. Hospitalized for alcoholism. Took on steady boyfriend and also a number of stray lovers. Became pregnant. Boyfriend deserted her.

AFRICAN MEN

Age	Occupation	Method	Symptoms
39	-	Burning	Told witness that he was not well and had seen a ghost.
16	-	Hanging	Had behaved oddly the previous day and spoken 'a lot of nonsense'.
50	-	Burning	Mentally defective, thought there were 'things in his head'. He was very violent, commanding these 'things' to get out of him. Set fire to his head in order to destroy 'the things'.
40	-	Poison	Heavy drinker – threatened to commit suicide many times, and on occasions play-acted at drinking caustic soda.
35	Labourer	Drowning	Appeared to lose his mind at times for last three months.
38	Labourer	Drowning	Complained that he was bewitched. Behaviour was abnormal. Spoke a lot of nonsense.
39	Unemployed	Jumping from height	Hospitalized as a mental patient. Jumped from fifth floor of hospital.
26	Labourer	Hanging	Institutionalized in mental hospital for nine months. Appeared normal for a few days after discharge, but then relapsed into former state.

Age	Occupation	Method	Symptoms
24	Unemployed	Hanging	Described as not right in his head. Wanted to assault father.
21	Unemployed	Threw himself before train	Institutionalized in mental hospital for four months. Wandered about on discharge.
20	Labourer	Threw himself before train	Reported as having become mentally deranged on taking up work in the city.
47	Labourer	Burning	Mentally ill and destitute. Lived in a room on his own. Found burning in his room by neighbours. They extinguished fire. He said he had burnt himself because he had no one. Hospital was informed, but ambulance arrived three days later, by which time he was dead.
40	Labourer	Hanging	Mentally disturbed, talked to himself.
46	Labourer	Threw himself before train	Lived in men's hostel in Umlazi. He was described as mentally unbalanced.
29	Unemployed	Drowning	Discharged from hospital where he was a TB patient. Very depressed. Talked of dying.
30	Labourer	Hanging	Mentally unsound. Treated by *inyanga*.

AFRICAN WOMEN

Age	Occupation	Method	Symptoms
25	Domestic servant	Burning	Lived with her family in township. Had three children by different lovers but all three deserted her. She was observed as going mad. She killed herself soon after a quarrel occurred between her children and her brother's children.

Age	Occupation	Method	Symptoms
40	Field labourer	Threw herself before train	Described as going out of her mind periodically
39	Domestic servant	Burning	Lived with two children. Used to suffer from bouts of hysteria.
50	Housewife	Hanging	Described as mentally ill.
45	Housewife	Drowning	Was mentally deranged. Used to disappear from home every now and again.
24	Domestic servant	Drowning	Suffered from insomnia. Believed that she was being bewitched by her brother-in-law's lover.
40	Unemployed	Drowning	Became mentally deranged – shouted and talked to herself.
18	Unemployed	Threw herself before train	Was mentally deranged – often wandered away from home.

COLOURED MEN

Age	Occupation	Method	Symptoms
24	Seaman	Burning	Mentally ill. Hospitalized for a month, then moved in with aunt. Went around begging for help.
36	-	Burning	Had become a recluse. Children used to run after him and tease him.

COLOURED WOMEN

Age	Occupation	Method	Symptoms
26	-	Burning	Heavy drinker – depressed – stated that she would burn herself to death to join her dead husband.
50	Housewife	Hanging	Lived with her daughter. Was described as of unsound mind. Used to wander away from home.
25	Unemployed	Burning	Lived with family. Used to sit around and stare vacantly.

Age	Occupation	Method	Symptoms
32	Housewife	Burning	Had six children by different men, none of whom supported them. Was living with lover, but was very depressed and often said she would kill herself.

INDIAN MEN

Age	Occupation	Method	Symptoms
26	Teacher	Poison	Good teacher, keen sportsman, studying for BA Degree, melancholic, treated for shock, under psychiatric observation, trouble with principal at school, wanted to resign, talked of suicide.
38	-	Poison	Acutely jealous of second wife, created trouble when her parents visited her - called her a prostitute and stated he was not responsible for her pregnancy. Developed violent temper, tantrums, assaulted wife. On the night he committed suicide he was particularly aggressive to wife and would not allow her to sleep, waking her each time she fell asleep.
50	-	Hanging	Moody and quarrelsome. In the habit of assaulting wife. Wife sought refuge with neighbour after being violently attacked by him. He hanged himself.
22	Student	Drowning	Writing his JC (Junior Certificate - public examination completing lower secondary school). Suffered mental strain as a result of overstudying. Became tense, restless. Felt persecuted by girls, said everyone was against him. Wouldn't dress, lost appetite. Took

Age	Occupation	Method	Symptoms
			on job as a clerk and then left it. Talked of committing suicide.
22	Unemployed	Threw himself before train	Mental patient at hospital. Complained that he was homesick. Discharged. Had bouts of violence when he assaulted his parents. Threatened to kill himself.
30	Unemployed	Threw himself before train	Was a recluse - talked to himself, swore at people and begged.
25	Unemployed	Drowning	Described as mentally unbalanced. Lived with parents. Father offered to take him to a doctor. Said it was a waste of time.

INDIAN WOMEN

Age	Occupation	Method	Symptoms
18	Housewife	Burning	Reported of unsound mind - violent and abusive.
45	Housewife	Burning	Husband said she was 'funny in her head'. Recently delivered her ninth child.
17	Housewife	Burning	Depressed without reason - went for a walk, returned home and set herself alight.
35	Housewife	Hanging	Had lapses of mental disorder.
22	Housewife	Burning	Had lapses of mental disorder when she complained that she was being attacked by strangers. Often said she would attend her own funeral, but would later deny all knowledge of such statements.

16 Social factors

STRESS IN THE MARITAL AND FAMILY SITUATION

Stress within the family, and more pointedly, conflict
between the spouses is the most common social setting
in which suicide occurs in Durban.   This is hardly
surprising since 91 per cent of all suicides during
1940-60 and 88 per cent during 1962-71 were of persons
living in families.   The incidence of living alone was
higher among White and African suicides - among
Africans because of migrant labour and restriction by
law of the number of African families allowed to reside
in the urban areas; among Whites partly because of the
larger number of aged suicides. Stress within the
family tended to claim the relatively young person -
under 40.
  Suicide occurs most generally because the family
ceases to be an institution of emotional and material
support.   Its immediate provocation appears to be the
termination, or threatened termination, of the relation
by one of the two presiding partners.   Black male
suicides are usually the aggressive partners in this
situation and their suicides occur when their women
finally refuse to be their victims.   White men by contrast are usually the 'victims' of their wives.
  The patterns are clearest with regard to Whites and
Indians, who constitute the largest proportions of the
Durban families.   While most Indian men had reduced
their families to destitution through long histories
of non-support and neglect, only one White husband had
stopped supporting his family, temporarily, while he
searched for a better job.   The family in that particular case was not destitute; the wife was working but
she refused to run the house on her income or help him
with his debts.   In most White situations of family or

marital stress, the wives appeared to be unco-operative,
and unsympathetic to their husband's financial or emotional problems.   A 34-year-old husband said he
suffered because his wife had refused to have sex
relations with him;   in another case, suicide was provoked by the wife starting divorce proceedings against
an alcoholic husband;   in a third case, the wife had
moved in with her recently widowed mother and overlooked
the consequent loneliness and sense of rejection
suffered by her husband;   in a fourth, the wife
appeared to have literally nagged the husband to death
through her near-neurotic jealousy because of the responsibilities he assumed for his widowed mother and
widowed sister-in-law.   In sixteen of the twenty-one
cases of White male suicides apparently due to domestic
disputes, the husbands had been reluctant divorcees or
their wives had abandoned them.

The conjugal partners among Indians and Whites are
generally married, among Coloureds and Africans they
are more often just living together.

(a)   The typical male syndrome

The typical male syndrome is that of a relatively young
man between 30 and 39 years old, alcoholic, unemployed
or casually employed, who contributes very irregularly
to the family upkeep and who uses up most of his money
on drink.   He is at times also a child-beater.   His
wife has reported him to the child welfare society and/
or the police, and he has had several official warnings,
but to no avail.   The overcharged, passionate, loveless relation falters through eight to ten years of
marital strain and then suddenly explodes when the
wife walks out of it, taking the children with her.
Her walking out is often preceded by a previous conflict in which he in fact had 'thrown' her and the
children out and locked the house on them.

The frequency of this syndrome appears to be related
to the intensity of male domination, and in turn to
socio-economic class.   Thus its incidence is highest
among Indians and Coloureds and among them in the lower
and relatively more traditional social ranks.   It is
rare among Whites, where the relation between the sexes
is relatively equalitarian, and among urban Africans
where the domestic relation is most often between
gainfully employed lovers.   All the Coloured men and
80 per cent of the married Indian males between 30 and
49 years of age whose suicide was apparently due to
family stress projected this syndrome.

(i) White

Physical assault and complete non-support of families
is rare among White male suicides.   Only five White
husbands whose suicides appeared to be due to domestic
disputes had directed aggression against their wives;
in three of these, the husbands had withdrawn material
support and in two subjected their wives to physical
assault.   In one case the husband transposed his
emotional state onto the wife and attacked it there.
In another, the wife's children (husband's step-
children) were the bone of contention, but the aggression was deflected to the wife.   In all five cases
the suicides occurred almost immediately after the
wives left the husbands.   Only in one case was
'desertion' precipitated by the husband putting his
wife and children out on the street.   In that case,
the husband had then been plunged into deep remorse,
and had tried desperately to regain his family.   He
had finally followed it to his wife's mother's house
and made a last desperate plea.   When that had failed
he had killed his wife and her mother before killing
himself.
     Antagonism and aggression against the mother-in-law
was not observed among Black male suicides, though it
was fairly common among White male suicides.

(ii) African

Approximately 20 per cent of those African male suicides,
about whose social situation some evidence was available,
were due to conflict in the 'family', mainly between
lovers.   In three cases suicide was apparently provoked by conflict between other members of the family,
between co-wives, and between a wife and her mother-in-
law.   The most usual picture was of a husband or lover
killing himself upon his 'spouse' finally refusing to
suffer his aggression any further and leaving him.   In
two cases the suicides killed their spouses before
killing themselves.   The conflict rarely reflected
economic non-support, probably because of its lesser
importance in the kipita situation.   Allegations of
adultery and of a cooling of affection, were predominant,
on the other hand.

(iii) Coloured

The Coloured men in this situation were in their
twenties, and with the exception of two - one living

with an Indian woman and the other with a Coloured -
married.   Without exception, they were alcoholic, and
they did not bring home their wages, so that the women
nagged and the men in return beat them.   The women
finally left and the suicide followed.

(iv) Indian

Self-abuse, through alcoholism, and family abuse,
physical assault and non-support begins early in
married life among Indian male suicides, and reaches
breaking-point five or six children later when the
wife finally, instead of 'crawling into his bed' when
his temper subsides, violates his authority and the
'sanctity of their home', calls in the help of relatives, friends and such public institutions as the
child welfare and police.   Feeling shamefully exposed
and utterly demolished, the husband locks himself in
the toilet or bedroom and hangs himself in the noose
of his wife's sari.

His act probably symbolizes his final submission to
female power, a power to which the Hindu man is particularly sensitive and which he readily recognizes as the
source of his being, but which he struggles to over-
power and keep subordinate throughout his adult life.
It may at the same time symbolize a return to the
womb, to the beginning, to a new being.   The sari
probably represents not only his wife, but also his
mother.   It was in his mother's best sari that he
was cradled as an infant and given his human name and
social identity.   On another level it may signify
the triumph of good over evil.   In Hindu folklore,
when the universe was threatened by an evil monster
and the gods could not save it, it was Devi Mahatmaya
(the supreme goddess) who did so, and it was with her
lasso that she overpowered him and quelled his evil.
So it is with the 'lasso' of the 'Devi' in his house
that he vanquishes the evil (*pasu*) within himself and
resurrects both his peace and the peace of his family
through his death.   'Your mother can now get R20 a
month maintenance', says a father to his son who is
about to hang himself with his wife's sari.   She
received practically nothing from him during her lifetime.

But the act may also symbolize the suicide's final
revenge, on his family and on his community.   In
Hindu folklore, this world and its inferior material
order exists because of the female creative impulse.
It is Shakli, the female power of the male theos that

stimulates its creation.   It is 'desiring', an intrinsically female quality that ensures its persistence,
but female power is dependent upon and works through
the male principle, and so it is that woman should be
subservient to man and live in awe and wonder of him.
In challenging the authority of her husband, a woman
challenges the very medium of her social existence, and
she must be punished.   No social status is as low and
as deprived in traditional Hindu society as that of the
widow.   Indeed death was preferable and *sati* eminently
honourable, for in life she continued parasitic and
aimless after the 'medium' of her existence, her
husband, had ceased to be.   'I am going to punish your
mother for reporting me to the court', proclaims a
husband, and the punishment he has in store for her is
a living death in widowhood.   He seems to be saying
to his wife: 'You have rejected my authority and
thereby rejected *all* authority.'   But the revenge is
not only against her.   He bequeaths his destitute
family to society and exposes it to the social malaise
that destitution breeds.

The suicide has in fact spent the bulk of his adult
life attempting to destroy society by refusing to
integrate its values and flouting its disciplines, and
he has done so in that area of authority and responsibility that is specifically his.   Since his wife is
the most proximate point through which he reaches
society, she is the most vulnerable.   His destruction
of society begins with his destruction of her.   In
five cases this was overtly demonstrated when the
husband's suicide was preceded by an attempt on the
wife's life.   The suicide desires to kill his wife in
order to possess her.   She symbolizes home, family,
life, creation, society.   Thus his mood during the act
of killing is an intense, uncontrollable diffusion of
love and hate.   It may also inhibit a sense of failed
mission: 'I love you very, very much.   I was always
wanting to kill you, but I didn't have the guts to do
it.   Now there's fire in my hand,' says a young
Indian suicide who makes an unsuccessful attempt on
his wife's life.

'Never had the guts', probably implies never had the
power, the opportunity, rather than simply, never had
the courage.   'The fire is in my hand' can mean that he
is in control (1) or alternately, he is powerless, and
his solution is superficial, not real, the intention is
in his hand not his heart and therefore he will not
succeed in consuming her or society but they have consumed
him and so he seeks death to obliterate the memory of
his failure.

The sense of failed mission is even more marked in
the case of the husband who finally admits that twenty-
one years of solid and consistent persecution has not
daunted his wife, and through her efforts his daughter
is about to be married.   The persistence of customary
forms, despite his effort to obliterate them, is too
much for him.   He burns the wedding invitations, sym-
bols of auspicious sociability, of family vitality and
community growth, and stabs his wife, the mother and
preserve of it all.
    The failure of these husbands to integrate the res-
ponsibilities of husbands and fathers may in the first
place be due to a serious defect in their social
development.   The boys never grew into men.   In constant search of the nurturing mother - the world is
symbolized as such in Hindu lore - they are shocked
into withdrawal when their wives in their dependence
upon them turn out to be dependent 'daughters' and
aggravate matters by crowding them with the demands of
screaming children.   Cheated, they seek comfort in
the bottle, a wholly unsatisfactory mother-substitute;
frustrated, they pursue their vendetta against family
and society, and then kill themselves in a final admission of hopelessness and meaninglessness.

(b)   Women

(i)   White

White women whose suicides were traced to trouble in
the family were usually between 48 and 53 years old,
almost 60 per cent being divorced or separated from
their husbands.   In most cases the suicides appeared
to have been brought about by the breach itself and
were usually precipitated by quarrels.   Edith, 49,
moves in with her sister after a separation order, but
unable to bear it, pleads with her husband to resume
their former relationship.   When he refuses she
commits suicide.   Such statements as: 'I love you
with all my heart.   I cannot live without you', 'I
am sorry I cannot go on any longer.   I shall be out
of my mind and you won't return', convey something of
the loneliness and despair of these women.

(ii)   African

The largest proportion of African women whose suicides
had been provoked in the family situation were not

formally married, but the relationship had persisted
long enough for the suicide to exercise a monopoly
over the spouse.   The woman in particular, having
enjoyed a longstanding relationship with a man, comes
to regard him as her legitimate husband, though his
legal wife is in the homeland and he visits her
periodically.   The man, however, though spending most
of his time with her, appears not to respect her as he
does his wife, who holds him to his cultural roots and
through whom he feels his on-going presence in children, livestock and land.   While African society has
come to accept the necessity for men to migrate to the
urban areas, it continues to be hesitant and critical
of the migrant woman.   Torn from her traditional
moorings and submerged in menial domesticity she comes
to be identified with the evils of the faithless urban
process and is used as such by the African male who is
counselled against her by his family as the *isifebe*,
the carrier of disease and the eater of his wealth.

   Though polygamy is traditional and a means of project-
ing male prestige and male power, the woman in town is
never an extension of that system into the urban area.
No tradition sanctions that bond, no gifts pass to
mark its beginning, no elders and age-mates meet to
witness and seal its union, and no community exists
to pamper it and patch its conflicts.   The woman, no
matter how faithful, is an *isifebe* and, as such,
suspect.   The man, rooted in a polygamous tradition,
will more often than not expend his ego through plural
kipita.   Yet the '*kipita* union' is founded on sex and
charged by sex so that the emotional and economic hold
of the one partner over the other depends on sexual
fidelity and when sex fails the only meaningful component in an otherwise wholly impersonal and exploita-
tive system disappears and the relation ends.

   Twenty-year-old Thokozile, a domestic servant who
had come into the urban area less than two years ago,
had been virtually living with Tenga for eighteen
months.   Though their relation was uneasy, it was
important to her, for it sustained her in the anonymity
of the wide, big, incomprehensible world to which she
had suddenly become exposed.   She didn't trust him,
but this was only a part of the incomprehensible situation, and she had survived in it by ignoring the
doubts and enjoying the warmth and tenderness of his
presence each time it had occurred.

   She had been listening to records with Tenga and
his friends one Sunday morning in his 'Khaya' behind a
warehouse in the centre of town.   Tenga's wife,

bedecked in tribal glory, baby on back, suddenly
appeared, bringing with her all the nostalgia of a
home lost and never to be regained.   The heady rhythm
stopped.   The room was filled with the radiance of
the meeting between husband and wife.   Thokozile did
not exist - there was no place for her.   Jealousy,
self-recrimination, anger, and finally hopelessness
pushed her out of the room.   She rushed in a little
later screaming and burning.

(iii) Coloured

Coloured women involved in domestic problems were
mostly in their twenties or thirties, more often in
their twenties.   Half of them had quarrelled with
their lovers or husbands over other women.   Vera was
heartbroken because her lover had taken on another
girl-friend.   Janet, 36, turned to drink when her
husband deserted her and gradually degenerated into a
tramp.

(iv)   Indian

Almost 40 per cent of the suicides of Indian women (45
cases between 1962 and 1970) were due to conflict
within the family.   They were all under 40 and, with
the exception of five, all were passive recipients of
male aggression.   In five cases the men were their
lovers, in the rest their husbands.   In five cases
the final provocation was the husband's flagrant
adultery or the lover's infidelity.   A young woman
caught her husband red-handed, on their bed with
another woman; in one case the 'other woman' had been
the suicide's younger sister.   Two of the suicides
had been let down by their African lovers - the
suicide of the one, a girl of 17 who had borne his
child, had been provoked by the arrival and hostility
of her lover's wife;   the other, a woman of 30 had
burnt herself in a passion of jealousy when she discovered that her lover had another mistress.
     Generally the suicides were precipitated by trivial
incidents - a wife reacting to a husband refusing her
permission to go to the cinema or visit her family, or
a friend, or a husband scolding or physically assaulting his wife because she had not prepared his bath
water, or had forgotten to wake him up on time, or
had not prepared the dish he had ordered, or had continued in gainful employment against his wishes, or
had not responded to a crying child.   Yet these

incidents were symptomatic of the abject dependency
and the excruciating subordination suffered by these
women to the extent where their simplest desires and
routine activities operated at the behest of others,
in particular that of their husbands.

Two of the suicides appeared to be acts of expiation, following the discovery of their adultery.   In
the one case the trespass had been forgiven after due
punishment - a beating and a period of temporary con-
finement to her mother's house.   The suicide occurred
when the chastised wife discovered her lover's faith-
lessness.

Young Indian girls, both married and unmarried,
have a markedly high suicide rate, particularly
apparent during 1940-60 (the 15-19 year age range had
a rate of 57.6 per 100,000). (2)   There is little
doubt that marriage in the traditional Indian setting
constitutes specialized hazards for the young girl.

Courtship until very recently was non-existent
among Indians and anything approximating to it was
viewed as 'bad'.   While this position has now
relaxed, most marriages continue to be arranged and
parents continue to live in fear of the shame to which
a daughter's indiscretion may expose them.   The young
girl thus stands in constant threat of bringing the
family into disrepute.   During most of the 1940-60
period, a fairly rigid separation of the sexes operated so that a young girl was isolated from all members
of the opposite sex save those with whom marriage was
not possible (male kin members).   She thus grew up
with little knowledge about the opposite sex, and this
was aggravated by her ignorance about sex generally.
Young girls continue to be told to keep away from boys,
often in an accusing tone which presupposes their guilt.
A girl is warned that something 'bad' will happen to
her, that she will bring shame to her family, that 'her
father will kill her'.   Little or no attempt is made
to define this 'bad' thing and often she has the
vaguest knowledge of its precise nature.   To safeguard her against such eventualities her freedom is
suddenly constricted - she may no longer engage in the
innocent pranks and excursions of childhood.   Her
whole being is permeated with a feeling of deep shame
of growing womanhood, and she feels violent rebellion
against it which, perforce, she must subdue and internalize, directing it against herself.   Her training
to take up the roles of daughter-in-law and housewife
is intensified, and the common chastisement for mis-
demeanours is 'wait until you get to your mother-in-
law's'.

Early marriage in such a situation can only
intensify the already brewing trauma.   It implies in
the first place that the young girl's difficult adjustment to womanhood is moved from familiar and relatively
sympathetic surroundings to strange and comparably
antagonistic ones.   More often than not, the mother-
in-law materializes into the promised bogeyman.   She
rarely concedes the fact that the daughter-in-law is
not quite a woman, that she is still a child in mind
and heart, and to a certain extent, in body; but
demands skilled adult performance which, if not immediately forthcoming, is met with impatience and strong
rebukes.   The young husband is often a stranger whose
relationship with his adolescent wife is very largely
influenced by the opinions of the womenfolk of his
family.   Under the circumstances, the young wife's
position is highly invidious.   There is a convergence
of the problems of growing up, sudden sex experience,
for which she has had no preparation, and of which her
knowledge has been purely accidental and often fantas-
tic, and adjustment to a household of antagonistic
women.   If she does not succeed in rising to all these
conflicts, she is flung into a state of extreme anomie.
Though inter-sexual mingling has relaxed the young
girl's sexual education, the family's fears about
sexual breaches have not changed.   The transition from
childhood to womanhood continues to be fraught with
conflict, and these conflicts account for the high
suicide rate of young Indian girls both married and
never-married.

(c)   Examples of cases

*(i) Suicide following routinized pattern of externalized
aggression*

External aggression reaches a point of insatiability A
45-year-old married Indian man, unemployed for a year.
Barely maintaining family.   Wife's suspicions of his
infidelity aggravate the strained relations.   He
assaults his wife, and threatens suicide.   Finally in
a burst of anger, he ejects his family and hangs himself.

*Externalized aggression is threatened with stronger
counter-aggression* A 40-year-old African man living
with a woman whom he frequently assaulted and barely
supported, hangs himself when she finally leaves him
despite his pleadings.

A 55-year-old White man, though separated from his
wife, is acutely jealous of her.   He torments her both
physically and mentally, forces her out of the house,
then pursues her and asks her to return.   When she
refuses, he tries to shoot her at her place of work
and then kills her.

A 35-year-old Indian alcoholic with seven children
who has threatened suicide on a number of occasions
previously, poisons himself when his wife leaves him
and charges him for failing to maintain their children.

(ii) Discovery of 'spouse's' infidelity

The disruption may come suddenly, following a shocking
discovery of e.g. infidelity, desertion, or, among
engaged couples, jilting.

A 35-year-old married African employed in an urban
area, discovers his wife's adultery when visiting home.
He returns to town in an apparently mentally disturbed
state and hangs himself in his room.

A 19-year-old Coloured woman, living with her lover,
burns herself when he breaks off their association.

A 17-year-old unmarried Indian woman burns herself
when her family discovers her pregnancy and her lover
denies responsibility.

(iii) Death of a loved one

A 76-year-old White widower, depressed since the death
of his wife, shoots himself.

A 24-year-old White woman poisons herself after the
death of her lover.

A 30-year-old Indian widow becomes 'mentally unbal-
anced' after the death of her husband and burns herself.

(iv) Disruptions in the joint or extended family

In the Indian joint family domestic disruptions extend
beyond friction between conjugal partners, and include
parents and siblings-in-law.   The young wife may find
herself completely dominated by such relations who in
some instances use the young husband as the agent of
their aggression.

A 14-year-old married Indian girl burns herself
because of ill-treatment by her husband and his family.
Among other things, they would not allow her to wear
jewellery and pretty clothes.

A 32-year-old Indian woman became desperately home-
sick, but her wealthy husband refused to allow her to
visit her home and parents in India.   She became
aggressive and when in anger he put her out of their
home, she jumped from the flat and killed herself.

FINANCIAL PROBLEMS, UNEMPLOYMENT AND FEAR OF ARREST

(a)   Financial problems and unemployment

Financial trouble, unemployment, a brush with the law,
or being caught in some compromising situation leading
to a feeling of shame and fear of reprisals, and
physical ill-health forcing dependence on others, are
some of the factors that may be classified under social
frustrations.   Suicide may follow sudden exposure to
such pressures, or may be due to such pressures cumulatively reaching an unbearable intensity.
     Problems of money and keep confront men more often
than they do women.   Unemployment is far more likely
to affect workers than persons in higher occupational
rungs.   Accordingly unemployment is far more often
associated with the suicides of Blacks than Whites;
conversely White suicides are far more often bothered
with financial problems than Blacks.

(i)   Unemployment

African men   A 40-year-old man, dismissed from his job
due to labour retrenchment, hanged himself.
     A 25-year-old unmarried man who failed to find
suitable employment, despite having a matric certificate, and suffering the humiliation of being dependent
on his mother and younger brothers, drowned himself.
     A 50-year-old unemployed man became worried about
his family and drowned himself.

White men   A 58-year-old married man couldn't find
suitable employment.   The fact that his wife, a nurse,
supported him aggravated matters.   He gassed himself.

Coloured men   A 48-year-old married general labourer
could not hold a steady job.   He hanged himself.
     A 27-year-old unemployed man became ashamed of
sponging on his brother.   He hanged himself.

(ii)   Financial problems

African men   A 25-year-old man was heard to say: 'I
wonder how a person can get some money.'   He hanged
himself.

White men   A 52-year-old unmarried man suffered from
insomnia when his business deteriorated;   he broke his
engagement and shot himself.

A 29-year-old business representative moved into a
new house with his family but couldn't meet payment
on debts incurred.   He shot himself.

(b)   Arrest, fear of arrest or caught in a shameful act

Arrest or being caught in a shameful act have a traumatic effect.   The offence may be purely technical, such
as breach of a pass law, or driving without a licence,
or it may be a 'moral' breach.   Sometimes it is merely
an allegation, resulting in detention on suspicion.
The confrontation with the police, fear of authority,
and the humiliation suffered all combine to make the
situation unbearable.   During both periods, more
Africans committed suicide in this situation than
members of any other race group.   This may partly be
due to the fact that far more Africans are exposed to
this situation than members of other groups, Africans
being liable to arrest for a large number of technical
offences.   Police treatment of African suspects is
reputed to be often quite brutal, and suicides of
prisoners in detention have been both suspected and
confirmed. (3)

African men   A 27-year-old man was found in a semi-
hysterical state following his detention and subsequent
release on suspicion of responsibility for the death of
an African woman knocked down by a bus.   A little
later he was found hanging.
    A 24-year-old man detained on suspicion of rape and
later released appeared to have been terribly shocked
by his detention.   He was found hanging soon thereafter.
    A 30-year-old man was visited by the police to
investigate a case of rape.   He excused himself to go
to the toilet and hanged himself there.
    A 27-year-old man was called by the police to make
a statement about a case of theft.   He reported that
the police did not believe him and imputed other crimes
to him.   He was found hanging shortly thereafter.
    A 23-year-old man was accosted by a White policeman
while travelling in a third-class coach.   The policeman walked by, then stopped, turned and slapped him.
His friend remonstrated but he was so petrified that
he flung himself out of the train and was killed.

African women   A 27-year-old woman was found by her
husband in bed with a visiting friend.   He called the
neighbours together to inform them of her adultery and

seek their advice. She slipped away from the
'tribunal' and burnt herself in the lavatory.

White men A 67-year-old man shot himself following a
complaint by two African women that he had exposed
himself indecently to them.

A 43-year-old man, arrested for drunkenness, had
to be 'pacified' by the police because according to
them, he became uncontrollably aggressive. He was
found hanging in his cell a few hours later.

A 49-year-old man was observed by a policeman
entering a cane field with an African woman. He was
arrested for intention to have sex relations with her
(contravening the Immorality Act). He pleaded that
in fact nothing had happened, but was arrested. He
shot himself.

Indian men A 22-year-old man, living with his uncle
who was good to him and who respected and trusted him,
hanged himself when the uncle caught him in his
daughter's room in a compromising situation.

Indian women A 40-year-old widow poisoned herself on
discovering that she was pregnant, after three years
of widowhood.

A 22-year-old woman burnt herself after admitting
her infidelity to her husband.

PHYSICAL ILLNESS AND OLD AGE

(a) Physical illness

(i) Whites

Physical incapacity or illness was the highest single
factor in the suicides of Whites. Among Blacks, it
was exceeded only by marital stress or rupture in a
valued relationship. Of the White suicides who
suffered physical ailment, 75 per cent were over 60
years old. If the association of illness with suicide
is restricted to the under sixties, then illness is
associated more often with Black suicide than White.
Among Blacks, illness is inevitably complicated by
the spectre of unemployment and poverty; among Whites
by helplessness, dependence, and loneliness.

Practically all White women suffering illness were
over 60, but an appreciable proportion of the White men
were younger: 62 per cent being in their fifties, 32

per cent in their forties, and 6 per cent in their early thirties. Sixty per cent were married; the rest were either widowed or divorced. Apart from eight who were pensioned, the rest held managerial or superivsory posts, or were technocrats or skilled artisans. Cancer, high blood pressure, diseases of the heart, liver and kidneys and duodenal ulcers were the usual complaints. They lived in fear of dying, had given up hope of becoming cured, and were petrified of being a burden to others.

A 47-year-old hotel manager suffered from bad nerves and began drinking heavily. Advised to go slow on drinking, his physical symptoms shifted to his head and stomach and he began to believe that he had cancer. He shot himself.

A 44-year-old electrician had a cancerous kidney removed. Convinced that the other would go the same way, he shot himself.

A 57-year-old man had had enteric fever for seventeen years, arthritis of both legs and bronchial pneumonia. He poisoned himself.

(ii) Africans

Illness was associated with the suicides of approximatèly 11 per cent of African men and 5 per cent of African women. They were all under 60, 80 per cent being in fact under 40. All except one – a shopkeeper – were labourers. Their suicide followed soon after the diagnosis of their illness, which was usually tuberculosis. Often they were unaware of their illness and the knowledge of it came traumatically when they presented themselves for compulsory health examination before contracting for labour. They were all married with dependents and the illness spelled an immediate cessation of earnings and disintegration of the male role, not only because of financial impotency but in some instances also because of feared sexual impotency.

39-year-old Goba is diagnosed as suffering from tuberculosis. He hangs himself.

47-year-old Cele is put off from work because of his illness. He throws himself before a moving train.

45-year-old Mwandla is suffering from tuberculosis and cannot have normal sex relations. He hangs himself.

African women suicides suffering from illness were generally older than the men. It was never clear what it was that they suffered from, but they usually

complained of aches and pains and said that they were
tired of living.

A 35-year-old woman told her husband that she was
tired of being a burden to him through illness.   She
burnt herself.

A 30-year-old domestic servant suffered from tuberculosis and lost her employment.   She was found hanging
in her room.

A 48-year-old housewife grew increasingly anxious
about her ailments.   She visited several *inyangas*, and
gave up hope of ever being cured - 'No one can cure me.
It is better to die'.   She burnt herself.

(iii)   Coloureds and Indians

Fifteen per cent of Indian men and 8 per cent of Indian
women suicides complained of physical incapacity and
illness.   They were all under 50, 80 per cent being
under 40.   Three were single, one widowed and the rest
married.   The nature of their illness was often inex-
plicit in the reports.   Diabetes, high blood pressure,
pneumonia, and tuberculosis featured when the ailments
were diagnosed.   Otherwise there were complaints of
headaches, backaches, stomach-aches and tiredness
about constant visits to doctors and moving in and out
of hospital.

Indian men   A 46-year-old barman, who had undergone
several operations and could not bear further pain,
poisoned himself.

A 43-year-old factory worker suffering from short
breath asked to be rubbed down with liniment, and then,
unable to bear further pain, drank the liniment and
killed himself.

Indian women   Manorama (22 year's old) had suffered
from stomach-aches and spells of coma since the age of
12.   She complained of a severe pain, said she
couldn't take it any more and killed herself with three
bottles of codeine and a fair quantity of wintergreen.

A 50-year-old crippled woman, abandoned in an old
age home by her family, drowned herself.

A 65-year-old married woman said that she could not
bear her ailments any longer and had thus set herself
alight.

Coloured A 36-year-old bricklayer suffered from fits
and became disabled as a result of a paralysed leg.
He burnt himself.

A 34-year-old woman complained of severe stomach-
aches. She burnt herself.

A 43-year-old woman suffered from high blood pressure
and said she couldn't take it any longer. She burnt
herself.

(b) Old age

The incidence of suicide among the aged is highest
among Whites. Eighteen per cent of the White men and
20 per cent of the White women who committed suicide
during 1962-70 were over 60. By contrast, 9 per cent
of Indian men and 3 per cent of Indian women, and
negligible proportions of Africans and Coloureds (seven
between the two groups) were over 60. The White
suicides invariably lived alone and suffered from
intense loneliness, pain and depression. The Blacks
lived with families. The White suicides were usually
widowed, invariably living away from relatives and
suffering physical pain and mental depression. The
Black suicides lived with their families, the men with
married sons and their wives, and the women, when
widowed, usually with daughters. There were nearly
always grandchildren about, and sociable neighbours in
very close proximity. Physical helplessness and a
dependence on others due to illness appeared to be the
main factor associated with their suicides. The White
suicides were not only physically ill, but also very
lonely.

The records are often silent about the feelings of
the Blacks, and the words left by the aged White give
only peripheral clues to their extremely distraught
conditions, yet these give some insight into their
tortured minds and painful bodies.

They are people who find themselves old, infirm,
alone; shunned by their former dependants, isolated
from society, and trapped in boarding houses and old
age homes. They are usually gentle and apologetic and
show a touching concern for the inconvenience their
acts may cause others and the mess they may leave
behind. A 72-year-old pensioner locks himself in the
bathroom, sits in the bath with the water running so
that no one will hear, shoots himself, closes the tap
and awaits his death. On the bathroom door he pins a
note for his daughter - 'Elaine don't open the door.
Phone police, phone Graham' (his son).

A 92-year-old White invalid writes, 'I am sorry about
all this mess.'   Another old man found sitting in his
bath, slashing his stomach, apologizes, and then with a
touch of humour explains to his landlady 'Your bloody
knife is blunt.'

An 85-year-old White lodger leaves a note for the
secretary of the hotel, 'I hope this won't trouble you
too much.'

An aged White husband writes to his wife, 'My dear,
I am sorry for all this trouble I have brought upon
you.   I want to thank you for the wonderful kind girl
and wife you have been.'

'I do not wish to be a burden on you', is a common
statement.   An 80-year-old sportingly declares, 'I
have had a good run for 80 years.   I don't want to be
a burden to anyone.'

Instructions to make funerals as simple as possible
convey a mixture of humility and guilt.   'Please bury
me in a plain black coffin, unpainted and the cheapest
that money can buy.   No flowers, no mourners'.   Guilt
predominates in such statements as: 'God forgive me
for what I may do and have mercy on my soul.'

Mental torture is expressed in such words as, 'My
brain is splitting, I go through sleepless night after
sleepless night', 'I have no intention to live and want
to blow my brains out', 'My head and nerves are bursting', 'I can't take any more, I have suffered too much
with my nerves'; anxiety in 'I can't breathe any more.
At each breath I think I will die'; physical pain in
'I can't after years suffer the pain I go through any
longer', 'My brain seems ready to snap', 'I have died
a thousand deaths, coughing and choking every night.
I would rather die once'.

Death for them appears to become a reality in the
deadness of night.   When life has been experienced as
action, independence, growth, work and the cumulative
rewards of work, inaction, helplessness, dependence are
in themselves death, and the suicidal act confirms
this.   Life ceases when work ceases.   The old White
man sits on the verandah of his old age home waiting;
'If they don't come for me in fifteen minutes they will
take me to Stellawood' (the cemetery).   Then he
states, 'I have nothing to live for', and shoots himself.

YOUTH

Teenage suicides invariably occur in situations of conflict with authority.   Teenagers are adults emotionally

and physically, but socially they are minors and dependent on parents who may impose their will upon them,
and constantly remind them of the returns they are
expected to make for services done.   The relationship
may be further strained when parents, frustrated in
their own ambitions, strive to realize these through
the children.   The pressure may explode in open conflict and settle down into a bearable bantering relation, or the children may find the home unbearable and
await the opportunity to leave it.   The suicide-prone
situation is probably the one in which the 'child'
internalizes parental values but finds them in conflict
with his own interests, or with the newly changed social
environment in which he must make his adult adjustment,
and is plunged into a state of guilt and confusion.
Repression of such internal conflict, most prevalent in
relations characterized by authoritarian distance where
'children' are incapable of talking things out with
parents, aggravates matters.

The apparent factors that drove the Durban teenagers
to suicide, according to the evidence of the Court
records, were disagreements with parents, usually over
their love relations, and to a lesser extent over
school work, anxiety over school work, anxiety over
unmarried pregnancy, or a sudden break in a valued
relationship, either through death or some other
factor.   Parents often objected to a 'young' love
relation because they considered it premature;   or
feared it would result in unmarried pregnancy, or
destroy a brilliant future and deprive them of the
returns they had expected from their children for whom
they had sacrificed so much.

In most cases the teenagers appeared to have experienced the parents as the most proximate point of an
overall crippling societal authority which they either
regretted deeply or rejected violently.   Their
suicide appeared to be an admission of their helplessness against that authority, and their failure to
realize new meaning, partly because of its vague definition, but primarily because of their emotional
involvement with traditional institutions.   They were
in an apparent state of unbearable tension between
'freedom' and authority, dependence and independence,
the past and the present and between the present and
the future which they awaited with mixed feelings.
Thus though they suffered a sense of suffocation because
of parental possessiveness, and of being strait-jacketed
into archaic forms they had outgrown, the only meaning
and security they knew was in terms of those forms, so

that if the past appeared outmoded, the new was strange
and ominous and the suicide appeared to have occurred
because they could not risk reaching out to it.

. Their suicide, it seems, works both to restitute the
traditional they had threatened to destroy - since they
and not it is destroyed - and to pave the way for the
new that they had hopelessly fought for, since in practically all cases the agents of societal convention,
the parents, are so shattered that it seems apparent
they can no longer impose traditional authority with
the same rigidity on their remaining children.

(a)   The Durban cases

During the forty years under review 128 teenagers committed suicide.   These constituted 12 per cent of all
suicides during 1940-60, and 8 per cent during 1962-70.
By far the highest proportion were Indian girls: 68
and 54 per cent respectively during the two periods.
Twenty-one per cent of the Indian girls who committed
suicide during 1962-70 were scholars, 18 per cent were
factory workers, two were domestics and the rest were
at home helping their mothers.   A small number, fifteen
in all, were married.

(i)   Fear of authority (Indian and African girls)

The suicide of Dolly, an Indian girl, occurred after
the principal discovered that she had played truant
from school and had gone to the cinema with a boy.
She was hauled out and put to shame before the whole
school.   The matter was then reported to her parents.
Unable to face further disgrace, she hanged herself.

Thoko, a 14-year-old African domestic servant,
hanged herself after burning her employer's ironing
board.

(ii) High parental expectations

Ambition of parents imposed on children is a frequent
factor in teenage suicides.   A significant proportion
of young Durban suicides appeared to have been provoked by the intense emotional stress created by
parental demands of 'high' educational achievement for
their children.   This was particularly marked among
Indians who place very high value on education and who
also had the highest scholar suicide rate.   The Mat-
riculation examination, because of its high failure

rate, induces annual stress and hurls an observable
section of the community into a state of nervous tension
at the time of writing, and anger and helpless dis-
appointment at the time of publication of results.

Eighteen-year-old Sivan breaks under the overpowering
ambition of his father. He cannot cope with his school
work and is convinced that he will not make the Matric
exam. In helplessness he turns away from school and
plays truant. Long and emotionally charged scenes
follow with his father, and finally in desperation he
hangs himself.

Eighteen-year-old Linda, a White student nurse,
failed her test and despaired of passing her final
exam. She worked herself into such a state of nervous
anxiety that she had to be hospitalized.   Unable to
face the exam room upon her discharge she strangled
herself.

An 18-year-old African girl, Rose, dropped out of
school despite her parents' protest and started having
a gay time, but then became stricken with remorse and
burnt herself after writing: 'I refused to be educated.
I bitched around with men. People who refuse to
listen to good advice end this way.'

(iii) Inability to relate to others

In some instances the young suicide, whatever his other
problems, appeared to have suffered from an inability
to break out of his shell and relate himself to people
apart from members of his family.

Nineteen-year-old Sigamony (Indian) is a very shy
petrol attendant, who hankers after the girl next door
but is unable even to raise his head and greet her.
He eats his heart out in silent torture when she becomes
engaged, and when the family receive her wedding card
he laboriously scratches out the name of the birdegroom
and inscribes his own in its place.   He then makes out
a new invitation card to his marriage with his 'dream
girl', goes out, gets drunk, and poisons himself.

*(iv) Conflict between parents and teenagers over choice
of marriage partner*

Opposition of parents to the choice of a marriage
partner often provokes the suicide of young Indians.
The making of a suitable match for children of
marriageable age continues to be the most important
parental function.   There is the greatest tension and
conflict when a 'child' chooses a partner from the

'wrong' social, language or religious group, and a
number of suicides are directly attributed to such
objections to the young people.   In three cases during
1962-70, such opposition resulted in the couples killing themselves together.

A 19-year-old Indian, Rajpathie, is in love with 23-
year-old Ronnie.   Ronnie is already married and there
is stringent opposition to their relationship.   They
tie their wrists together, jump into the harbour and
drown.

Seventeen-year-old Valiamma and 19-year-old Ahmed
meet in the factory where the two are employed.   They
fall in love but know that their parents will never
consent to the marriage because of their religious and
language differences.   They take a room in a hotel,
drink poison and die.

(v)   Unmarried pregnancy

This plunges young teenagers into the most devastating
conditions of stress.   In extreme cases young girls
may place the blame elsewhere in order to appear as
victims of rape, and the boys may attempt to slip out
of the situation by denying paternity.   In a small
number of cases, suicide appears the only escape, both
girls and boys resorting to this, though it is commoner
among the girls.

During 1940-60, the largest number of suicides provoked by this factor was that of Indian girls, during
1962-70 it was of African girls. That Indian girls
should be so provoked is understandable in view of the
relatively strict control that is exercised over
meetings between the opposite sexes, but it is surprising among Africans since African attitudes to courtship
are very relaxed, and the majority of African births
in Durban are out of wedlock. (4) It reveals that
though urban African life exists in a state of gross
disintegration, Africans continue to value traditional
norms and are extremely sensitive to their violation.

Traditional African society recognizes petting,
but at the same time jealously guards the virginity of
the young girl.   Courtship is institutionalized
through a public ceremony involving the two partners
and controlled by the peer-groups of the couple.   Any
breach of sexual rules brings shame not only to the
couple but to the respective peer groups, particularly
that of the girl, and her group will go naked to the
umdeni (homestead) of the offending suitor and wail
at his door and demand that they be cleansed by the

payment of a beast.   Interviews with tribal Zulu women
revealed that these customs still continue and though
the unmarried pregnancy rate is high it is deprecated
because of the strength of traditional values.   Hence
we have a situation in Zulu society where on the one
hand the objective conditions have so changed that it
is almost impossible to regulate sexual relations and
to restrict pregnancy and procreation within the marital
state; and yet on the other hand the values observed
in the past continue to be treasured in the present.
The consequent feelings of guilt and shame following
transgression are aggravated by the economic problems
that children born out of wedlock impose on the *umdeni*
or homestead.

A young girl who conforms to traditional sexual
structures and marries respectably, brings not only
cattle and wealth to her parental *umdeni,* but she
establishes firm economic and social rights for her
children in her father's *umdeni.*   Children born outside marriage are without rights in any *umdeni.*   They
are deprecated as *ivezandlebe* (5) in their mother's
umdeni, and if their maternal grandparents love them
too much they stand in danger of evoking the envy of
their cousins who may see them as a threat to their
inheritance.   Children born of an adulterous union
are likewise derogated as *umtwana wesiblahla* - children
of the bush.   Such attitudes and their associated
values continue to influence the lives of African
people despite their urbanization and christianization,
so that in African congregations the 'illegitimate'
child is baptized separately from the legitimate child
and both the child's mother and maternal grandmother
are punished in public by being temporarily suspended
from wearing the uniform of the church.

There is a high incidence of abandoned African
children throughout the country and investigations
show that this is in the main due to the mother's
feeling of shame, her fear that the children will not
be acceptable in the *umdeni* and fear of the unmanage-
able economic burdens that they will constitute in
the urban townships.

The woman living with a lover also suffers a mixture
of guilt and shame (for abandoning traditional mores)
and insecurity, for she does not know how long the
liaison will last.   Discussion with a group of thirty-
five African workers (June 1972) in the age range
34-40, convalescing in a Zululand hospital, revealed
the unanimous attitude that women in the city were no
good, that though they would sleep with them, they
would not consider marrying them.

In terms of personality, one may deem young girls
whose suicide is apparently precipitated by unmarried
pregnancy to have highly developed superegos. They
may be seen as consumed by guilt and fear of anticipated reprisals. But the element of altruism is
probably strong and fundamental, so that the suicide
is seen as an act that exonerates the 'group' from
blame for the transgressions. Thus a young unmarried
pregnant Indian girl told her brother that she had
burnt herself because she did not wish to disgrace
her family.

The Indian attitude to unmarried pregnancy is rigid
and unrelenting towards all infringements of sex taboos
and young people are keenly aware of this. The
following statement of a 23-year-old Indian youth,
who hanged himself allegedly because of his depression
over a love affair, is significant in this context:
'Our race is very sensitive about love.'

The attitude of the other ethnic groups is far
more relaxed. In addition, the relatively more
informal and equalitarian relations between mother and
daughter and husband and wife among Whites, allows for
a freer exchange of confidences and guidance in
problems. The Indian attitude by contrast is harsh,
abortion often inaccessible, or the type resorted to
ineffectual. The mother, because of her own state of
dependence on in-laws and husband, is mortally afraid
of the blame that accrues to her and thus often lacks
the strength to support the young girl in her calamity.
In many instances, parents are quite unaware of their
daughter's pregnancy until after suicide.

Indian girls A 14-year-old girl, left in charge of
the house and young children while both parents worked,
drowned herself when she discovered she was pregnant.

A 15-year-old girl burnt herself when her family
discovered her pregnancy and chastised her severely.

(vi) Failure to find new meaning

The need to assert independence, through new ties, new
values, new norms, and the inability to do so without
parental approval and support is often an important
factor in teenage suicides.

Manickum Manickum, a young Indian girl, has a job as
domestic help, minding the children and looking after
the house while her mistress teaches at a school.
She lives with her own family and travels daily to

work.   As often happens in Indian families engaging
Indian domestic help, she is treated very much as part
of the family by her employer, going out with them to
the cinema or an occasional play.   The result is that
not only is her standard of living distinct and
different from that of her family's, but she also
assumes in some respects her employer's middle-class
norms.   Her attitude as a young unmarried girl towards
members of the opposite sex, for instance, is far
more relaxed than her family is prepared to tolerate
and on this specific issue friction begins to build up
between her and her mother.   Manickum asserts her
right to fall in love and have a boyfriend and rejects
her parents' attempts to assert their traditional
rights in this matter.

Her employer, though treating her as a member of
the family, does not feel the responsibility of a
mother towards her.   Had she done so, she would not
have allowed her to be dated.   Her main interest lies
in ensuring that Manickum performs her domestic duties
efficiently, and so long as she does this, she says
nothing about the dates.   Manickum interprets this as
approval, and deludes herself into thinking that her
behaviour is in accord with her employer-cum-guardian's
values and dismisses her own parents' stringent objections to her late home-comings, with impunity.   Her
relations with her mother cool to the point where they
stop speaking to each other.   Manickum, comfortable
in the support of her employer, does not appear to be
disturbed by this.   She becomes bemused and shocked
however when her employer joins her mother in criticizing her, partly because of the growing deterioration in her work performance, but primarily because
she begins to fear that the precedent Manickum is
setting will adversely influence her own daughters.

Manickum begins to feel herself being pushed into
isolation, and the pushing is completed when she has
a serious quarrel with her boyfriend.   She finds herself suddenly entirely alone and without any moral
support.   The small confidence she had in her own
innovations explodes.   She blames her mother for her
distraught state, screams 'You must be glad now as my
boyfriend doesn't want me any more.   It's all broken',
and sobs into her pillow.   Her mother lashes back
'That's what comes of not listening to your parents.'
An impassioned battle of words follows, during which
her mother tells her 'If you don't want to live with
us why don't you just pack your clothes and go.'   This
has a searing effect.   Her mother walks away sobbing

hysterically.   Blocked from expressing all further
aggression, and feeling grievously wronged in view
of all the financial assistance she has given her
family for years, she locks herself in the bathroom
and a little later is heard screaming and shouting
'Mother, come and see, I am burning for you.'   Mother,
in Hindu theology, also represents society.   Thus if
one wishes to interpret her gesture within the
Durkheim frame, she may be heard as saying - 'Society,
come and see, I am burning for you.'

To her parents, it had seemed that Manickum had
been trying for months to burn society, to burn her
home and family by taking on a boyfriend and entering
into a liaison outside the confines of social prescriptions.   For months, it seemed, Manickum and her
mother had been locked in a duel of 'who would burn
who first.'   Had Manickum fallen pregnant, she would
certainly have burnt her family, for she would have
'cut off their noses.'   Her self-burning had thus
saved them the impending disgrace.

But Manickum's act was not entirely altruistic.   It
was as importantly an act of revenge.   She had not
desired her death.   Death had been imposed upon her.
She in fact wanted desperately to live, and to live in
terms of a definition no longer burdened by the stric-
tures she had outgrown.   Unfortunately she never
realized the nature of this definition and just when
it seemed that she was beginning to do so, it spoiled,
and became unintelligible, throwing her into an unbearable, normless limbo.

While her self-destruction symbolized the redemption
of society it in effect did not redeem her family.
It is unlikely that suicide ever serves this purpose
for the surviving kinsmen of the suicide.   They become
trapped in the whirls of stigma associated with the
act in the social mind, and are obsessed by its encum-
bent guilt.   While society defines the act, and the
situations in which it may and even should occur, it
officially deprecates it, and holds all those involved
in it guilty.   Thus the relatives are haunted by the
death, and the guilt of the death, and rationalize it
by minimizing the provocations of the deceased, pleading that the act is inexplicable and that the suicide
had no reason to resort to it.   Nearly always the
same statements are made: 'She was such a happy girl.
We never dreamed she would do such a thing.'   On
further questioning they would admit that she had
threatened suicide before, even made an attempt, 'but
we thought she was just fooling or trying to frighten

us. We never thought she would actually do it.   What
reason did she have?   We were a happy family.'

Rungi Sixteen-year-old Rungi hanged herself with her
tie from the rafter of the toilet.   She was in Standard 8 at school.   Her mother does not know why she
did it, yet her mother's long rambling account of her,
suggests that she was afraid of becoming her mother
and despaired that she would be anything else.
   'I can't say why she did it.   No there was no
trouble, no boy, nothing like that - nobody scolded
her. Why anybody must scold her?   She was a very nice
girl and she was the only girl, so everybody liked her
and gave her what she wanted.   You must see her
clothes.   Aiyo, I can't even close the trunk.   I
packed them all away.   What she can want?   Everything
she want, we give her.   No, nobody had quarrelled
with her.   My sons want anything, they ask me.   They
won't ask her, why, because she little short tempered.
She was very religious.   Every day, she will pray
after coming home from school.   She pray just like
me, to Perumalsami and Angalesperi and Mariama.   But
she don't get spirit (6) like me.   Since she died I
never get spirit, I never asked God why it happened.
I just don't have the mind.   I don't know why.   I
can't tell God why you did it?   No I can't say that.
I must think of the other children.   I must pray for
them now.   I take the needle every year.   I stopped
it this year for the first time in 9 years, not because
I don't want to, because in our religion, we mustn't
when someone dies.   Two months before she died she
had her sixteenth birthday party.   She said she must
have it, and said I must tell her brother to give her
his first pay for the party.   How much I told her to
wait till she is 21, but she said no, she won't have a
party then, she wanted it now.   So my son give her
his pay packet.   He is a page.   He got R16.   He said
that's all I can give.   You must put the rest.   She
bought a midi dress and expensive shoes.   We put a
tent outside.   She invited all our relatives.   Such
a good party she had.   There was a funeral that same
day.   People near us and I said how you will have
party when they have funeral and she said "we can't
stop now.   Never mind we won't put the music high."
Till six o'clock (p.m.) we had the party.   It began to
rain.   She took everybody in the garage and they were
dancing.
   Her cousin came everyday and they will go to school
together.   She always came out first.   Her elder

brother failed.   Then he got fed up, because she was
beating and so he left school.
     She always told me "one thing I'll never work for
White people like you do.   I'll do typing or teaching
or anything, but I'll not work so hard and break my
back."   She did all the housework.   She cleaned and
scrubbed, washed clothes and cooked.   She was very
clever.
     The day she died, I had just come from hospital.
I had had an operation and I was in my room.   She
cleaned the house and prepared my bath water.   She
had a bath and her hair was wet.   She didn't say anything to me.   I heard my son shouting.   I can't tell
why she did it.   It must be God asked her.   It was a
religious day on which it happened.   It was amavasi
[a Hindu period of fasting and spiritual cleansing].'

(vii)   Introjection and revenge

The suicides of young teenagers often resemble the psychological model of introjection and the sociological
model of revenge or 'samsonic' suicide. (7)   In the
first, the suicide introjects the external source of
aggression into his personality and in killing the self
there is the symbolic killing of that external source.
In the second, the suicidal act is interpreted more
generally as a means of revenge on the surviving
aggressor.

African boy   A 13-year-old boy is questioned by his
father about some missing money which he suspects his
son has stolen, and threatens to call in the *isangoma*
(Zulu diviner) to divine the truth.   The boy is found
hanging from a tree a little later.

European boy   A 16-year-old boy asks his guardian - his
aunt, for permission to spend the night with a friend.
His aunt refuses, and warns that he must be home at
10.30 p.m.   He returns home at the appointed time.
His aunt was up to meet him.   There is an exchange of
words between them.   He goes into the kitchen, and
returns in a state of collapse.   He has taken poison.

Indian boy   The mother of an 11-year-old boy asks him
to fetch their goats.   He refuses.   She threatens to
beat him.   He picks up stones to strike her.   She
then beats him with a stick.   He cries and is later
found hanging from a tree. (8)

Coloured girl   A 17-year-old girl dressed to go to
church asked her mother for some money.   An argument
followed.   The girl then sulked and said she wouldn't
go to church.   A little later she was found hanging.

Indian girl   A 19-year-old girl looked after the house
and her younger siblings while her parents worked.
Her mother returned from work one evening and finding
the house untidy, and the children dirty, scolded her.
She bore the chastisement in silence, attended to the
neglected duties and then drank some poison and died.

(viii) Failure to find security in the family

The Court record in the case of 14-year-old Gail who
committed suicide through poisoning, describes her as
clearing up the table after dinner and the family
laughing at her unsteady gait as she did so, thinking
that she was putting on an act.   The laughter ends
and is replaced by a sharp rebuke when she drops and
breaks a dish.   'Mummy does not know I am sick and
dying', says Gail, and then collapses on the floor
and is dead in a short while.

'Mummy' apparently never understood that Gail began
dying at the age of three, when in quick succession
she lost her father, when he died, and then her mother,
when she remarried and devoted herself to the children
born of that marriage.   Suffering insecurity and an
unbearable sense of being unwanted and unloved, death
appeared the only way out.

Her 'dying' was intercepted for a short while, when
she formed a strong attachment with a boy in the
neighbourhood.   She told his mother that she wanted
to leave home and live with him, that she wished she
would fall pregnant, because then she would have to
move in with them.

Gail's mother however, intercepted the process of
'living' and in that sense brought on the death by
strongly objecting to her relationship with the boy
and obtaining a court order restraining him from seeing
her.

17 The construction of suicide models

The information abstracted from the Inquest Court records can be used to construct models of typical Durban suicides by race and sex. The credibility of these models depends on the quality of the Court records. The models are closer to the 'truth' for non-Africans than for Africans.

AFRICAN MODELS

(a) Men

The more usual African male suicide is between 25 and 35 years old, employed as a labourer or domestic worker and living in a compound or on his employer's premises. He is married, but his wife and children live in the 'homeland' or rural area. He is involved in the city, in a passionate, emotionally corroding and insecure relation. His suicide often follows a break in this relation. The other factors likely to provoke his suicide are the trauma of an arrest or a serious brush with someone in authority - 20 and 14 per cent of the cases respectively. Informants usually describe the African suicide to have been a person easily roused to anger. He most usually hangs himself (71 per cent of the cases) or throws himself before a moving train (13 per cent of the cases).

(b) Women

The African female suicide is invariably a domestic worker and her suicide is provoked by a traumatic break with her lover. She is usually in her thirties and rarely over 35.   She is emotionally distressed (35 per cent of the cases), restless, nervous and depressed (27 per cent of the cases) and has taken to excessive drinking (20 per cent of the cases).   She is at times described as breaking out into bouts of violence (12 per cent of the cases) and her suicide often occurs on the crest of a violent outburst (32 per cent of the cases), following a quarrel (52 per cent of the cases) during which she may have suffered an assault (33 per cent of the cases), usually at the hand of her lover. Her suicidal act is violent and impulsive, and one gains the impression that she would regret it if she survived.

African suicides rarely leave notes, partly because of the impulsiveness of their acts, but probably also because of their higher rate of illiteracy and the lower presence of the writing habit in their socio-economic and cultural milieu.

WHITE MODELS

The White suicide is usually between 50 and 59 years old, the men tending to be younger than the women.

(a)   Men

The White male suicide is usually between 50 and 59 years old, and is more likely to be physically ill (31 per cent of the cases) than emotionally depressed (22 per cent of the cases).   The most usual precipi-tating factor is a serious break in a valued relation. The break itself occurs because he can no longer cope with his material responsibilities and because his wife fails to support him.   His notes express relief, or plead for forgiveness.   He most usually shoots himself.   The whole pattern of his act - writing of suicide notes (he is the greatest contributor to the suicide notes in the Durban Inquest Court records), a history of previous attempts or threats (most common in his case) and the committing of the act in private, and away from his family and friends - suggests care-ful planning and reflecting.   His is not an impulsive act.

(b)   Women

She is both physically ill and emotionally distressed,
the first condition often producing the second.   A
sudden break in a valued relation, usually through
death, aggravates the condition and suicide results,
most usually through an overdose of barbituates.

COLOURED MODELS

(a)   Men

He is between 35 and 49 years old, alcoholic (80 per
cent of the cases), emotionally distressed (33 per cent
of the cases) or in poor physical health (20 per cent
of the cases).   He has suffered a serious break in a
valued relationship (26 per cent of the cases).   He
is indifferent about privacy and either hangs or
poisons himself.

(b)   Women

The Coloured female suicide is under 30.   She has
undergone prolonged suffering due to a brewing rupture
in a meaningful and emotionally supportive relation
with a lover or husband.   Her suicide occurs when she
finally admits that the relationship has ended and she
has no means of saving it.   Her act usually erupts
after a serious quarrel, usuably with her lover.   She
lashes out against him as if in a last bid to save the
relationship and then, exhuasted, turns her rage upon
herself as the only 'victim' over whom she has any control or right.   She usually blames her tragedy on the
world.   Her suicide occurs at home, usually in the
presence of others (50 per cent of the cases) and she
draws deliberate attention to herself (50 per cent of
the cases).   She appears to have neither the time nor
the inclination to write notes, having declared herself
publicly.

INDIAN MODELS

(a)   Men

He is either between 20 and 29 years old or 45 and 59
years old.   In the latter age range he suffers from

depression, ill-health, a loss of status and a sense
of helplessness and uselessness. He is an alcoholic
(25 per cent of the cases), is alienated from both his
family and his work so that he neither understands
these nor knows how to cope with them. He has often
stopped supporting his family and his quarrelling
with his wife has become chronic. A serious quarrel
or the demeaning effect of a sharp warning from someone in authority are the most usual events precipi-
tating his suicide. He usually hangs himself, and
his hanging usually follows an act of violence against
some member of his family.

(b) Women

She is between 15 and 25 years old (57 of the cases).
Her suicide symbolizes the final explosion in a long-
threatened break in a relationship which contains her
entire life. The break may be with husband, lover,
parents or parents-in-law. Her act is impulsive,
there is little evidence of planning or meditation
and it usually erupts in the midst of a family flare-
up. Like the Coloured woman, she draws attention to
her act. She appears to be contrite after the act.

African, Indian and Coloured women suicides, it seems,
did not intend to kill themselves. Their suicides
appear as cries for help, and for greater human consideration, and their deaths often seem to have been
unintended and 'accidental'. Suicide appears to be
far more meditated and intended in the case of White
women.

18 Selected cases in greater depth

TEMBE

Case 190/71 of a 28-year-old African woman is a typical example of the peripheral nature of an Inquest Court investigation, particularly in respect of Africans. The available information is recorded accordingly:

Name:	Tembe Shange
Age:	about 28 years old
Cause of death:	'extensive tertiary burns' (there was no evidence of how, when, or where deceased came to be burnt)
Admitted to hospital:	9 January 1971 - sisted visited her 10 January 1971
Time of death:	8 February 1971
Body identified by sister:	10 February 1971
Sister's affidavit:	15 February 1971
Post mortem signed:	16 February 1971. (The body had been refrigerated upon death.)
Post mortem reveals:	'These burns appear to be several weeks old showing evidence of healing at edges.' 'cut down wounds on both ankles.'

Tembe's 21-year-old sister Rose, working in a Durban suburb, visited her in hospital on 10 January 1971, on hearing that Tembe had burnt herself and was in hospital (affidavit 15 February 1971]. Rose says she did not know her sister's boy friend but that her sister had told her that she had burnt herself after a quarrel with her boy friend. The investigating officer did not ask

160

who had given her the news.   On 5 July 1971 the
investigating officer states there is no trace of who
brought Tembe to Hospital.   Investigating officer
puts in affidavit that all attempts to trace boy friend
has failed.   On 14 October 1971, verdict is given in
open court, but no next of kin are present.

The recorded information in this case is much too
thin to allow the researcher to make any valid interpretation of the causal situation of the suicide.   One
familiar with the life of migrant labourers, the
insecurity of the *kipita* (1) relation, the illegal
occupation by one of the partners of the room in which
it has to be maintained - the furtive slinking in by
night, the fear of police raids, of discovery by the
employer (2) would read more into it, and even from
such thin material, restructure a plausible 'reality'.

The researcher of this volume can claim intimate
knowledge of the Indian situation only.   Having been
born into it, and shaped by it, she may speak of an
'intuitive', 'sixth sense' understanding which will
come to her assistance when she attempts to fill in the
missing links.   But when the 'cultural' or 'class'
situation is different such attempts may result in
disaster, and must thus be handled with the greatest
of caution.

Accordingly, the interpretations that follow are
closer to the truth in the Indian cases.   The interpretations of the selected White cases are better than
those of African and Coloured because the recorded
evidence is better in their respect.

Five of the cases in this chapter are traced back
to the personal situations of the suicides - to their
homes and to those persons who were most intimately
related to them and were part of the suicide act.
This results in a better grasp of the 'concrete',
'real-life' suicide.   The grasp would be improved
considerably if the real-life situation was presented
in even greater depth - if the interviewers probed the
formative years of the suicide, analysed his relations
with his parents and peers, and recorded the impressions
he left with his teachers, employers, otc.   This is a
technique which other researchers may pursue more
exhaustively.   This study merely indicates it.

RUNGA

Thirty-two-year-old Runga had reached the end of his
tether.   He was unemployed and had a fine of R40

pending for failing to stop at a stop street.   His rent
was unpaid, his family stood in danger of being thrown
out on the street; his wife had not cooked any supper,
since there was nothing to cook in the house.   Unable
to face his responsibilities, he was made 'without face'.
He could not 'face' his wife and was surly to her.   He
was far too stricken with shame to concede to her
request that he take her to her brother's so that she
could borrow money for rent.   He was equally ashamed
to accept the bottle of tea she put in his car.   So he
threw it out of the window while she watched from the
kitchen and wept.
   In her testimony, his wife said that they had been
happily married and she could not understand why he had
done such a thing.

AMRIT

Amrit's suicide may be interpreted as revenge in an un-
obtrusive and almost imperceptible way, on a society
that had never allowed him to be himself.   He travelled
150 miles from home and killed himself with carbon
monoxide poison which he released from his car.   He
was in debt to the sum of R3000.
   My name is Amrit .   My address.... My body must
   be given to my wife Jessmonie in .   I had to come
   here to commit suicide to make it easy for my family
   because all my family [brothers, sisters, etc.] live
   here.   My wife is at home [150 miles inland].   I
   did not tell her where I am going.   Please inform
   Dera upstairs where my car is parked.   Thank you.
   I came here at 1 a.m.
   The letter together with the information from the
Inquest Court, gives the story of a man who failed to
fit into the shopkeeping tradition of his family, and
was too weak and ill-equipped to branch off into something on his own.   His first marriage was his first
attempt at rebellion but it failed.   The continued
objections of his family so played on his mind that he
left his wife and two children, though he continued to
support them, and married a woman chosen by his family.
Businesswise, he struggled along and so long as he had
the support of other members of the family, his income
and expenditure balanced, but when left to his own
resources, his business faltered, and to save utter
ruin, he sold out eight years ago and moved into a
country town where there would be less competition.
He still found himself in debt.   He borrowed from his

brother.   His wife Jessmonie testified: 'my brother
pressed him for money he owed him, so he transferred
his car in his name.'
   This is the sum total of the story gleaned from the
Inquest Court record.   Sufficient to indicate something of the suicide's personality, his continued
dependence, material and emotional, on the family of
his orientation, and his inability to maintain a
family or business on his own resources.   These however are the bare bones and the man, Amrit, his
passions and pains, the conflicts he suffers due to
the forced separation from the woman of his choice,
and his children, his state of turmoil and happiness
during the years when he lived with her despite the
objections of his family - the effect of these objections on his mind - deeper still, his relations with
his parents, with his brothers and sisters, his aunts,
uncles and cousins who formed the large extended
family in which he very probably lived, remain hidden.
He obviously became the 'problem' in the large household, the constant talking point, and point of common
concern, pursued by the others, both young and old.
His self-respect in that situation could not but have
slowly receded as he became a 'delinquent', first in
the eyes of his elders, then his peers, and finally
the younger members.   The more they attempted to draw
him in and to integrate him, the greater must have been
his feeling of being pushed out.   One may surmise that
had he succeeded in escaping into the family he had
founded, his suicide may not have occurred.   But the
recriminations of a burdened conscience probably
tracked him down and flogged him to death.

MANIKUM

The circumstances preceding the suicide of Manikum are
drawn together from the evidence recorded in the court
file, of his wife Devi, his brother Thagie and his
niece Neela.
   Thirty-four-year-old Manikum travelled thirty-six
miles each day, leaving home at dawn and returning at
11 p.m., to keep his job as a chef in a White hotel.
He consequently saw very little of his wife and three
young children.
   The police called on him one day at his place of work
with a radio, which he recognized as being the one he
had bought from a customer for R8 a few weeks previously, and charged him with receiving stolen property.

They told him that they had obtained the radio from
Kenneth, who lived in his neighbourhood.   Manikum
was acutely ashamed and distressed, but what worried
him most was how the radio had reached Kenneth.   That
evening he and his brother Thagie, questioned his
wife, Devi.

Devi said in her evidence that her husband was very
angry and very upset.   'He asked how Kenny got the
radio.   I said I lent the radio to my brother.   He
didn't believe me.   He said I was a liar.   Then
Thagie started with me.   They said I must go straight
away to Umzinto so they can ask my brother about it.
How I can go, just like that.   I said I can't go.
Then Thagie hit me.   Next day I laid a charge against
him.'

Thagie said that his brother told him that he suspected his wife was having an affair with Kenny and
when the police found the radio with Kenny, he felt
his suspicions confirmed.   'He was shaking and very
upset.   He started crying.   I told him to pull up
and went with him to see his wife.   She kept saying
she gave the radio to her brother.   We told her we'll
go to Umzinto and ask her brother.   She refused to
come.   I said "what you frightened of?   You must be
guilty."   She started using big mouth then.   I gave
her a smack that is all.   We then left her.   She was
shouting after us: "When you return your life will
be misery."   We went to speak to my father about the
trouble.   He said to get a lawyer but Manikum said he
had already pleaded guilty.   But Manikum wanted to
make sure that his wife was lying.   So we drove to
Umzinto.   Devi's mother said Devi never come to see
her.   Manikum said she was always saying she was
coming to see her.   Where did she go then?   Then he
asked Devi's brother about the radio.   He said he
knew nothing about the radio.   We returned with Devi's
aunt and young brother and told Devi that she was lying.

Neela said that there was a bit of trouble after
Devi's aunt and brother came.   They scolded Devi and
took Manikum's part.   Devi said that her husband went
to work in the morning as usual, but retired early.
'I saw he was not feeling very well, so I remained
quiet - also he was angry with me about the radio
matter and not talking to me.'   Thagie said that for
the first time since working at the hotel, Manikum had
an argument with one of the fellow-workers who assaulted
him.   Manikum had then left the hotel and gone home.

Neela said that Manikum was very quiet and went to
lie down on his bed.   At 4 p.m., he asked for a cup of

tea which she made and gave him.   She said there was
a bad feeling in the whole house.   Devi had got fed
up with her son Peter and given him a hiding, so Peter
was screaming.   They hadn't observed Manikum go to
the toilet.   The second child Stella had come in then
and said her father was standing in the toilet and not
speaking to her.   When they went to see, they found
him hanging from the electric light tube, on his nylon
shirt.

   This is the evidence of the Inquest Court.   According to this evidence, Manikum hanged himself because of
the confirmation of his wife's infidelity.   But his
wife's infidelity, the breach in his personal relation
was the final factor in a whole series of factors that
cumulatively drove him to suicide.   Waitering is one
of the poorest-paid and least attractive occupations in
Durban.   The hours of work are most uncongenial and
since most hotels cater exclusively for Whites, and
are far from the Black townships, waiters have to
travel far to work, and keep late hours, often returning home in the early hours of the morning.   Apart
from the low pay, the occupation is not very conducive
to marriage.   His waitering duties probably so claimed
him that he could be neither an effective husband nor
a good father.   At the root of his wife's infidelity
was probably also a shocking confirmation of his own
'impotency'.

ANNA

Twenty-nine-year-old Anna is found in a pink chiffon
night dress, with a scorched hole and traces of powder
in the region of her abdomen.   Andrius, her husband
and a member of the police force testified that they
had been married for eleven years, and had been childhood sweethearts.   There were no children from the
marriage.   This worried his wife very much and she
used to weep easily.   Two years before her death, she
had an operation and had become more hopeful about
having a child.   Andrius had, in the meanwhile, struck
up a relationship with Julia, an old family friend.
They had been intimate with each other for the last
two years.   Julia used to visit him in his home when
his wife was away and had borne him a child.   He con-
fided this to his African maid, Linda.   Linda also
stated that her master used to bring Julia home when
her mistress was away and they used to be intimate in
the master's bedroom.   She said that her mistress had

found clips and hair pins on her bed on several occasions and questioned her about them, but she, Linda, had refused to confirm her suspicions. She testified that her master had also made sexual advances to her and had offered 'to buy her cookie'. (3)

Anna's suspicions about her husband were probably confirmed by some remarks made, or confidences exchanged within her hearing, between Julia and her husband while spending an evening with Julia. Anna, in great distress, had walked out of the 'party'. Andrius testified that he had found her quite ill when he had come home and had had to rush her to hospital. She had taken an overdose of barbiturates. According to him, she had later appeared contrite and promised never again to make an attempt on her life.

Anna had thereafter begged that they should leave Durban and the begging had become the more persistent after her discovery of his fatherhood. 'The business of my child by Julia was heavy on my conscience', testified Andrius. 'I spoke to my wife about this. For the first time I admitted that Julia's youngest year-and-a-half-old child was mine. She cried a lot, but said that she was happy I had confessed and that she forgave me.'

Two of Anna's nieces were holidaying with them at the time of Anna's suicide. That evening Andrius had come home to find the three of them dancing in the living room. This, he said, was unusual. The nieces went out with friends later. Andrius and Anna relaxed after dinner. She again brought up the subject of their leaving Durban. He again told her that they could not because of his work. There was again the usual scene and she had begun crying. He had to return to duty and so had left her.

The nieces returned home at about 10.30 p.m., but no one answered the doorbell, though the lights were on and the radio was playing in Anna's bedroom. They then knocked on the bedroom window, which was open, and when they still did not get a reply, they peered in and saw Anna slumped and bleeding profusely. They then climbed through the window and discovered that she was dead. They immediately phoned Andrius at the police station.

The situation interpreted from the case records suggests a state of violent conflict between Anna and her husband over his infidelity. While the husband in his evidence suggests that his wife accepted the other woman, this is highly improbable. Her persistent pleadings that they leave Durban establishes that she

found the relationship unbearable and wished to be rid
of it.   The conflict over the dinner table at Julia's
house, the recorded attempt at a previous suicide and
her nagging cross-questioning of her maid Linda, all
confirm a highly distraught mind.

Far from accepting his fatherhood, she probably saw
it as illegal, immoral, and above all an assault on
her own passion to become a mother.   She had become
hopeful about motherhood after her operation, but he
had deprived her of that hope, and fulfilled it in Julia
who had the child which ought to have been hers.

She wished to leave Durban with her husband so that
he could be returned to her again, and she be rid of
both the woman and the child, who were a daily reminder
of her own infertility.   But Andrius refused her pleas.
There must have been many scenes between husband and
wife about leaving Durban.   Andrius's latest refusal
must have appeared to Anna as final.   Believing herself
doomed to loveless sterility, she killed herself.

ALFIE AND LORNA

Twenty-two-year-old Lorna and twenty-one-year-old Alfie
wanted to die.

Alfie, lonely, withdrawn and apparently gentle, found
himself ineffective and incapable of achieving the
things he desired.   He desperately wanted to marry
Nancy, but though she returned his love, she refused to
marry him, saying in her testimony - 'I was married
before.   Our love had cooled.   I was afraid that if
I married Alfie, the same would happen again.'   Alfie
found that he could not persuade her to change her mind.

He felt dominated and 'bossed' around by his parents
but found that he could not muster sufficient courage
to tell them off.   He told Nancy, 'If I get sufficiently
drunk I'll tell off my parents on Saturday.'   He had
wanted to take Nancy home to meet them, but they had put
him off saying that there wasn't enough room in the
house since his sister was staying with them.

Nancy was estranged both from her husband, who had
gone off to England, and her wealthy parents.   They
cared for her young daughter Lauren, as she suffered
from fits.   Alfie wasn't working at the time of his
death and she was virtually supporting him.

Alfie had invited Nancy to die with him, but she
said in her testimony, that though she loved him
deeply, 'I had my daughter to think of.   I told him so.
He wanted us to jump from the window of his 10th storey

flat.   He got on the ledge and had wanted to jump himself.   I screamed and pleaded and he got off.   He
had bought a gun and he carried a cord with him.   He
told me that he had tried out the cord and it took 15
minutes to pass out.   He told me: "You should not be
surprised if you arrive in my room and fine me hanging".'
     This type of desire for death is present in twenty-
two-year-old Lorna four years before her death. (4)
She had admitted being unhappy since the divorce of
her parents and felt uninvolved and unimportant.   'I
felt, well, look at me - I am nothing.   So I can do
what I like'.   So she became a drug addict and in her
drugged state she lost consciousness of the difference
between being or not being.   She took dexedrine
tablets.   'I raved out of my mind, couldn't sleep for
days though the effect was rather fabulous.'   She
believed that she had been raped at thirteen.   'I was
given barbiturates by a gorilla.   I don't think I
should call him that ... when I came to, I was in a
strange flat with strange people and a very strange man
sort of hovering over me'.
     Her great shock came when her twin brother died.
He was the only point of security, bound to her from
birth.   'The death broke me up, I think I counter
compensated and got myself pregnant'.   But she was
not allowed to keep her baby, so she left home and
became more addicted to drugs than ever before.   She
had a safe source, but was obliged to sleep with him
in return.   This she hated.   Then she was arrested
and imprisoned.   'The walls kept coming down to the
floor and it seemed I was just getting crushed and I
remember sitting there and screaming "just let me out
of here.   Let me just see the air."   You can't see
the night or bloody day in this place.   Then from jail
I was carted off to court where they first sent me off
to two months mental observation at the fort.   Prison
was such a strange atmosphere because there are some
incredible people, people I never really mixed with
before.   So off I went not really knowing what to
expect and I was put in a ward for incurables.   On my
first morning I woke up and saw all these incredible
faces peering through my observation window and I
thought, "Oh God, I will never be able to live through
this and I thought this is the end for me".'   Her
parents came to her rescue and her lawyer got her off
with an admission of guilt.
     'After my release from the mental hospital I started
trying to commit suicide regularly.   When a situation
goes beyond my control, I resort to cutting my wrists

up or taking an overdoes of pills .... Days and
nights drugged up to the eyeballs not knowing whether
it was day or night.   You lie there and stare at the
ceiling for days.   What is there to stop for?   To
get a job? get married?   Oh God, no, I want to run
from things like that.   I can never lead a normal
life.   I'm on the outside ... I'm on outside.'
     She went on to receive intensive psychiatric treat-
ment, and then in a frame of acute indecision, got
married.   The marriage did not last.   The psychiatric
treatment did not help, there was nothing to keep her
to life which had in fact expelled her from it through
the recurrent shocks it had given her.   She jumped
from the twenty-sixth storey and died, as she had
wanted to.

RAJGOPAUL

The Inquest Court records the death of Rajgopaul,
unemployed Indian male of Road No.   , House No.   ,
Chatsworth, on July 1971 through hanging.   It also
records the evidence of his wife Parvathie (55) and his
daughter Muni.
     Parvathie stated that they had 9 children, 3 girls
and 6 boys, of which 6 were married and living away
from them.   They had moved from Mtubatuba to her
mother's home in Merebank eleven years ago because of
her husband's ill health.   Last year they had all
moved to Chatsworth, being forced to do so because of
Group Areas.   Deceased was unemployed for the last
2 years and said that he would not live long and God
would take him away.   He did not threaten suicide.
On 9 April 1971 a washing line pole was erected in the
yard on the instructions of the deceased by his son.
On 10 April 1971 his wife was lying in bed, feeling
somewhat off-colour, when deceased asked her to eat
with him.   She declined, but joined him when he
insisted.   Deceased thereafter moved about the house,
chatting to his aged mother-in-law and his daughter
who was visiting them.   They saw him apparently standing
against the washing pole but on further investigation
found him to be hanging by a rope from the pole.   He
was dead.
     This case was followed up with a visit to the
family.   They lived in a fairly attractive economic
home.   Parvathie was in, her mother was away.   Her
eldest son was visiting her.   Parvathie was not very
communicative and what she had to say did not add much

to her evidence in Court.   The additional information
gleaned from this visit was that Rajgopaul had worked
as a field labourer in Mtubatuba until he had been
stopped by poor health.   The family had moved to
Merebank, to Parvathie's mother's home, as a temporary
measure, but the arrangement had become permanent and
this had drastically changed Rajgopaul's status in
the family.   His eldest son said that his father did
not like staying with his grandmother.   Parvathie
interrupted and said not to say he had trouble with
mother.   According to his son, the root cause of
Rajgopaul's problems had been economic and he apolo-
gised for his own failure to help his father.   His
mother explained: 'The money he get is too little for
his own wife and children.'

Their neighbour admitted somewhat reluctantly that
the old lady and Parvathie were sharp with him at
times.   'You can't blame them two.   When the man
doesn't work and is sick all the time and living on
his mother-in-law, you can't expect anything else.'

One can surmise from this that Rajgopaul suffered a
complete sense of role disintegration as the years
confirmed that his family would be permanently dependent on his wife's people, and this finally drove him
to his suicide.   He did not wish to commit suicide on
his own however, and in a sense sought his family's
co-operation.   Thus he asked his son to put up a pole
in the garden, ostensibly for a clothes line.   He
persuaded his wife to have a 'last supper' with him.
'I was sick then and I said leave me alone.   I don't
want to eat, but he forced me and that night we sat
down and eat together.'   He settled down to a long
friendly chat with his mother-in-law, something he had
not done for some time.   He also discussed many little
problems with his married daughter who had come to
visit them.   Then having taken leave of all, and in
a sense made his peace with those he was about to shock,
he had that night hanged himself.

His death was an escape from his deteriorating role.
From provider of bread (no matter how humble) and
patriarch, he had become converted into a 'parasite'.

CHRISTINA

Forty-two-year-old Christina is described as having
died from an overdose of self-administered sleeping
pills.   The evidence of her half-brother, a railway
worker, gives some insight into her background.   There

is no evidence of any other relative.   The half-
brother's evidence suggests that she had drifted into
Durban from a Northern Natal town after three husbands,
three divorces and two lovers.   She had two children
from the first marriage.   The court records do not
indicate their whereabouts at the time of her death,
or the factors leading to her first divorce.   Her
second husband, according to her half-brother, was a
drunk, and the third had been both drunk and unfaithful, and she had left him after a month.   She had
then lived consecutively with two lovers and had taken
on a third one, 27-year-old Dawie at the time of her
death.

Dawie according to the evidence of his mother,
Clara, was not very employable.   He drank too much.
He would take on a job and drop it.   It appeared that
he had got used to sponging on his mother.   There were
brief spells, when he got hold of some other woman,
and relieved her of the burden.   But this did not
last long, because of his quarrelsome nature.

Christina and Dawie had drifted into each other two
months before her death in the passage of a Durban
rooming house in the central business area of the city.
Dawie had moved into a room in the block with his
mother and her lover Dirkie that very morning.
Christina had a problem, her cat had to be spayed and
Dawie made a prompt offer and took it to the vet.
That evening he moved into her room and relieved his
mother of his uncomfortable presence.

In the two months that followed, Dawie and his
'family' and Christina became very much a part of the
hostel community.   Living in the same passage and
sharing a common bathroom and toilet, were Dot,
Marietjie, Pieter, Karel.   Jamie and Fanie had two
young children and they rented two rooms.   Jamie was
employed in the customs department.   The evidence
does not give us any other information about the rest
of the 'clan'.   Christina cooked a meal a day for
Karel, who paid her R10 per month in return.

The evidence suggests that the members of the 'clan'
moved fairly freely into each other's rooms, and the
children had the run of the place.   One gains the
impression that they had jolly times together and they
got involved in one another's violent quarrels.

Karel said of Christina that she was a good sort.
He felt that Dawie had some sort of a hold on her.
Dawie's mother said that she was a strange, sad, but
good-hearted woman.   Jamie testified that she was
often under the influence of drugs and he had warned

her not to come into his rooms and make love while in
that condition.   One assumes that she and Dawie had
probably come near to doing something like that on
some occasion.   He testified 'On one occasion while
drugged, she fell in my room and her dress went up,
exposing her naked person and this was seen by my
little son.   But she was a very nice person when not
under influence of drugs.'   Fanie said that Christina
tolerated all Dawie's nonsense somehow.   She believed
that Dawie was unfaithful to her and was also sleeping
with Marietjie.   This both angered and depressed her.
Dawie, from available reports, exploited her thoroughly.
His mother, Clara said she did not know what they lived
on, but they appeared to get their drink and drugs.
Dawie in one of his drunken states, got involved in a
violent quarrel with Marietjie and assaulted her.   She
called in the police, who arrested him.   Christina
bailed him out.   Clara said that her son and Christina
often quarrelled, but Christina always took him back.
John, the African caretaker, testified that Dawie quite
often beat Christina.   He would then go to Clara and
say: 'Baas is beating missus too much.   She can come
stay by you?'   Dawie's mother always took her in on
those occasions and Christina would sleep in their
room.
     The day before Christina's death, the 'clan' was
having a ball.   In the middle of it all Christina
persuaded Karel to take her to a place in the Indian
area, to get some pills from her doctor.   The others
accompanied them, waiting outside, while Christina
went in, ostensibly to her doctor.   They then went to
a bar.   Karel did some more errands that day for
other members of the 'clan'.   After driving around
quite a bit, they settled in at another bar.
     Clara says that Christina was very depressed at that
point.   She did not eat the food they had ordered.
Dawie persuaded her to do so and, when she refused,
became angry and stuffed some in her mouth.   Christina
left the table and vomited in the lavatory.   Someone
had said 'Shame on you' to Dawie.   'But you can't do
much to Dawie', Clara said, 'once he wants to do a
thing, he will do it.   He is a man like that'.
Christina had begun to cry and said that she wished
she was dead.   She had probably moaned about her life
and accused Dawie, provoking him into slapping her.
The manager asked them to leave.   The party had
ended.
     Dawie said that they had all returned to the rooming
house and spent some time in Christina's room.   The

others had left after a while but Clara and Dirk had
remained.   He and Christina had gone to sleep on the
bed.   Clara and Dirk had retired on the floor on a
foam mattress.   There is no explanation in the
records as to why they had not gone to their own room.

Fanie said that she had seen Christina go to the
bathroom late that night.   Dawie reports that she had
told him at some stage that night that she had taken
an overdose of sleeping pills and she was going to
sleep forever.   He had not taken much notice of it,
but at one stage he had felt her uncomfortably cold
against him.   He had called to his mother and said:
'This woman is getting cold.'   She had got up, adjusted
her blanket and gone to sleep.   In the morning they
realized that she was dead.

The 'Christian clan' represents the very small group of
Whites who have abdicated their roles as custodians of
civilization in Africa.   Since there is no other recognized role for them, unless they joined the Blacks,
which under the present system they would be prevented
from doing by law, they move in a world of their own
which stands far more apart from respectable White
society than does any comparable Black group from
respectable Black society.

19 Case studies

1 KRIS

Kris, 26-year-old Indian male, hanged himself in his
bedroom on 10 February 1971.   According to the court
record, Kris lived with his 'wife' and two children
with his mother.   They were not formally married.
They occupied one room in the house, but cooked separately on a common stove.   His mother testified that
she scolded her daughter Dolly on the morning of 10
February 1971 for not cleaning the stove, but her
'daughter-in-law' Santoshamah started swearing at her.
She complained to Kris who scolded his 'wife'.
Santoshamah stated that he had unfairly taken his
mother's part and in anger had gone off to *her* mother
with the two children.   She returned a little later
with her mother and an argument had followed in which
Santoshamah's mother had threatened to 'fix up' her
'son-in-law'.   They then left.   The time was 11 a.m.
Dolly corroborates her mother's testimony.

His brother, Sonny, testified that he went to borrow
a broom from his brother at 2 p.m. and found the door
locked.   He peeped in, and saw his brother lying in
bed, and not wantin to disturb him left.   At 4 p.m.
one of his brother's friends came to see him.   He went
to call his brother, but finding no response to his
knocking, peeped through the fanlight and saw him
hanging from a sari.

Santoshamah's evidence is brief.   She says that she
was at her mother's when her young brother-in-law came
to tell her that her husband was dead.   She states
that they were happy together, but there was interference from the family.

The report suggests an unhappy 'marriage', the
unhappiness being aggravated by the 'interference' of

Kris's family.   It seems that if the couple had lived
on their own some of the conflict may have been avoided.
Family pressure and poverty appear to be the two
factors that killed him.

The house where Kris lived is built below the road,
a near-perpendicular flight of steps leads down to it.
A young man was beating a young woman on the pavement
at the crest of the steps.   Neighbours watched and
despite the crying and screaming, none came to help,
but on seeing me and confusing me with 'authority', the
young man abruptly stopped his beating and slunk away.

'He's hurt your lip,' I remarked.   She lowered her
head and presenting it to me said, 'Just see.   Feel
here.'   There was a lump on the crown.   'You must
report him,' I advised.   'How many times I reported
him.   He frights for nobody.   My child is sick.   I
asked him for money.   He told me, "Fuck off."   Where
I am going to go.   He's not married to me too.'

'Where's your mother?'

'I got no mother.   I got father only.'

She was slovenly and unkempt, but attractively
plumpish.   She said her name was Angelay.   We had
walked down the steps and into the house.   A thin
shrewd-faced young woman with a child buckled to her
waist met us in the doorway.   She was Dolly.   The room
was drab.   A cupboard and two studio couches filled
all save a narrow walking space.   The kitchen stood
exposed and untidy through the doorless doorway, and
Muniamah, Kris's mother, emerged from it, tall and
gaunt, wiping her face with the end of her sari.   We
sat down on the studio couches.   Dolly and Angelay
remained standing, with one silent child-in-arms and
another at the skirts.   I asked Muniamah why they
didn't restrain Sonny from beating Angelay.   'You can
stop him you think?' Dolly answered.   'Nobody can
block him.   He hit my mother too when she block him.'
'You'll see we'll have trouble the whole night and
there will be another suicide here', Muniamah proph-
esied sombrely.

Kris is one of eight children of whom Dolly, the
eldest, is 31.   The youngest is a year old.   One
other daughter is married and living with her in-laws.
Sonny and Kris had both brought home girls, Angelay and
Santoshamah respectively;   they moved into the only
two bedrooms upstairs, and began to live with the
family as wives and daughters-in-law.   Muniamah said
there had never been either money or time to get them
married.   The girls kept falling pregnant.   'You
can't have ceremony when you like that - not in our
ways.'

When Kris was alive, his parents, Dolly and her three
children, Muniamah's baby and three other unmarried
sons, two of whom, Bala and Jaya, are working, slept in
the small living room downstairs.   Now some of them
sleep in Kris's bedroom.   Sonny and his father worked
for the Corporation and earned R55 per month each.
Kris was a conductor.   Bala and Jaya worked in a shoe
factory.   They earned R40 a month each.

The married couples bought and cooked their own food
but used the common family stove.   Sonny gave his
mother R4 a month when he could, his wife took R35 to
buy food and pay instalments on furniture.   But the
money placed in her charge did not come easily.   Sonny,
aware of his weakness for drink, had arranged for
Angelay to come to the pay office each pay day so that
she could take charge of the money.

Angelay had gone that morning as arranged and waited
with others.   'One man was there - decent man, and he
was speaking decently to me, so I gave answer.   Just
then Sonny came.   "Why you standing next to that man?'
he said.   How much shame I felt.   He is jealous for
nothing.   He gave me some money and said I must go.
He'll give me more later.   I told him to give the
money.   I can pay accounts, but he was getting angry
and so I came away.   But he drank up half the money
before he came home.   I asked him for the money.   My
child is sick.   I got to buy medicine.'   Angelay
couldn't continue any further.   She began sobbing.
'He is only hitting me.'

'Why don't you get them married?', I asked Muniamah.
'Where's the money?', was her reply.   'Why don't you
get married?', I asked Angelay this time.

'How many times I tell him', she replied, 'but he
won't take brain.   What can you do?   The welfare too
told him - you got two children now, you must get
married.   How much brain they give him.   But he won't
take it.'

We talked about Kris.   Muniamah blamed it all on her
daughter-in-law, Santoshamah.   'He brought the girl.
We can't say no.   Your son brings.   You got to take
her as daughter-in-law.   But she never liked us.'
Dolly butts in and says 'If we gave him tea, she'll say
"don't drink, they putting things inside to pull you
their way".'   Muniamah continues 'He can't sit next
to me, my own son, she won't like it.   She wanted him
to stay with her mother.   He said "How I am going to
go?   She like, she can go and stay there.   I won't go."
She was Christian.   What I can say?   They wanted him
to be Christian.   He said he won't be Christian.'
'That all the trouble' Dolly emphasized.

Dolly went on to recount how on the day of Kris's
death Santoshamah had started fighting with them early
in the morning, how she had given her mother her big
mouth and then gone off to her (Santoshamah's) mother's
house and returned with the mother, and the mother had
then given them all 'big mouth' and threatened that
she would bring gangsters to beat them up. Muniamah
supported her and said that they had in fact engaged
gangsters to beat up her younger son in the bus.

Recalling the suicide, Muniamah said that she had
found Kris dead when she returned from visiting her
relatives. His wife had refused to participate in
the funeral ceremony. 'She stay with him. How she can
refuse to do ceremony. We forced her. So she stayed
and after sixteen days she left. I haven't seen her
since then. I don't want to see her. The children
come. I see them. If they don't come....' She
dismissed them in her mind and with the gesture of her
body indicated that it would not matter.

They took me to Angelay's room with obvious pride.
There was as much furniture in the room as there was
space - a laminated bedroom suite, a child's pink cot.
'We had so much trouble, fitting it.' The sheets were
fashionably striped, but the room was drab, untidy.

Santoshamah's people live in a large, brightly-
furnished house and have a comfortable income.
Santoshamah draws R26 a month widow's grant. Her
children are clean and well cared for. The house
stands out in splendid contrast against the drab dis-
order of Kris's household.

Santoshamah's mother says that Muniamah gets the
trance. On the day of the suicide her daughter came
home about 9 or 10 a.m., very upset because Dolly and
Muniamah had said 'one thing to her that no human
being can bear'. 'I was so upset I took my daughter
and went to their house to ask about the trouble, but
Muniamah, instead of talking decently, just kept saying
one word: "Ask your daughter." What I must ask my
daughter! I can see her troubles. In a house like
that, anyone can see her troubles. You saw the
house - that Dolly got three children by three men and
she is the big boss all the time. I asked Muniamah
who come first for you, your daughter or your daughter-
in-law? That Dolly got no shame, all that children
and not married but still bossing everybody and only
her word is listened to. You can see yourself what
kind of people they are. I told my daughter, no good
talking to them and we came away.... At 5 o'clock we
get the message that he was dead. What kind people,

they did not even take him down.   My son had to go and
break the door and cut the sari.   His body was still
warm.

And my daughter - how you think she is feeling eh?
But they sweared her such a way - no feeling they had.
They said she must stay in their house.   She didn't
want to stay but they forced her and they made her do
all that ceremony.   How much she saying, she Christian,
she not Hindu, but they made her do it'.

Muniamah predicts that there will be another suicide
in her family, and that probably sums up the picture.
Whatever the personality factors that contributed to
Kris's suicide, Kris lived in a suicidal situation.
Angelay and Sonny are living in that situation now, and
they know it - a situation of poverty, overcrowding and
the resultant brawling.   Sonny's work is hard and
unpleasant, yet he earns so little that he must remain
without any private pleasures if his family is
to subsist, and if he dies, more than half his present
income will be secured to Angelay in a welfare grant,
and she will be spared quarrelling over it with a
drunken husband.

2 SAVI

Savi, a 16-year-old Indian girl, died on 15 May 1970
as a result of second-degree self-inflicted burns.
From the affidavits submitted by her father and by witnesses to the death, and from interviews with these and
other persons with whom Savi was involved during her
lifetime, the following story emerges.

Savi's father is a club steward.   At the time of
her suicide he earned R7 per week and had to keep a
family of seven on it.   The money was barely enough
to maintain their frugal diet.   Christmas or Diwali
made little difference to their lives.   The family had
never ventured out to the centre of town at night and
Savi's father does not think that Savi had ever seen
the Christmas illuminations in the city, or the permanent illuminations on the beach front.   He thinks that
she did go to the cinema, once or twice.   'Sister it
is hard.   Busfare is too much - you don't know one
person you meeting.   It is dangerous.'   Munusami is
in his late forties, his wife is slightly younger.
Both are illiterate in English.   Their house has very
little furniture and there are no curtains in the
window.   They have five children, of whom Savi was the
eldest.   The younger children are at school, but it is

unlikely that they will remain there long.   Savi left
after four years and began helping the family by washing
clothes in the neighbourhood, earning twenty-five cents
a time.   She rarely earned more than fifty cents a day,
and didn't seem to want to earn any more.   She was
never in a hurry to leave one place of washing for the
next.   The neighbours report that she would dawdle and
was pleased to stay and chat, and drink a cup of tea
and eat a slice of bread.

Her mother says that they did not like her to go out
washing.   The money helped, but she was a grown-up
young girl.   'What people will think, and today's
times are bad.   One thing you hear about young girls
today, you never hear before.   But you can't hold back
today's time girls.   Savi say she want to go, she go.
No one can stop her.   She get cross and make noise.
On that day she died also, how much her father told her
in the morning, don't go.   Stay and help your mother.
But she say she must go.'   According to her mother,
Savi gave her more than half of the money she earned.
The rest she spent on herself, making small purchases
from the bag vendor.   'Why must tell lies - since she
left school and working we bought nothing for her.
She bought everything her own money, and she buy for me
too sometimes,' her mother reports.

Chengiah testified that Savi left home with him at
5 a.m. on 14 May 1970.   She told him that she was
going to do washing and she would then go on to her
maternal grandmother's house and return the following
day.

Sherifa Bi states in her affidavit that Savi came to
her house at about 6.30 a.m.   She was sweeping the
yard at the time and her daughter-in-law, Hawa, was
still in her bedroom.   Her husband and son had already
left for work.   This was the second time Savi had come
to her house.   Sherifa Bi knew her to be very poor.
The first time she had come she had pleaded for washing, saying that her father was unemployed and they
were starving.

Twenty-year-old Neelamba testified that she was
washing clothes with her cousin when Savi passed by.
They did not speak to her for Savi had once stolen
Neelamba's skirt.   She had returned it when confronted
with the theft, but since then there was a coolness
between them.   The two girls put out their washing to
dry, but when they returned to take if off the line,
Neelamba's washing was missing.   She raised an alarm.
Her mother, Manikum, became particularly excited.   It
did not take them long to fix their suspicions on Savi

and they dispersed in all directions to track her down.
Manikum traced her to Sherifa Bi's and descended upon
her in the full state of her anger.   Her loud ringing
tones brought several neighbours to the scene.   She
sent one of them home to call Neelamba, who arrived
with two cousins.   They all poured their righteous
indignation on the helpless girl in the presence, as
it seemed to her, of the whole world.   She was exposed
and trapped and without face.

Manikum was asking Sherifa Bi for the house key.
Hawa was locking the kitchen door and rooting herself
firmly in front of it.   Manikum was locking the front
door door and passing the key through the window to
Neelamba, and Sherifa was shouting: 'Close the window -
you can't trust her.'   Manikum was shouting: 'Keep
her locked up until I fetch the Police.'   Savi broke
down and sobbed hysterically,   'Don't call the police,
please don't call the police.'   Neelamba retorted,
'Hey don't act now.   So much buck to steal.   No buck
for police,' and she began regaling the neighbours on
how 'the dirty little rogue' had stolen her clothes
from the line.

Savi in the meanwhile had changed her tactic from
pleading to attacking.   She made a feeble attempt to
shake off the outrage from herself and stick it on to
Neelamba.   'You bitch, don't disgrace me,' she screamed
and now the thought raged in her mind that Neelamba was
to blame, that Neelamba had started it all and they
should turn against Neelamba and leave her alone.   But
she could enlist no support.   Neelamba slapped her face.
Savi retaliated and the two girls were locked in a face-
scratching, hair-pulling huddle.   Somebody pulled Savi
away and flung her against the wall.   Incensed, Savi
took hold of the kettle of boiling water on the stove
but it seemed as if a hundred hands bore down on her
and pressed her to the ground and held her there in the
muck and the mire.   In her intense and unbearable
degradation she had only one thought - to escape from
that degradation.   'I want to go to the toilet,' she
pleaded.   They were suspicious, but they let her go,
and directed her upstairs to the bathroom.   'Follow
her', a voice shouted but she succeeded in getting
upstairs and locking herself in the bathroom.   How
could she escape the police, the people, the horror of
it all.   She saw a bottle of paraffin and some matches.
She poured the paraffin over herself and then struck a
match.   There was a burst of flame.   She screamed.

One can guess her feelings when she finds herself
suddenly aflame - shock, physical pain, terror.   Where

before she had wanted to escape the others, to seal herself from them, she now rushes towards them, a flaming
torch running and falling down the stairs.   Somebody
brings a blanket and she is wrapped in it, like a child.
Where before there had been accusations of theft, now
there was a flood of concern.

The concern follows her to hospital.   Why did she
do it?   What could she say?   In the face of that concern, and the fears, of the people, the police, the
shame, the prison, things of the past, she may well
have regretted the fire, and yet could she not have
seen the fire as good, as having brought her a consideration which otherwise may have been denied her?   Without it she may well have been locked up, branded as a
theif and ceased to be a person.

In her small closed-in world, of the numbered roads
and the numbered units and the many people squeezed
together in houses that piled up and stretched out, the
dubbing of Savi as a thief would have travelled quickly
and as in a whispering game, her 'sin' would have been
distorted and magnified and she would have been converted into a bad girl shunned by all.   But now they were
sorry for her and Neelamba was a bitch for bitching her
to death.

3 RADHA

Radha, 43, killed herself one morning by jumping from
her twelfth-storey window.   The evidence of her husband
and children portrays a very unhappy woman, who had
left her village in India and come to live in South
Africa twenty years ago.   She had never adapted to the
country, and could not even speak the current language
of communication.   She remained closed in the mores of
her Hindu village.   Her daughter testified: 'My
mother was deeply religious, she rarely went out and
spent most of her time praying and reading religious
literature.' So long as her husband and children
shared those mores with her, she felt secure, isolated
as she was from the rest of her society of adoption.
When, however, they abandoned those mores, and assumed
those of the strange wicked society, life became intolerable and unworthy of living.   She wanted to destroy
that society.   A month before her death, she told her
husband that she felt she was chopping people's heads
off.   In Hindu mythology, the Goddess Kali, or
Wagheshwari, sits in judgment over society and devours
it when it becomes evil.   One may interpret that

Radha in terms of her internalized norms and mores saw
her husband and children as having become corrupt and
in need of destruction.   Unable to destroy them, she
destroys herself.   The investigating officer summarized
the situation accordingly:

'It is obvious that there was domestic trouble and
that the husband has been visiting a Coloured woman
for years.   This as well as her children's love
affairs must have played on her mind and eventually
led her to take her own life.   The family is well
aware that if this is known by the public, they
would be held in disgrace by people of their own
caste and they were obviously trying to avoid this.'

The husband in his first testimony stated that his
wife had been ill for the last twelve years, that they
were perfectly happy, that she had neither shown any
signs of unhappiness nor expressed a desire to end her
life.   He denied that there had ever been any domestic
trouble between them.   In a second testimony, two days
later, he stated that he was in love with a Coloured
woman whom he had been visiting for the last twenty
years with his wife's knowledge.   He said she had
raised no objections, 'although it is looked upon as a
disgrace for me, a Gujerati Hindu to associate with
people of another nation or caste (Jaat).   This woman
never visited my flat, but her son did.   I had no
children by her.'

Radha's 23-year-old daughter testified that she had
a Muslim boyfriend, but as far as she knew, her mother
did not know of this.   'It is against our custom and
religion to marry Muslims.   This is not due to class
differences, but because we belong to different
"nations".   My mother would never have agreed to the
marriage.   My brother's Hindustani-speaking girlfriend
visited our flat.   My mother never objected.'

In her first statement to the police she had said
that she had never heard arguments between her parents,
but in a subsequent statement, two weeks later, she
admitted that they often quarrelled over minor things,
that they had been unhappy in their marriage and for
the last few years her father hardly spoke to her
mother.

Radha's son testified that there was invariably a
quarrel when his mother asked his father for money to
buy a sari or something.   He said that his mother
regretted very much that she did not speak English.

Radha's suicide appears to be saying: 'This world is
corrupt.   It is not worthy of my existence.'   Radha's
world was her family, and it was the 'corruption' of

her husband and children, their abandoning of the narrow, but the only, system of mores that had any meaning for her, that apparently drove her to suicide.

4   MALIGA

Maliga, though reported as 27 years old in the Inquest Court record, was in fact 25 years old, the second child in a family of four daughters and two sons.   Her father's income as a chef was so inadequate that it did not even meet the family's minimum requirements and her mother was forced to supplement his earnings by going out washing clothes in private families.   The two elder girls, one of whom was Maliga, were left in charge of the four younger children and the household chores.   Sivam, the elder, sharp-eyed and sharp-tongued, divided the chores so that most of them fell on the gentle, uncomplaining, withdrawn Maliga.   Since the age of six, Maliga had cooked and served the food, scrubbed the floors, washed and ironed the clothes, and looked after the babies.   The two girls had doted in particular on the two younger children, both boys, and Maliga had formed a strong attachment for Thagie.

Maliga's parental family was only a part of a larger kinship system that included her uncles and aunts and cousins from both her father's and mother's sides. Her maternal grandfather and both her paternal grandparents had emigrated from India, but though both pairs of grandparents were deceased, the kinship ties had continued strong and there was a lot of giving and receiving of help and quarrelling on appropriate occasions.

When Maliga's father's sister, her *ata*, fell ill, Maliga was sent to look after her.   She was 15 then, and it was then that her 21-year-old cousin, Munsame, 'had spoilt her' (made her pregnant).   When Maliga's mother discovered her pregnancy, she beat her long and hard and threatened to kill her.   Maliga left home that evening, convinced that she had perpetrated the most shameful deed, and in despair arrived at her maternal uncle's home.   He contacted Munsame and arranged for her to go and live with his family. Munsame was happy to marry her, but according to custom the marriage could not be performed while she was pregnant.   Thus after the baby was born, by which time Maliga's family's anger had also cooled and she was reconciled with it, the couple was taken to the temple and their marriage solemnized.   But Maliga's mother

never forgave her the breach and continued to blame her
for having brought misery on to herself. When I spoke
to Maliga's mother months after her funeral, she said,
'He spoilt my child. I could not give her to somebody else', and then, smiling coyly into her blouse,
she said with moral righteousness that she had arranged
the marriages of her three other daughters, and they
had had nice weddings and nice presents. 'He gave
Maliga nothing.' When asked about their marriage,
Munsame said: 'You see I spoilt her. So we just had
ceremony.'

Munsame's mother had died in the meanwhile, so that
Maliga was left in complete charge of the household
responsibilities. Some few years and three children
later, the Naidoos were served with eviction notices
since the area in which they lived was declared White.
The family split. Munsame and Maliga took on a room
with their children. They found they could not make
ends meet on his wages, so Maliga found work as a
cleaner in a butcher's shop, but found she had to leave
work within months for she had fallen pregnant again.
They changed rooms three more times in two years, being
hounded out each time by the Group Areas Act. Each
time they paid R3-4 per month. Eventually they were
given a home at R9 a month. They had not known such
luxury before, a kitchen, a sitting room and two bedrooms upstairs, all in concrete. They were proud of
the house, but since it was 'so large' and they had so
many relations, they felt both obliged and to some
extent happy to take them in. Maliga was happy to
have her two young brothers, Logie and Thagie, live with
them. Munsame was happier to take in his unmarried
brother Kista, and his younger married brother Deva and
his wife and child. But after Maliga's death,
Munsame said: 'Since we came to this house we never
had peace. One relation come and want to stay with us.
One time it is his relation, 'nother time it is hers.'

Deva and his family occupied the 'spare' room -
Munsame and his family occupied the other bedroom and
the three men slept in the sitting room. Maliga kept
house for all of them and when money was short for rent
or food, they helped out. Thagie bought a studio
couch for the sitting room and a table and dresser for
the kitchen.

In four years Maliga went twice into town. The
marketing was done by the men. She never once visited
a cinema. Occasionally she visited her mother and
sisters but Munsame did not approve of this and invariably there was trouble when she went to them. He

claimed that they had biting tongues and they kept
criticizing him to his wife, accusing him of being
lazy and a won't-work.

Maliga's three sisters were respectably married, all
had husbands with regular work, all had houses
scattered in the various units, each identical to
Maliga's. But there the similarity ended. Maliga's
home was drab; theirs bright, furnished with sparkling
lino on the floors, and glittering display cabinets.
They had wired their homes for electricity and had
electric stoves and fridges. All three girls were
gainfully occupied and had domestic servants.
Maliga's mother, Lutchme, a widow, was living alone in
her double-storeyed house with her youngest child, a
6-year-old daughter. She was proud of her three
daughers but not of Maliga, though Maliga looked after
her two sons. Lutchme, of course, never saw it that
way. As far as she was concerned, she had lent the
Naidoos her two sons out of the kindness of her heart
to help them out. She never lost an opportunity to
remind Maliga of the 'hole' into which she had fallen
through her own doings or to recount to her the new
things that the other girls had bought for themselves,
and the purchases that the husbands had made to make
their homes grand.

Maliga's only indulgence was cheap colour prints of
Indian film stars. Munsame smoked and drank and that
made a big hole in their income. Maliga's sister,
Savithri, claimed that he was a *ganja rooker* (hemp
smoker). Her sisters passed on the clothes that their
children shared, and the saris they discarded. They
had also given her the four new saris that constituted
her going-out wardrobe.

Her relatives visited her often and though she was
pleased to see them she never enjoyed the visits for
they usually broke out in fierce quarrelling between
her husband and them. They pointed out all their
shortcomings and Munsame could not stand this. After
they left, Maliga was made the target of his hostile
reaction to them. Maliga's sister says that this
hurt her very much. 'It must hurt anyone, if you
keep swearing about your people to them. How much
Maliga love us and do things for us. Maliga was
quiet but inside her heart would be crying. She said
she couldn't think any more, about anything - all the
trouble was stuck in her heart and each time her heart
beat it was like the trouble beating her.' Maliga
had six children by now.

Each Friday Maliga washed her God lamp and decorated

it with Kunqoo because this was what married woman did,
because it was holy to do so.   God as such had little
meaning for her, and she began to discover Him in Jesus,
the God of her sister-in-law.   A month before her
suicide she was converted to Christianity and shortly
thereafter when the bag man came she bought two more
coloured prints and hung Jesus in between the film
stars.

Munsame describes the conversion accordingly:
'My brother and his wife were living with us and she
was a Christian.   So I don't know what the two
womans was speaking.   Before that she was praying
and doing everything by her God lamp and so when she
change and told me she changed, I said you know
these things, you always pray, and to make everything one way, I also changed.   I used to read from
the Bible one verse before going to sleep.   Then
she get happy.'

Munsame's brother, Kista, broke his leg about this
time and became very crabby and demanding.   Maliga's
mother, Lutchme, increased her attacks on Munsame.
She accused him of spoiling her son Logie, who had
begun to accompany Munsame to the market where they
earned money through casual chores.   Munsame began
assaulting Maliga.   Maliga had differences with her
sister-in-law and so Munsame's brother, Deva, vacated
the spare bedroom and left with his family.   Munsame,
in retaliation it seemed, picked a quarrel with
Maliga's brother, Thagie, the one to whom she was
particularly attached.   Both her brothers left and
suddenly they were alone with the children and Kista,
trapped with his crippled leg.

Munsame began nagging Maliga about the R7 he claimed
she had given to Thagie.   On Tuesday morning he had
asked her to get that money and produce it in the
evening.

'I didn't scold or anything.   I just said we need
money and she had taken and given her brother our
money....   That is all I told her.   She just took
the baby and went.   She never went without all the
children.   I don't know, some devil got her or
what.   She left all the children, just took the
baby and went.   I said where you going?   She won't
talk.   She said nothing.   She went....   I got to
tell her bring the money.   How we going to eat -
all the children?'

Lutchme says that her daughter came to her that day
with the baby.   She claims that she spoke of no
trouble, that she chatted aimlessly about many small

things.   She visited the next-door neighbour and then
went on to visit her husband's eldest brother, Jack,
living close to her mother.   Jack's wife said she was
pleasant, and mentioned no trouble.   She said they
were surprised to see her with just the baby, and in
fact she very rarely visited them.

Munsame says that Maliga arrived home late that
evening and he did not talk to her.   He claims that
she was stuck up with him.   At the crack of dawn on
Friday however, he asked about the money, and she
became very cheeky - what money? she had challenged.
Hadn't Thagie bought the table and dresser in the kitchen
and the studio couch?   Munsame says: 'I admit I got
angry, not to say her brother didn't help.   But I was
talking about my money and when she spoke like that it
made me angry and in my anger I said things to her.
They were not in my heart.   They were only on my
tongue.   She didn't answer back.   I told her to make
me some tea.'   She went down, passing Kista on the way
as she entered the kitchen.

Kista said he had been awakened by the noise.   The
children were quiet.   The children always went quiet
when big people quarrelled.   He saw Maliga pass him
and go into the kitchen and from where he was lying he
could see her light the primus and put on the kettle
to boil.   He then saw Munsame come down and go out
into the yard to wash his face at the tap.   He
returned and sat in the sitting room opposite him.
They did not talk.   He saw Maliga take the bottle of
paraffin and run upstairs.   Munsame ran after her,
snatched the bottle from her hand and dragged her down
into the sitting room.   She was struggling all the
time, and breaking loose from him, ran out into the
backyard.   He ran after her, caught hold of her, and
forced her into the kitchen.   He placed the paraffin
bottle under the kitchen table.   Later he regretted
this and said that he ought to have thrown out the
paraffin.   'But I didn't think she'll do such a thing.
I closed the door and left her in the kitchen.   I went
back into the sitting room and sat down.'   Kista says
he saw Maliga take the paraffin bottle from under the
table and alerted Munsame.   By the time he reached
her she had poured the paraffin on her head and
clothes.   He gave her a few smacks and brought her
into the sitting room.   She started going upstairs but
stopped half way up and sat down on the stairs.   They
did not notice at what point Maliga went upstairs, but
they were suddenly alerted by a great screaming.
Munsame says he rushed up and found Maliga in flames in

their bedroom. He rushed her down the stairs, trying
all the while to beat down the flames with his hands
but he felt them just leaping up into his face and
scorching his arms. She fell on the landing against
the hall stand. Joey and his 8-year-old brother ran
out and called for help. Two men who were passing by
came, and they managed to put out the fire.

Maliga's mother, Lutchme

Maliga's mother was not at home when I called. I asked
a neighbour standing outside about her. He was
receiving a key from a child as I talked to him and
said she was Lutchme's daughter. An old lady came
up just then, also looking for Lutchme. The old man
told me it was her mother - Maliga's granny. As we
waited we saw a tall, straight figure in the distance
in a black sari, tied in South-Indian peasant style,
and long-sleeved white blouse. Lutchme collected her
key and welcomed us into her home.
    I explained that I was trying to understand why
people committed suicide. She appeared not to understand. 'You know, people who take their own life.'
'Oh yes. I know, they go hang themselves or drink
poison and all that. Very bad to do like that. Why
must do it? I stayed with my husband so long. He
hit me. Never mind what he do to me, I don't do such
a thing.' Lutchme was passing judgment on her daughter
unsolicited, and also interpreting her suicide as
caused by her husband's ill treatment of her. She was
in addition generalizing that it was normal, or the way
of men to misuse women, that this was life, and it had
to be tolerated.
    I mentioned her daughter and asked why did she think
she had committed suicide. Lutchme began weeping.
I waited until she wiped away her tears with the end of
her sari. I asked, 'Wasn't Maliga happy?' 'What
happy?' she retorted 'with that husband! How can be
happy? Always trouble. Munsame and Kista! They
took the life out of her. I got all her clothes.
They bought her nothing. You want to see?' She did
not wait for my reply, but went upstairs, and returned
shortly with a neat bundle which she placed on the
table and untied. There was a blouse, an under-
petticoat, and three saris - a black nylon embroidered
in white, a floral nylon and a red sari. All three
were splattered with the red kunkun powder (1) that had
been wrapped with them. From the end of the red sari

Lutchme untied Maliga's thalie. (2) Maliga's grandmother began to groan and sobbed silently.

Maliga's house

I visited her house six months later. Maliga's husband
opened the door. His arm was badly burnt, the skin
shrivelled and dead in parts and in others not at all,
so that there were patches of white. He was slight in
stature and looked younger than his 33 years. His
dark face was handsome, his eyes red. He admitted,
with just a trace of embarrassment and apology, that
he had been drinking the night before. The sitting
room was small - a studio couch, a radiogram, a kitchen
table, three kitchen chairs and an old sideboard made
up the furniture. The wall was green with coloured
pictures of Indian film stars and in between these were
two pictures of Christ. There was a new copy of the
Bible on the sideboard. The one bedroom upstairs was
occupied by an 'aunty' and her four children. Munsame
claimed that the aunty helped him with the housework,
but there was no sign of aunty or any of her family.
The room held 'aunty's' furniture as well as his wardrobe. There were two beds in his bedroom, with a
mattress and a blanket on each, but no bed linen.
There was a dismantled bed standing against the wall
and a dressing table. A passage of about three feet
remained in between all the furniture.
    Munsame described the events that led to Maliga's
death. His manner was polite, humble and did not
reveal his emotion, except when he said: 'I should
have smashed that bottle.' He looked after the
children, washed and cooked for them. He said he
worked at the fish stall and earned R9 a week, all of
which he used to give to Maliga. He was all praises
for his wife: 'All the time she lived with me I never
saw her do anything out of the way. She never went
here or there without my permission. She looked after
all of us nicely. She was very pretty. I wanted to
buy furniture for the house but she stopped me.'

Sivam

Sivam is Maliga's eldest sister. Her husband is a
foreman in a tin factory. He pays the rent, buys the
food and clothes and gives her R10 a month. 'Is that
enough?' I ask. 'Too much,' she replies with an

expansive gesture of hand and a proud rolling of eyes.
She is an animated young woman in a mini, holding her
baby in her arms.   Three other children sit on chairs,
one of them Maliga's, with a strong resemblance to
Joey.   'He don't like to go to his father's house',
she tells me - 'Ask him,' and then proceeds to ask
herself.   The boy says he doesn't want to go to his
father.   She proceeds to tell me how Munsame abused
Maliga and turns for confirmation to the little boy.
'Didn't your father hit your mother?   Didn't Thagie
Ana buy the studio couch?'   The boy confirmed each
point dutifully.   She said that Joey had come home
yesterday to fetch his brother, but he had refused to
go.   'I told Joey that they mustn't think that we had
no right over them.   They were my sister's children
and we had every right over them.'   Then she went on to
say 'I can take the two little girls, specially that
Audrey.   Never mind she's black but I like her face',
and her eyes animated with the pleasure the child gave
her.   'I can keep her like gold.'

20 Suicide notes

The Durban Inquest Court records contained 241 suicide notes, of which 134 were written between 1940 and 1960 and 107 between 1962 and 1970.   The majority of the notes were written by Whites and by men (see Table 64).
   The suicide note is the closest one can get to the mind of the suicide in a sociological study based largely on Inquest Court records.   It is an invaluable document, not only because it gives direct access to the suicide but also because it is the suicide's last considered communication to the world.   As such, it is the most authentic summary available of the suicide's life, the situations through which he related to society, the interactions that prompted his act, and the final factor/factors that precipitated it.
   Both psychologists and sociologists distinguish between apparent motives and real motives, between rational, conscious factors and unconscious, irrational ones, and strongly suggest that it is the conscious, rational self that commits the suicide.   Yet the Durban suicide notes, in keeping with the findings of several other studies, (1) project the rational and coherent state of the writers, even of those writers certified as psychotics.
   Though Durkheim and Menninger offer two distinct interpretations of suicide: Durkheim, as the effect of the social environment; Menninger, as the function of the death instinct inherent in man, the typologies they construct closely resemble each other.   Thus when Menninger defines suicide as 'the wish to kill' (corresponding with conscious hate) he describes syndromes which equate with Durkheim's anomic suicide.   Likewise his definition of suicide as the 'wish to be killed' (corresponding with conscious guilt) and the 'wish to die' (conscious helplessness) resembles Durkheim's

altruistic and egoistic suicide, as is observed in the
following comparison:

The Wish to Kill (2)	Anomic Suicide (3)
1 Symptoms: rage at the approach of threats.	1 Symptoms: the suicide is exasperated, blasphemous and directs violent re-crimination against life in general.
2 Wish to eliminate the source of the threatened deprival.	2 Threats and accusations are directed against the particular person(s) to whom the suicide's un-happiness is imputed.
3 'The wish to kill', un-expectedly robbed of certain external occa-sions or objects of un-conscious gratification may be turned back upon the person of the 'wisher' and carried into effect by the suicide.	3 Feelings of exasperation are expressed at loss of control over situation of which he felt himself master. He revolts against the cause of his ruin whether real or imaginary. If he rec-ognizes himself as res-ponsible for his disaster he takes it out on him-self.
4 Suicide may be preceded by homicide.	4 Suicide may be preceded by homicide. (5)

The Wish to Die (6)	Egoistic Suicide (7)
1 Capacity for dealing with reality is poorly devel-oped - suicide expresses himself against life and eulogizes death.	1 Withdrawal from life. 'Melancholic languor which relaxes all the springs of action.' In-difference to work and all public interests.
2 Menninger refers to lit-erary works which con-tain this wish. Phil-osophic pessimism. Wish to return to the womb. Victim indulges in introspection.	2 Durkheim refers to lit-erary works expressing this wish.
	3 Indulgence in self-introspection, thought,

inner life, self-observation, self analysis. Self-concentration deepens the gulf between self and society. He is enamoured of himself and so detaches himself from society. Retreats from outside world into himself. If he loves, it is to dwell on love, not to give himself in love. A calm melancholy marks his last moments. He may make minute observations of his last moments. 'Melancholic languor which relaxes all the springs of action.'

The Wish to be Killed

1 Being killed is the extreme form of submission and essence of masochism. It is the desire to derive satisfaction by punishment of self. The conscience leads the individual to suffer strong guilt feelings which demand punishment of the self. (8)

2 Martyrdom is associated with this type. (10)

Altruistic Suicide

1 Source is violent emotion. In obligatory suicide, it is controlled by reason and will. The suicide has serene conviction derived from a feeling of duty. It is an active suicide in contrast to the depressive state of the egoist. He kills himself at the command of his conscience. Burst of faith and enthusiasm carries him to his death. (9)

The similarities between the two sets of typologies tend to be confirmed by the fact that the suicide notes from the Durban Inquest Court records could be classified interchangeably in either of the two sets - Durkheim's or Menninger's.

INTERPRETING THE MEANING OF SUICIDE FROM SUICIDE NOTES

The unique insight that a suicide note gives is, however, weakened when the notes are thus categorized into
sociological or psychological slots.   It is more useful to take each note at its face value and to interpret the suicide's world view from it.   The note may
thereafter be classified into some scheme, new or
existing, and the classification will then be less
contrived.
    Jack Douglas identifies four meaning-patterns in
suicide - a means of transferring the soul from this
world to the other world, a means of transforming the
situational self into the substantial self in this
world or the other world, a means of achieving fellow-
feeling and a means of getting revenge.   These meaning-
patterns are contained in their broad characteristics
in the Durkheim-Menninger typologies.   The first two,
in the wish to die or egoism, the third in the 'wish
to be killed' or altruism and the last in the 'wish to
kill' or anomie.   The awareness of these meaning-
patterns emphasizes the importance of knowing and
understanding the real-life suicide.
    The Durban suicide notes strike a note not so much
of tragedy as of relief.   The writers often appear to
look forward to death.   The moods struck vary from
relief, apology, shame, abject self-condemnation to
hostile aggression, but in practically all instances
they express the desire to be relieved from the sorry
state of affairs in which the writers find themselves.
Death does not appear to have the same implications
for them as it has for people involved with life and
caught up in its activities.   In many cases, death
conjures up visions of a real, divine freedom, of new
opportunities and at least the prospect of eternal
rest.   The last may be likened to the state of salvation offered by Hinduism and Buddhism - Moksha,
Nirvana, a state of non-birth, non-life, non-pain and,
as such, the ultimate that a human can reach.   Thus
he who is saved is he who will never again be whipped
up on the wheel of karma, of life and action and be
exposed to the pains of birth and death.
    The genuine suicide thus appears to see life not as
the living see it, as man's most precious possession to
which he clings at all costs, but as the preferable
state of non-life to which he aspires.   Thus he aban-
dons the compulsion to live.   'I have come to this
world, I must live, if life is poison, I must drink'
(Hindi ditty).

Jerry Jacobs (11) classifies the notes he studied
in the Los Angeles area into first-form notes, sorry
illness notes, not sorry illness notes, direct accusation notes, will and testament notes and notes of
instruction. He suggests that the notes in themselves
explain their suicides and it is not necessary to go
outside them to search for their meaning. While this
may be true, most suicide notes are short, some are
written in a hurry, or in cases of poisoning, while
the drug is acting, and come to an abrupt end. It is
inconceivable that these notes communicate all that
the suicide intended to communicate. It seems too,
that the suicide is under pressure to summarize his
feelings. Just as he does not wish to impose his
presence any further on life, so he does not wish to
impose his thoughts unduly. Thus many notes are
cryptic. The researcher, moreover, knows more than the
contents of the notes. He knows the circumstances in
which the suicide occurred and may also have had access
to the history of the suicide. The meaning of the
note is thus enhanced if he uses all this information
to 'interpret' the note, not in terms of any ready-made
scheme, but in terms of the suicide's own assessment of
his life situation.

The Durban suicide notes have been analysed and
classified into:

1 The passive death wish notes - 'I am tired, I can't
take any more, I wish to sleep'.

2 The active death wish notes which (a) reject the
world - 'I wish to die, the world is not worth my
life', or (b) 'I wish to die because I am not worthy
of this world'.

3 'You have killed me' notes.

4 The resurrection notes which (a) wreak revenge,
(b) transform the self into a worthier self, (c) offer
the self as a sacrifice, (d) join the beloved in a new
life.

The four classes may also be identified with Durkheim's
egoistic suicide (class 1), altruistic (class 2(b)) and
anomic (classes 3 and 4(b)), but such broad categoriza-
tions are not very useful.

1 Passive death wish notes - 'I am tired, I can't take
life any longer'

The pain-wracked, nerve-ravaged suicide is listless,
tired, disinterested. He is weary of life and has no
interest in any kind of future. He is often apologetic

and begs forgiveness of those whom he leaves behind.
The one single statement he seems to be making is:
'I am tired, I want to sleep.' For him suicide is a
happy relief from a miserable existence. His own
description of his inner state, his pain and internal
mental misery is so explicit that to impute any other
undertones or overtones appears extraneous and contrived. As he puts it himself, he is 'sick', 'a
burden on others', his body is in a state of 'unbearable
pain', his emotions 'extended to the utmost limits -
and taut with the strain', he wishes only to be
'relieved of the torture'.

Even society acknowledges this state, and while some
half-acknowledge the humanity of euthanasia, others are
known to have actually practised it. The suicide in
this condition does not conceive his act as tragic,
pathetic or abnormal, but as a real and logical solution. He has realized a fundamental of life, that
death is inevitable, and discovered that his body is
useless and his emotions no longer responsive to life.
He plans his death, and salvages whatever dignity he
can in preference to continuing a slow and ignoble
disintegration. While the mood of these suicides
resembles Durkheim's egoism and Menninger's 'wish to
die', they do not reject life, and do not voluntarily
or actively choose death. They in fact have only the
one reasonable choice, death. Thus the 83-year-old
man says, 'I have lived long enough. I am not well.
Bury me next to my wife.' He has no recriminations
against life. He does not choose death in preference
to life, death is all he has.

His statement, moreover, though short, is so lucid
that it seems quite unnecessary to seek any other
psychological or sociological explanations for his act.
Eighty-three years is a good spell and if at 83 the
body begins to disintegrate there is little logic in
propping it up. Thus the wisdom of the statement,
'Better to die in your boots than coughing in bed.
Cheerio all my pals', and the irritation of the old man
who, disturbed in his act by the landlady, retorts
'Your bloody knife is blunt.' For these people, death
is the rational end.

This is the general condition of this class of notes,
but each case is marked by its own additional complex-
ities.

To magistrate

'Dear Sir, This letter is to put my dearest husband at
rest as no one can be better to me than he has been to
me.

I can't carry on any longer, but *please* have me
cooked and my ashes scattered around. I do hope the
other roses don't die and please don't think that I
have any drink in me. I don't want to be buried in
my dad's grave as I don't think it is right to pay
R100 to open a grave when R3.40c can be scattered. My
body is only here. My breath has been taken.

This is my last will so please carry it out.'

To husband

'My dearest, Please don't condemn me or hate me but I
am very tired of life. My only wish is cook me and
put the ashes in next day. I know I am very weak and
you have been a very patient husband. I can't carry
on any more. My life hasn't been all roses. I did
my best. Please look after my dear old mother and
comfort her. There are a great many more wicked
persons than me, so please don't think too bad of me.
I don't want any one at my funeral but Mama and yourself and David and Mary.

I have written a letter to the magistrate, so you
are not blamed, as you have been a wonderful husband
to me. As a wife, I can only be a housekeeper.

Please understand and don't condemn me too much.
Oh, don't put me in Dad's grave. You know what I
want.'

A 60-year-old White man: 'Please forgive me for doing
this but I cannot struggle any more. Life is abso-
lutely empty. You made me so happy and I have been
such a nuisance to everyone and you've all been too
kind my family and all my friends. God bless you.'

A 65-year-old White man: 'I pray God will some day
forgive me for what I am about to do but my health
seems to have gone. I seem to have little ability
to do anything but get deeper and deeper in debt. I
spent sleepless nights and can't see any other way.
Thank you for being a wonderful wife. I hope you'll
remarry someday, that you will find someone better
able to take care of you.'

A 55-year-old White man: 'Dear Kenny, I have no
will but trust you to share everything that is mine
with Derek and Timothy. I would like the house paid-

off before selling and sharing the money out.   Otherwise you must keep everything you have given me as
well.   Please forgive me but I can't stand anymore of
this illness.   Thank you for all your love, and kindness.   This is best for you.   Don't be sad as I will
be at peace.   Love to all my loved ones.'

2(a)   Active death wish notes - 'I wish to Die - the
World is not Worth my Life'

In contrast with the people who realize that they cannot cling on to life any more, that they have in terms
of all physical laws of nature reached the end of their
tether, there are the others, often young people who
feel that life is not worthy of them.   They may be
categorized as 'egoistic'.   They either reject the
world or consider themselves as apart from it.   The
operative themes of their letters are: 'I am fed up
with life.   The world is not worth the trouble of
living', or 'I am no good for the world'¡   'no good'
probably concealing 'too good'.   The writers of some
of these letters had been diagnosed as emotionally disturbed, as psychotic or neurotic.
    Rejection of the world - 'The world is not worth my
life' - this was expressed in a number of the Durban
letters, e.g. 'This is the last day I call you.   I am
fed up with life' (30-year-old African man), 'I am fed
up of life' (26-year-old Indian man), 'I am disgusted
with life.   I am bitterly miserable' (33-year-old
White man), 'The reason why I have come to take this
step is that I am simply fed up of life and there
seems nothing to look forward in life' (40-year-old
Indian man).

Letter 1

'I am just tired of sitting in the wheel chair day in
and day out.   My sisters all have big cars and plenty
of money but never can offer a ride or a bit of outing
to me.'   The writer is bitter about his deprivations.
Others have and he does not have.   Such an iniquitous
world is not worth his life.

Letter 2

'I am taking my own life which I hate to but I find
this world is very cruel.   I have tried to lead a
normal life but there is always something that beats
me.'

Letter 3

A 30-year-old Indian man: 'In the event of my passing
over don't think it's 'fowl' play because I'm not a
rooster nor was there a chicken or hen with me.   Got
that!   Don't worry about doctors because the drug is
very powerful and no earthly being or apparatus will
help.   Rather inject morphine or a patent life ending
drug.   You cannot save me.   Don't say what my wife
or family intend saying or want to say.   They will
fabricate and fabricate so that although I am dead or
dying they will prove their innocence.   My wife
believes in 99% witchcraft, spiritualism and other
phenomena like her most enchanting dreams and her
rotten coolie temple at Carlton Road, Mayville.   No
paper, cannot say much.   My belief is 000000%, witchcraft is 100%.   Wife is 100% witchcraft, God is
000000% Tata everybody.   My wife's lamenting was
jealousy, mine was progress and not retrogress.'
   In the first sentence, the writer clarifies that he
has not eeen murdered (foul play) nor is his death due
to complications with women - ('I'm not a rooster, nor
was there a chicken or hen with me.').   His light-
hearted, joking mood makes the point that life is
worth so little to him, that he can dismiss it as a
joke.   His mood at the same time stresses his contempt for the world and this contempt is more explicit
in the succeeding sentences when he rejects the power
of humans to help.   They failed him in life and he
does not want them to mess up his death, because they
cannot save him.   In the sentences that follow, he
blames his wife and family (probably her family) for
his poor world view.   It is her small mind, steeped
in witchcraft and obsessed with jealousy, that has
tainted his world and made it useless.   As distinct
from his wife and the world she defines, he is progressive and must thus move on and out of its crippling
confines, into infinity - 000000% which is his belief,
infinite, and which is God, infinite.

Letter 4

The following letter of a 35-year-old African suggests
that he is running away from life to escape the long
arm of the law.   His criticisms of the society which
prosecutes him, unjustifiably, is found in the letter,
but feelings about his innocence are clear.   His whole
attitude is philosophical, an admission of his helplessness in an evil world controlled by an alien government
and its police.

'The house caught fire from me
with a big mistake
In a devilish way
I slept there and smoked.
The cigarettes fell on the masonite
So the government is going to sentence me to death
with a blue jacket and I will die in trouble
Don must not worry
David knows nothing
I give a watch to my brother
They must look after Lilian Mchunu
To her I am married
I give all my articles, I possess
To my wife
To be taken home
I pass my best wishes
I am at the ground
Where I am
Nkosi who is working for the construction
Must give Juliet 50 cents
That is her money.'

Letter 5

The following two notes were written by persons diagnosed as psychotics or neurotics:
   'I have found myself wanting for my mind to simply
cease, intermittently for many years.   This is the
dead end situation.   There have been aggravating
things from time to time (like the present sickening
situation with this intolerant, hysterical, deranged
woman who appeared up to recently charming, amusing,
stimulating, likeable), but the main overshadowing
background has been the desire to cease.   I cease.'
The writer has wanted to die for some time.   He has
found the world unworthy of his life, and his latest
relation with this 'deranged woman' has confirmed the
hopeless nature of his existence.   The woman, at
time pleasing, at times repulsive, is probably both
real and symbolic, an actual woman he knew, or the
fickle, intolerable, undependable world which elates
him the one moment and depresses him the next.   The
world is a 'dead end' situation, and not for him.
   A 35-year-old White woman signing herself sarcasti-
cally as 'Vanity' writes: 'My sincerity may be doubt-
ful and my endeavour proved to be nil but the disintegration of soul or psyche by over analysis is obvious.
I have lived for twenty-one years, I am of ordinary
education with a desire for a full and useful life, but

now I am reduced to a state where outwardly I am selfish,
with interests in keeping myself tidy, and seeking other
people's favour. No matter how conscientious I may be
to co-operate, the powers that be scientific or provi-
dential prevent me from the exact continuity of well
being with those about me. The brain has been subjected to such a vigorous analysis by sound processes in
timing of noise to correspond with that of my brains
deliverance of ordinary speech that such noises even as
dogs barking (a frequency much higher than that of
human ears) may be used' The letter becomes incoherent.
There is mention of sound in insects - her interest in
psychology 'which through scientific testing and use of
her as a guinea pig, has become implanted in my mind at
the cost of disintegrating my human relationship'.
She has feelings of persecution - 'No doctors can ever
help me in what is beyond their imagination or mental
cycle of thought. They can't alleviate the persecution and out of timeness with other human society
which varies with the brain's variation in registering
consciousness'. She suggests that 'whether my
behaviour is explained away scientifically or ethically
as the fate of the damned, it will not help me in
'living a useless existence of inharmony'.
Whatever the nature of in-depth analysis, here at
least is one comment from the 'inside' - from a
psychotic. She seems to be saying: over-analysis is
destroying my soul and psyche. I cannot recognize
myself anymore. I may not be what I appear to be (I
am presenting to you my situational rather than substantial self). (12) I may be a failure, but at
least I was a whole person until you started taking me
apart. Now I am a confused mess of disintegrated
pieces. I no longer know myself. Whatever I do is
misinterpreted. If I am tidy, I am told that I am
obsessed with my appearance, if I please and love
others, I am told that I am fawning on them.
Doctors are incapable of understanding and helping
her. It is as if she were saying: 'My problem founts
from the fact that I am not in rhythm, in touch, or in
sympathy with society. Since I am not with society,
I am persecuted by society. Doctors can't help me
because it is beyond them to know the precise rate at
which I can adjust to social demands. They work in
terms of generalizations that don't apply to me and
vary with each person. (They can't alleviate the
persecution and out of timeness with other human
society which varies with the brain's variation in
registering consciousness.) Psychologists categorize

me as neurotic, moralists as damned, but this does not
help me, and I continue to live a useless existence of
inharmony.   Thus it is better for me to die, because
the world is not worth my soul or psyche.'

2(b)   'I wish to die.   I am not worthy of this world.
I am a failure'

Letter 1

'I have not brought anyone any happiness and so I think
it is better that I now say goodbye.   Please forgive
me and don't believe all you hear as a lot of untruths
will be told.   My biggest fault was that I just talked
idly without thinking what I was saying.   You deserve
someone much nicer than me and I hope you may eventually
find him.   Sorry to do this but there is no other way.'
He sees himself as not knowing how to behave in this
world and therefore causing unhappiness to others, of
spoiling the world.

Letter 2

The following letter and the act that follows almost
immediately on writing the letter, express two moods.
The suicide begins with hope in himself and asks to be
readmitted to his wife's favours, and through them,
into the world.   The hopeful mood however, is quickly
conquered by an overpowering feeling of helplessness in
the self, resulting in suicide: '2 am, sweetheart
note time, I will undergo treatment that you always
wanted if it will bring you back to me.   You make
arrangements and I will be with you.   Whatever you
decide.   Will do anything to get you back.   After
treatment can always start again.   After you receive
letter I will 'phone you.   Don't put phone down.'
He starts writing another letter but does not go
further than the salutations.
    Above all this suicide wants to resume his relation-
ship with his wife, who represents his entire world.
He does not want to die, he wants to live, but he cannot live without her support.   She, however, cannot
give him that support because of his weakness and his
worthlessness, his total inability to 'reform'.   He
sees himself as trapped in his own weakness, and doomed
to become dissolved by the disorganized routine that
has taken over his life, and which is unworthy of his
wife and her world.

Letter 3

Self-blame, however, is often accompanied by an undertone of blaming others as is evident in the following
letter by a 46-year-old White man, a railway worker,
who finds that he just cannot cope with the rising
expectations of his family, nor with the pace of
their successes. He writes to his wife: 'Don't forget none of it has been your fault. My darling
Sheila, I am writing this in the boys' room. I am
sorry I could not give you and the kids a better life.
I know I have been a bloody fool because not many could
have you and kids like ours. Please congratulate K
for me and I hope he passes his Matric. Also please
tell M I am sorry for all the trouble caused. But by
doing this I think you and the kids will be better off
(as K says). Please also apologise to them. Bye-
bye my love. I wish you and the kids all the best of
luck because you really deserve it. Sorry for
writing in such a hurry but I am shaking. Oh my love
darling. I know what you have been to me but sorry
I was a bloody fool. Please look after the boys and
M. I can't write any more. Love.'
   His letter is a table of self-recriminations. He
blames himself for not giving his wife and children a
better life, for failing a wonderful family. But the
self-recrimination is underlined with bitterness,
against his family, against K who has apparently told
him that they would be better off without him, and
confirmed his feeling of being a drag on his family.
There is an undertone that it is they who gave him his
poor self-image, made him feel worthless. Thus his
statement: 'Don't forget, none of it has been your
fault', is probably double-barrelled: 'Look all this
is your fault. I am dying because you wish me dead.'

Letter 4

In the following letter, written by an aggressive
patriarch, self-blame is suppressed by the claim that
he is 'redeeming' his wife by ridding her of himself,
her persecutor. The writer, a 28-year-old African
writes: 'Goodbye love - enjoy yourself and remain
well. May God remain with you and spare you. You
must not walk about. You must not die because I am
the person who kills you. I the one who kills you is
no longer around. I have killed myself.' The key
point is made in the statement: 'I am the person who
kills you' and the meaning of his action is contained

in the very next sentence: 'I the one who kills you is
no longer around. I have killed myself'. The implication of the letter is probably: 'I was a nuisance
to you in life but now I am killing myself and through
my death I am no longer a nuisance. I redeem your
life. You don't have to walk about any more.' It is
also probably: 'you don't have to be without support -
loaf around, be a tramp, left destitute and without
roots.' The court records reveal that he had tormented
his wife, coming home drunk, beating her, often pushing
her out of their home, and forcing her thereby to sleep
with neighbours and friends. His message: 'Enjoy
yourself and remain well', is an admission that he did
not make this possible for her. Yet his note is
written in an imperious way. It was he who deprived
her of this freedom, and it is he who is returning
this freedom to her. While not making any abject
admissions of his worthlessness, he admits that he is
incapable of making her happy, that he has in fact
failed her.

3 Notes that accuse and wreak revenge - 'I didn't wish
to die - you killed me - you will suffer through my
death'

Probably all suicides contain elements of accusation
and revenge against the social survivors. Whatever
the fundamental intention or meaning of the act, the
act in itself is the most eloquent accusation against
society; and the definition of the suicide as a quirk
is a social defence against this accusation and protection against the guilt and remorse it provokes. It
transforms the surviving 'scapegoat' into a 'murderer',
and at the same time acts as a force that transforms
the powerless into a new state of supernatural power-
fulness, through which justice is restituted and the
persecutor punished. Accusation and revenge letters
often also conceive death as resurrection, in which
the person, ineffective in life, becomes effective in
death.
   In the first letter that follows, the writer
emphasizes accusation and the revenge element is almost
imperceptible, in the second letter the accusation
aspect is as specific as the revenge aspect.

Letter 1

A 37-year-old doctor writes: 'My darling, this will
solve your problem better than anything else I can
think of.   I trust you will be financially reimbursed
for all you have contributed over the years.   I am
afraid I am unable to live without you and the children.   When they are older please explain things to
them.   I adore them and am ashamed to inflict this
stigma on them.   Please treat them with kindness and
don't shout too much.   Don't forget the model aero-
plane we promised Steve.   Fortunately my position is
such no real loss will be incurred.   Much as you
detest the family please don't desert my mother who
will need all the support she can get.   Love to you,
Mum and Dad, and thank them particularly for their
encouragement over later years.'
     It is a letter of a husband to a wife whom he had
experienced as demanding and possessive.   She exercised
her rights over him partly because of her economic contribution to the family.   The last conflict had been
provoked by his need to fulfil his duties to his
brother's widow.   She had objected to the time he
gave to his parental family and 'hounded' him out of
life.

Letter 2

A 25-year-old Indian man says: 'Dearest K.G., Sorry
to hit your aunt but she got big mouth I am going to
leave you for her big mouth I had to shut her up.
Sunday, for your Ma's sake I left her.   I only have
respect for your mother.   If your Ma wasn't there I
should give her good doing up.   I am committing
suicide.   I came here specially for giving her hiding.
You'll say I am a liar, rogue, so good-bye.   No one
will come to you all for anything from today.   I am
no bother to you all.   I do not have a father.   What
did you all give me?   Nothing - That all.   So long.'
     The young writer of this letter had become deeply
attached and dependent on his friend's family.   They,
however, had used him as something of a doormat and
though usually quiet, uncomplaining and obliging, he
had become incensed at the jibes of the aunt, so that
in one surprising moment, he broke through all his
restraints and hit her.   The incident provoked a
great family furore.   Everybody turned against him
and he became a confused mixture of guilt and revenge.
He knew that in terms of prevailing structures he

ought not to have hit the aunt but she ought not to
have provoked him, ought not to have 'used her big
mouth', ought not to have hurt him so insensitively.
But he is powerless to impress upon them the magnitude
of their crime against him.   He impresses this upon
them by his dramatic self-killing.   That self-killing
also converts them into murderers.   They murder him,
he does not kill himself.

Letter 3

A 26-year-old White woman: 'My ticket is up.   You
only felt sorry for me and don't love me, so I am
leaving life and taking our baby with me.'   The letter
is written by a pregnant woman to her lover.   She had
attempted suicide on several other occasions and had
been abandoned by lovers before.   Her suicide in fact
had little to do with him and she knew this, yet she
accuses him of her death.   In doing so, she uses him
as a scapegoat.   He represents her relation with
society and in placing blame on him she blames that
situation which insensitive in itself, will be sensitive
and conscience-stricken in him.

4(a)   Death as resurrection

Practically all religious systems interpret death as the
path to immortality.   The idea of resurrection after
death is persuasive and many suicide notes impress that
their writers have died in order to be reborn in a
purer or more powerful form.
      Death by this interpretation is not a mode of doing
away with oneself, not an act whereby one ceases to
exist, but rather an act that produces a new existence,
a new self.   Jack Douglas identifies the suicide act
as a transition from the temporal existence into a
permanent, immortal, eternal one.   In this context
suicide has a logical and rational meaning for the
suicide himself.
      Christ is the classical model of this pursuit for
resurrection and immortality through death.   He is
the incipient suicide, who pursues death in life, and
Judas is probably not so much a traitor as the instrument through whom he fulfils his goal.   In that sense,
he is a true disciple of Christ, who makes the supreme
sacrifice to Christ - offers his life for him, not in
pride or glory, but in the ignominy of his suicide, so
that Christ's martyrdom will not lose an atom of its
radiance to Judas's.

The Christ-complex is a mixture of altruism, egoism
and anomie. He wishes to die, to be killed and to
kill. He wishes to die (egoistic), to be liberated
from this world (to die), to join his Father, to be
resurrected in the God-world; in the Christian context, to become Himself. He wishes to be killed
(altruistic) so that through his killing, all those he
intends to save will be saved, so that through the
shock, the Christian community will be found. Simultaneously, he wishes to kill (anomie) all those who
stood for evil, the Pharisees in particular, against
whom his anger throughout his short life is strong and
vigorous but whose duplicity he will not disdain to
match. Instead he wills his death and resists all
attempts to save him, so that his persecution will
stand exposed, and those who brought it about stand
eternally damned.

In the three Indian religions, Hinduism, Buddhism
and Jainism, the idea is strong that 'life' or meaningful existence only begins after death, after the
meaningless material illusory *maya* (existence) of this
world has passed away. Thus in Jainism the monk is
in fact an incipient suicide; he so tortures and
torments his physical body that there appears to be a
deliberate attempt to snuff it, or push it out of
existence, so that the soul may be liberated.

While the idea of life after death is present in
Judaism and Islam, it does not take the theological
dimensions found in Christianity and Hinduism, nor is
it characterized by the surety of eternal life after
death, by the example of God (Christ in Christianity,
Krishna in Hinduism) assuming the form of man and then
'passing on' to be resurrected into 'Christ'. If it
happened to Christ and Krishna, it could happen to Don
and Perumal. This may be a contributing factor to the
lower suicide rates of Jews and Muslims.

The largest number of the Durban suicide notes
express belief in life after death and impress the
idea that life inhibits a secret power which the person
releases upon his death. This power could win back
for him that which he lost in life, or gain for him that
which he could not gain in life - love, prestige, honour.
The writers of such notes are never Jews or Muslims.

4(b) Revenge through resurrection

In the preceding suicides, particularly class 3, death
wreaked revenge in itself by invoking guilt, pity,

sorrow, etc.   In the following suicides, the idea is
projected that the person becomes transformed in death
and acts upon this world in that transformed state.

Letter 1

Dhanama (18 years old) lived in such poor conditions
that there is not even an address reflected in the
Inquest Court record.   She shared a room in a poor
Durban suburb with her mother and brother.   Her father
had left the family; her mother had been forced to
take in washing, she herself had enrolled for shorthand
and typing on a part-time basis.   Her body was found
in a small room, with no electricity, one bed, a table
and a primus.   Dhanama's mother, left destitute by
her husband, had moved with the children to her
parental home in Merebank.   Though her parents were
deceased, her brothers were alive and they were duty
bound to care for her, which they did.   But after a
year, Dhanama's mother had moved with her children to
their own 'home'.   Dhanama had visited her uncles on
the day of her suicide and had asked them for money to
buy books.   An altercation had occurred and she had
returned home very depressed.
     Soon after that she had burnt herself to death, but
before doing so, she had written a four-page note, the
time on the note is 4.30 p.m.   On top of the note it
says: 'Please find a cheque in my handbag in the
middle zipper.'   The note is not addressed to anybody,
it is simply an explanation for the tragedy.   It
starts thus: 'The reason for this tragedy is that
because I went to Merebank and I heard a lot of unnecessary false rumour about me, that I am talking a lot
with boys.   This word has been spoken since Friday
and before that nothing of this sort was declared.   I
wonder what is the background to all this scandals?
Just because people are beginning to become friendly
and united, heaven knows that I am not their hindrance.
Just to find a mere excuse they say that I speak a lot
with boys and why shouldn't they declare it while I
was there.   They always like to speak behind my
innocent back.   Now it is told to Uncle.   I was told
not to come to this house anymore - they are talking,
I am walking up and down all the time.   I am told I
must not go to Sunday school in Merebank but instead I
should go to the Somsteu Road.   I don't possess a
father who could also buy a nice house.   I can't stick
anymore nonsense.   I can't be kept hidden.   But I am
just a teenager.   I am not consciousness of anything,

crime or falsehood. They have usurped the authority
of Christ's disciples. The people who spoke lies
about me and scandalised about me, they shall be
thrown into burning hell, and thank God, their house,
they will not carry with them.
I have lived a life of an innocent and no one can
put a finger at me and say I am bad. It wouldn't be
very long they shall plead for mercy just for accusing
me for all fake things. Guilty conscience pricks the
person who scandalized about me.'
     The letter, written on sheets torn out of an exer-
cise book, accuses her uncles for her death (they have
usurped the authority of Christ's disciples, exceeded
the authority of the church and indicted her character
maliciously and quite unjustifiably), declares her
innocence ('I have lived a life of an innocent and no
one can put a finger at me and say I am bad'), and
promises revenge in the last sentence.
     The letter simultaneously explains her suicide as
an act to overcome her poverty, dependence, pain and
deprivation, it is an act that liberates her from her
small, helpless, insignificant, ordinary self and
transforms her into an all-powerful spiritual self
sitting alongside God and dispensing His justice on the
world and upon all her tormentors. In the note itself
she graduates from the mental state of a helpless
defeated mortal ('I am just a teenager') to an invin-
cible immortal ('They shall be thrown into burning
hell'). Thus she broods on her life-situation,
analyses her conflicts with her extended family, and
convinces herself that her uncles are guilty and she
is innocent. She raises herself out of her worldly
form and condemns the villains and pronounces a living
hell upon them. She analyses the reasons for their
evil and concludes that it is due to: (a) jealousy,
(b) her uncles' need for unity which can only be
achieved by finding a target to unite against, and (c)
the fact that she does not have a father and is thus
vulnerable to their authority ('I wonder what is the
background to all these reckless scandals? All this
is because ... of jealousy, because people are becoming
friendly and united.... I am not their hindrance ...
I don't possess a father who can also buy a nice house').
     House recurs in the letter. House is central to
Dhanama's affliction. It represents her whole world,
security, independence, respectability, rootedness -
father and family. Deprived of her own home, her
family broken, her uncles' house had represented home
and family to her and indeed she had a right to it, for

it was her maternal grandparents' home, inherited by
her uncles. It contained her cousins whose companionship she enjoyed and uncles and aunts who had given
her support. But suddenly she found herself excluded
from that home - the only world she knew. She was
pushed out of their house ('I was told not to come to
this house anymore'), off the street ('I am walking up
and down all the time') and out of the neighbourhood
('I must not go to Sunday school in Merebank but instead
I should go to Somsteu Road'). They have made her
into an outcast, but from self-pity she graduates into
judge. She declares that she will not allow such
injustice and such evil behaviour - 'I cannot stick
anymore nonsense ... I cannot be kept hindered ... but
I am just a teenager', and an innocent and pure one
and so she will be resurrected. 'I am not conscious
of anything - crime or falsehood.' In death, she will
step out of her helpless temporal mould and assume the
all-powerful spiritual one. On the threshold of that
all-powerful self, she declares: 'The people who spoke
lies about me and scandalized about me, they shall be
thrown into burning hell, and thank God, their house,
they will never carry with them.'

Letter 2

A 30-year-old Coloured woman writes: 'Dear concerned,
Should anything happen to me you must know that Raphael
Clark is responsible for me. Having gone to my
parents home and took me from them just to come and
make me a dog. He hits me when it suits him, says
things to me. Well if he hasn't got a heart on him.
I have. So I am tired of being made his slave for
four years. Today he can blow me around if he likes
because another woman is better than me. He has had
the rope for too long and has danced his music for too
long. He doesn't want to leave me alone cause he
won't get another fool like me, well, guilty conscience
will prick him that it will drive him to pull his head
off. I am so very sorry to being the horse to get
sjambocked that I can't stand it any more. So goodbye
to a life that's miserable and to be in tears every day
that God gives you. God you must make Raphael Clark
suffer the same way as I did. Bury me in my white
dress and I don't care what you say to my parents.'
    Raphael has dehumanized her. He has made her into
a dog. He has made her into his slave. He has made
her into his horse and he has sjambocked her, he has
hit her, he has said things to her. He has been

heartless, he has been without any sensitivity or any
humanity. She has finally risen up against him and
refused to tolerate his dehumanization of her any
further. But she will wreak divine revenge upon him,
through the supernatural power she will acquire at
death when she becomes united with God. Thus he will
suffer as she suffered.

Both in this letter and in the preceding one there
is reference to the 'guilty conscience that will prick';
in this letter that conscience will drive him to 'pull
his head off'. Both these people see the guilty conscience as an independent reality that can be penetrated and manipulated against its possessor. Thus the
suicide not only becomes part of God through death, but
also part of the living person whose conscience she
prods.

Letter 3

A 17-year-old Indian girl writes to her parents: 'I am
so sorry for falling in love and making mistakes.
Since yesterday lived in darkness. Now I got no face
in the world to live. He had a girlfriend next door,
why did he come here and do unnecessary things with me.
My heart was boiling since the things were returned.
Forgive me for what I have done. All my dresses and
engagement presents are given to poor children in any
society. He will never live in happiness in this
world. I have done all this in a temper. He will
never live in happiness after taking my life.'

Her second letter is to her fiancé: 'My dearest
loving future, over five months have passed with
sorrows and tears every minute, day and night, since
you agreed to marry me. Your family disliked me, but
you said you are only for me. We were in love and
promised to commit suicide if we cannot marry. All
of a sudden you broke your promise. The things came
back and what face I have left in the world, after
they saw us arm in arm kissing. Get married but you
will live in hell after doing all this to me. I kept
your secrets and made the greatest mistake by falling
in love with you but you did a crime, you will never
live in happiness. Your loving.'

The young girl was engaged to be married but then
her fiancé broke the engagement. Her suicide occurred
immediately thereafter. She refers to him as her
'dearest loving future'; suggesting thereby that he
was her entire future life, indeed since she had been
engaged to him and they had been observed kissing,

there would be little chance of her becoming engaged
again in terms of Indian orthodoxy, and if there is no
marriage ahead, there is no life ahead.   His desertion
spelled her social death, and paved the way for her
physical death - left her without 'face', that is
dignity, pride, self-confidence, the elemental part of
her physical existence.   It left her heart boiling.
Life under these conditions is impossible and her
suicide completes the physical aspect of it.   At the
same time, it resurrects her in a new and powerful form
in which she can curse and pursue him.   There is
however, the hope that moved by her death, he will join
her in death, as they had once pledged to do.   The
pledge had been made in the belief that in death they
would be resurrected to 'live' in strength and
happiness.   In her 'curse' upon him there is also the
invitation to fulfil his pledge and follow her in
death,   She sees death as giving her power over her
lover, to possess and pursue him, invading his heart
and soul, and tormenting him to fulfil his promise or
be forever cursed.

Letter 4

The letters of Jimmy Brown which he wrote to his 'wife'
and of which he filed copies with the coroner, project
a complexity of emotions, ranging from sacrifice to
revenge to resurrection.   They tell the story of an
introverted young man who emigrated to South Africa from
Britain, became successful in business, fell in love
and then committed suicide.
On his first trip to South Africa he meets Cheryl
but is unable to tell her that he is married.   He
does so in the first of the letters filed at the
Inquest Court and written on board ship while returning
to Britain: 'I should have told you before we embraced
that I was married, but I could not do so.   I was
afraid that you would misunderstand.'   He continues
to unravel the steps that led to his marriage.   'I
was home from combat duty.   We were at a party.   I
was boozed up.   I had avoided sex all along and was
afraid of it.   I had been engaged before but the girl
had died, and there had been little between us.   I
returned to my base after the party.   When I was back
home two months later, she told me she was pregnant.
She told me that I was the father and it had happened
at the party.   I was shocked, but I believed her.
There was only one thing I could do.   The child had to
have a name and so I married her.   I left England the

same night.   We never shared a bed throughout our
marriage.   She continued to live with her parents.
I went to see the baby when it was grown and I became
fond of the kiddie as it grew.

'When the war ended, she and the kiddie joined me
and we set up home.   The kiddie and I were pals, but
there were constant quarrels between her mother and me.
Then one day she told me that I was not the father of
the kiddie, that in fact there had never been anything
between us.   I was shocked.   I had a blood test done.
The kiddie's blood and mine did not match.   I had not
betrayed myself over any woman.   I left her and the
kiddie and went to Europe, then to Canada and the
States.   I returned to see the kiddie in between and
I saw to all their material needs.   The last time I
returned to our home, I caught her, in our house, with
a man.   We had a terrible row.   She left with the
kiddie.   I tracked them down and put the kiddie in a
boarding school.   I couldn't forgive her.   She had
been guilty of infamy of the worst kind.   She had
played me a sucker and fool.   I believed then that I
could never trust a woman.   I decided against annulling
the marriage.   The kiddie had my name and I didn't
want his name to be dragged to court.   Instead I came
to South Africa.'

The letter goes on to describe his meeting with Cheryl:
'I fell in love with you the first moment I saw you.
You were walking in the park with your hunter.   Your
blue coat was buttoned up to your chin.   I took photo-
graphs of you that day in the hot house.   Then later
I stole my first kiss in my hotel room.   I didn't
want to frighten you so I just brushed your lips.
Then I took you to meet my mother.

'I want to marry you.   I am taking steps to have my
marriage annulled.   I have never known such joy, as I
have found in you.   I beg only that you accept my
explanation, that you know how deeply I love you; that
I come to you pure, not having known any other woman
before.   There have been only two women in my life –
my mother and now you.'

Cherly returned his love and indicated her desire to
marry him.   He returned to South Africa and entered
into a period of passionate courtship with her.   The
death of his father had left both mother and son in a
very shocked state and in their grief they had clung to
each other.   Jimmy's doubly distraught state had
pushed him into excessive dependence upon her.   His
mother in turn had transferred her emotional links from
her husband to her son, and so treasured that dependence.

She could not brook competition from Cheryl.   She feared
her and in her fear hated her.   Jimmy, determined that
nothing would stand in the way of his new-found happiness, broke with his mother, and justified the break to
Cheryl in a letter: 'She is trying to possess me
completely, body and soul.   I will not be possessed by
her.   She wants me to be around as if I were her
husband.   I find it revolting.'

    They moved to Durban and began living together as
husband and wife.   He recalls the union nostalgically,
in a letter written to lament their parting.   'I had
made our flat ready.   I came to fetch you at the
station.   Our first stop was at the jewellers.   You
chose a wedding ring.   I slipped it on your finger in
the taxi.   We kissed and became husband and wife before
God.   I carried you across the threshold into our
home.   There was a radiance on your face I had never
seen before.   You smothered me with your kisses and
said that you had a home and a husband now.   Then you
had cast a disapproving eye at the twin beds.   I had
told you we would use only the one bed.   I had kissed
your wedding ring.   We became husband and wife that
night.'

    The happiness did not last.   Whatever Cheryl's con-
tributions to the breach, Jimmy's are apparent in his
letters.   He was too possessive, too jealous, and too
much up in the clouds.   Above all, it seems that 'he
was in love with love and not with her', an accusation
he made against her in a letter.   It was as if he had
projected his own idealized, not real, self on her, and
was worshipping that self there.   His relation with
her remained over-romanticized.   He sent her 'sweetheart roses' daily.   He spoke of their life as their
'honey garden'.   She became irritated, impatient.
She wanted to have a child.   His response was that
children must be born in wedlock: 'I am honour bound
to prevent you from having a child, no matter how
strong your desire for motherhood.   The sacredness of
sex in the production of a child has a special meaning
for me.   It belongs to God.   We need a special
sanction from God to create a child.'

    His hypocricy revolted her.   She wanted him to be
flesh and blood and a man about the house.   She found
instead that he relished ideas. 'During one of their
quarrels she had shouted at him.   'Go back to England.
Don't live with your memories.'

    The first serious break occurred on a Christmas Eve.
He wrote to her: 'You got drunk.   A lady does not get
drunk.   You behaved badly, like your low friends.

You let me down in public.   I could not bear it.   You
then walked out on me and went off to Debbie's.   That
night I had a nightmare.   I traded you with a prostitute, and then we were dead.   The next day I atoned
for all our misery.   I traded you with a prostitute.
Jimmy, while in one sense exulting in his sexual
relation with Cheryl ('You have transformed me from a
constrained living creature into a man of flesh and
blood') is guilt-stricken in another.   He has never
been liberated from his qualms and fears about sex, and
the dream, appears to symbolize this.   Thus he trades
her with a prostitute and dies.   That is, his relation
with her is reduced to the sin of their sex.   He has
lost his 'purity', though he pretends he hasn't, and
thus in 'trading' Cheryl with the prostitute in the
morning, he admits this and thereby atones.
Cheryl returns to him temporarily in the early hours
of the morning.   'I was full of gratitude.   I helped
you to undress and I made you lie down beside me.   I
did not wish to force myself upon you.   I left you to
make up your own mind.'   The reconciliation is short-
lived.   He writes to her after another quarrel 'I
begged you to stay.   You refused.   You went to your
lawyer and on his advice, took off your ring and flung
it at me.   They tell me you look terrible these days.
Your eyes are flabby and baggy - why do you keep away
then?   I plead to you on my bended knee, to come back.
I cannot live without you.   I don't sleep at night - I
write, or watch the sea to keep myself.'
These entreaties fail.   Cheryl does not return.
He stubbornly refuses to consider that the fault may
lie either in himself or in Cheryl, places it in
Cheryl's friend Debbie and insinuates a lesbian relationship between the two.   'I curse the day Debbie
came into your life.   She is rotten to the core....
You have replaced me with a girlfriend.   How foul!
The things you women get up to.   Debbie is enticing
you into her dirty world.   Don't enter it.   Come here,
my darling, I can't live without you.   I watch the
door night after night.'
Cursing Debbie does not help.   He begins to attack
Cheryl and thereby draws dangerously close to attacking
himself, for in Cheryl he sees his idealized self-
image.   It is as if that self-image, nurtured in
Cheryl, is disintegrating.   He accuses her of ingrati-
tude and infidelity and draws a degraded image of her:
'I did the sewing and the washing.   I taught you to
cook and drive.   You needed kindness, devotion and
someone to look after you.   All these I have tried to

give you.   What do you want?   Independence?   Good
food and dancing without paying for it?   I thought you
were above such human faults....   They say that you
are depressed, that you are drinking too much, that you
have dyed your hair.   Am I to believe this?   I don't
think you are eating your heart over me.   If you
recalled the sacred moments of our fusion as husband
and wife, you would return for the sake of that sacredness.'   He becomes openly abusive, and borders on the
fringe of blackmail: 'If the people in your firm came
to know of your unmarried association with me your
name would stink.   Wake up woman you're half dead.'
And again in despair: 'I must have you.   Another
woman won't do.   I wish I could get you out of my
mind.'

He begins to wonder if after all the trouble does
not lie in the way they had approached their union.
'We must start again.   The trouble is that we drifted
apart and became absorbed in our separate worlds.'
He turns upon himself.   'I succeeded in business; how
did I fail in marriage?'   And finally he turns upon
himself, not aggressively, but in a sort of masochistic
enjoyment of his inward turning.   It is as if he has
become his own object, and he observes his 'delicious
agony' from outside himself.

'I have had 113 days of anguish.   You have ordered
me to keep away until you are ready.   I can't bear
this.   You say you can't bear being in our flat for
two days.   Think of my agony.   I have to live in it,
alone and without you.   It is unbearable.   I am
going mad.   I have stopped answering the phone....
You have shut the door with a last exultant inexorable
clash.   Nothing is real.   Nothing touches me.   I
have forgotten to do all happy things.   I can only
weep.   Only a short while ago I was a married man.
Now I am forced to live the life of a bachelor.   I am
starving for you.   My hunger is deep rooted.   Even
you cannot reach into its dark recesses....   You were
my wife for 688 days.   I have gone through tortuous
hell since you left.   I wish I had not been so
scrupulous and given you a child.   That child would
have held us together.   What fools we men are to cling
to our wives who treat us like dirt.

'I am now dominated by a destructive force which I
cannot resist.   All my plans for the future crumble
before my eyes.   I want to destroy and wreck everything.   I saw death at Dunkirk.   It meant nothing to
me.   I faced it, I stared at it, I saw it floating in
the sea, or lying in the ship.   I saw it from the air,

from the sea, from the land.... I don't want sympathy
or pity. I am too numb. I no longer possess the
inclination for anything. I am just very livid and
now want to get away from it all. I am finished.
Facts will soon speak for themselves.' He loves her
and at the same time hates her for what she has done to
him and made him do. She turned a proud and happy
man into a tragic failure. 'You will never forget me.
I am your other self.' The only way he can get away
from her is to kill himself. He will thereby also
wreak revenge on her for having lived in sin with him,
and for having caused his death. He writes: 'There
is juncture at which the question of dying and living
loses it's significance. At this critical juncture
one still fights to live - but one's success is measured
then, not by whether one survives, but by which greater
catastrophe one can bear.'

   Two notes follow this letter. The first is very
short, encloses a cheque for R30, and assumes a Christ-
posture: 'If there is any kindness I can show or do,
speak now, as I shall never again pass your way after
July, 14th.' The last is his suicide letter. The
letter expresses sacrifice, blame, revenge and assumption of supernatural power.

Sacrifice 'Today is your birthday. It is my death
day. I give you my life as your birthday present.
The newspaper will splash the event and you will have
some sudden fame. I pay this terrible price because
of my love for you. I should go to you, speak to you
and command you to return, but I am a gentleman. I
cannot do that. I leave you a third of all that I
possess. I desired marriage, not sacrifice but you
desired sacrifice and now I willingly sacrifice my life
to you.'

Blame 'Few women are gifted with powers such as yours
to drive a man to suicide. You are guilty of the
worst kind of crime. With the kind of financial
backing I had, I could have been at the top of my firm
in a year. You didn't give me a sporting chance. I
need you, but all I have are memories that backfire
and torture me. This is a terrible price to pay for
my love for you.'

Revenge and supernatural destiny 'My demise will break
you. I can never forgive you. My mother will be
shocked to death. You must read my last letters to
her. I shall ask A to explain everything to her. I
am leaving copies of my letters to you for the coroner.'

These statements and instructions inform her that she will not escape blame and punishment from this world. The statements that follow establish the supernatural powers he will assume to punish her from the other world.

'You will have to account to God for your deeds.   I will tell God how I helped to save 700 men.   You will tell him how you killed a son, and his mother with shock.   Don't use the name Cheryl.   It spells suicide, mine, or murder, at your hands, in high heaven.   I'll be tried at sea, but you will never look upon the sea again without seeing me in it.   For the sea is my memorial for all time.   You will read ND on every car plate, as 'Now Dead'.   You will never be lonely for I shall always be with you.

Salvation - I am leaving at 5 a.m.   I go to the City of the Blessed where God himself dries all tears.'   He signs the letter: 'Unto eternity - Jimmy.'

His body was found at 7.40 a.m., fully clothed, including a raincoat, his head facing the sea, the water lapping his head and feet, arms outstretched.   A note, a red rose and cigarette lighter were found in his pocket in a wrapping of cellophane.   The note read: 'Cherry, goodby my darling - to eternity.   Daybreak 1955.'

Letter 5

Revenge: *I am powerful in life.   You dared to question that power.   In death I am ever more powerful.*

A Durban swami gained god-like stature in Durban's Hindu community and was accepted as a guru, or divine intreater to his followers.   His power, however, also attracted hostility and resulted in divisions within his rank, particularly over the administration of the Order's property.   He also became the centre of a scandal involving affairs with women - forbidden to swamis.   He died suddenly following numerous phone calls and letters threatening his life.   A lengthy inquiry fails to establish murder and suicide is strongly suspected.   Whatever the cause of his death, the letter he leaves behind is preoccupied with his funeral arrangements and is heavily suggestive of vengeance against his opponents, who were also the leading officials of his organization.   The object of his death appears to be to testify his innocence: 'I have no regrets.   I have given my very best to God and my people', and to point out his enemies and place them beyond the pale of redemption.

The dead, out of the way and beyond harming the living, are usually not only forgiven their sins by survivors, but are also remembered endearingly in terms of their goodness. Funeral orations often transform humble lives into super souls. The swami could thus have expected not only his redemption in this world, but also his elevation into a veritable god.   That in itself would demolish his opponents. In other words, that which he could not achieve in life, through tireless persuasion, defence of his actions and attacks on his enemies, he would achieve through death.

As he had expected, and indicated in his letter, his death aroused great public interest and his opponents became the victims of public and self-recrimination. They were charged with murder and while defending themselves successfully against this, they could not quite escape their own self-accusation, that they had through their vindictiveness killed a good man, very probably a saint.

The repeated and explicit instructions to exclude those 'members of his family [Order] whom he had renounced' from his funeral rites, and the selection of others to officiate at these rites, not only emphasized the finite nature of their expulsion from his 'grace' but also deprived them of their moment of glory.   His funeral, as he had both anticipated and planned ('my funeral may be delayed if need be so as to make it both convenient and possible for distant branches and members to attend.   I wish this to be done for the sake of all my children'), was one of the largest Durban had known.   It was thus as if he had deliberately staged the Organization's greatest moment and then deprived the castaways of all glory.   Thus he wrote: 'There may be confusion as to how to dispose of the body and I do not wish to have any disagreements over this body on my death.   Over the past two years there has been much bitterness and the Centre has been torn in two; therefore I wish that the Committee of the Centre has no authority or say whatsoever over my funeral or in any memorial service and it be left with no undertaking in this matter whatsoever nor consulted in any way.'   The letter thereafter, after repeating again that the committee shall have no jurisdiction whatsoever, proceeds to select and appoint by name those who shall be charged with the important duty of disposing of his body.   These included those members of the Committee who had remained loyal to him: 'My dearly beloved ones who have stood till the very end, braving all odds.'

To them, and them only, does he grant the privilege of
placing flowers on his body, of conducting a 'simple
service', of feeding the poor, particularly poor
African children, after ten days.   'All this is to be
arranged by those I named with the co-operation of
those members and branches who were with me till the
very end....   My pall bearers are to be selected from
amongst those who had been with me and served me till
the end.   This could be changed by regular intervals
so as to give as many of my dear ones as possible an
opportunity.   This could be arranged in advance.'
    The large attendance at his funeral also struck home
the point that he, and not the Organization or the
officials, was the all-powerful factor, and his death
struck their own death knell.   That death knell
becomes all the more forbidding with his promise to his
supporters that 'my spirit shall be with you for ever
and ever.   I shall never leave you for I have stood
with you when I was alive and I shall do so after
death.'   By the same token, his enemies could expect
his spirit to stand against them even more powerfully
in death, despite this declaration, 'I have no bitter
feelings against those who have reviled and attacked me
in every possible manner.'   This statement, apparently
forgiving, also has the effect of raising his stature
in the public eye and simultaneously reducing that of
his enemies.   His innocence is confirmed by the
statement: 'I have no regrets.   I have given my very
best to God and my people.'

4(c)   Reunion through resurrection

Letter 1

Rebirth and refuge are the goals of the following
suicide of a 13-year-old White boy: 'I am sorry for
what I have done.   I did it because there was no room
for me on this earth.   I was always told I am a big,
fat, over-eating monkey, I got big frog feet.   I am
sorry forgive me.   I think God will know my problems.
His reasons for leaving this world are so explicit as
almost to hit society under the belt.   Mum, Dad and
God form the trinity, the three individuals who understand and care for him.   They alone are not cruel,
they alone love him but this trinity does not exercise
power in this world.   It cannot protect him from the
taunts of those who dehumanize, disintegrate, destroy
and transform him from what he is, a human being, into

something which he is not, a monkey with the feet of a frog. He is not only dehumanized but also dismembered, distorted and though Mum, Dad and God know this and understand this, they are helpless in this world. Hence he must move out of it and make his way to heaven where their authority exists. There is no expression of revenge in this letter; only the desire for a heavenly refuge.

Letter 2

A 50-year-old White woman: 'Please forgive me for what I have done. I have taken 20 pills. Dad has been here and he says he will never come back to me, so I have done what is best. I love him with all my heart and cannot live without him. I am sorry I cannot go on any longer. I shall be out of my mind. Love to Granny and pray for me. God bless the family and I love you all. Please sign all my money to your Dad so he can fix attorney affairs.'

Her life is centred on her relationship with her husband. When he breaks that relation, she realizes that she is powerless, to do anything about it in this world, but through her death she may reawaken something in him. The fact that she leaves all she has to her estranged husband supports this interpretation. He cannot refuse her gift in her death, although in her life he refused her love. In taking her gift he in a sense symbolically takes her too. Death is thus the necessary sacrifice she makes in order to repossess him.

4(d)   Suicide as sacrifice

The idea that through death the suicide transforms himself into an offering to the beloved was present in a number of Durban letters.

Letter 1

A 21-year-old Indian woman writes: 'Dear Dev, I do hope that this will at least bring you peace and happiness to satisfy your heart. I do hope that you will forgive me for what I have done to you. Dev don't carry my coffin please. I don' think that you should carry my coffin after what I have done to you. I loved you so much that for your happiness I am giving you my life. I do hope you every success in your

future life.   Don't cry over me, don't worry to spend
a penny.   One favour, please put the wedding ring in
my mouth.   (Signed).'   The letter indicates an
experience of deep but turbulent love, probably due
to physical frustrations.   The demands of their
physical bodies stood in their way.   Thus she destroys
that body in order to liberate and give him her true
self.   It was her physical body that caused him pain.
So she requests that he should not carry her coffin.
The ring symbolized their physical union and thus it
should be placed in her mouth to be consumed with her
physical body.   Her body is finally the sacrificial
offering.   In Hindu lore, the idea that through such
an offering the inner essence is liberated is common.

Letter 2

An Indian man writes: 'It is all in a state which
started long ago in 1938.   My brother was happy or
not, I don't know, but I grew up and had bouts of
depression.   God blessed me with intelligence, and I
was not wild and raw.   I got through Matric and I
felt it was the end of the world.   My ambition was to
be a lawyer - but circumstances did not permit, and I
became a teacher.   I fell in love and married.   We
were very happy for a short while, except my mother
who was very unhappy.   My other family members were
happy/unhappy even my wife, unhappy.   Only one way out
one man had to make the sacrifice.   I had to bring the
families together that were incompatible.   Then I had
to separate them.   I studied hard, couldn't make the
grade, except in my studies.   End of the year I will
write an exam, I hope today will be curtains which will
close a chapter in the life of somebody who is not fit
to live.   I had to make the decision for a number of
reasons.   People who hate and love me should try and
forgive me.   This is the only way out.   Evidence of
what is said and done are in the brief case.   Nega-
tives are to be found and I don't want anyone to know
except my wife.   The drug tablet is taking effect, I
don't know how it will work.   It is getting very
serious now.   I am going out.   I am.'   The letter
ends abruptly as the writer is overcome by the drug.
     The letter is a brief résumé of the writer's life,
an admission of its failure in two respects - education
and marriage.   The orthodox values of his community
have deep roots in him, yet in his youth he had tried
to escape them.   He had married for love, against the
advice of his family and the dictates of the stars that

traditionally would have guided the choice of a marriage
partner.   He had thereby brought together two incompatible families, only to plunge them into conflict:
'I had to bring the families together that were incompatible....   Then I had to separate them.'   His
marriage had forced him to assume economic responsibilities earlier than he had planned, so that he had to give
up his ambition to be a lawyer and become a teacher.

He had failed his family in two ways: by following
the dictates of his passion instead of submitting to the
dharma (sanctions) of his religious faith and community,
he had destroyed harmony in his home; by not succeeding
as a lawyer, he had failed to raise their social standards.   His marriage in fact had lowered their existing
social status.   'One way out and one man had to make
the sacrifice.'   He makes it, in order to liberate the
family from their existing conflict and degradation.

4(e) Suicide to join the dear departed

The obvious reason for the suicides of some is that they
cannot continue to live without the person they loved
dearly.   Death paves the way to reunion.

A 57-year-old White man: 'Darling son, I will die
loving you, to join your mother and my parents.   Auntie
Dolly has plenty of diamonds for you.   Her money too
she will leave for you.   Tell the Jewish society to
bury me as I am a Jew.   Good-bye.   God bless you.'

'To Whom it May Concern.   All my entire estate be
donated to X.   Pay for my funeral and also Mrs P's
who died on 28.1.63.   Anything left over to be given
to Doroty P. daughter of Mrs P. who lives with her
aunt.   The savings book and pension funds also to
Doroty P.   If possible bury me in the same grave as
Mrs P.   Thanking you.   My brother must handle my
affairs.   I can't live without Mrs P.'

Conclusion

Suicide continues to shock and fascinate: it will continue to be judged simultaneously as an act of inexorable courage and unforgivable cowardice, since life is viewed both as a most precious gift and the most severe test of human endurance.

The fundamental sociological interest in suicide probably arises from the belief that the suicide has another perception into the meaning of life, one that is available neither to the prophet nor the philosopher, let alone the 'ordinary' man. The social scientist attempts to grasp that perception from the very restricted data available to him, that of case histories and official statistics. Strangely, and against the logic of the very method he professes to use, he often attempts to understand this phenomenon by using the one set of data to the exclusion of the other. Thus he concentrates on the particular, on case histories, as does Karl Menninger, and rejects or underplays the importance of the statistical or general; or he rejects the particular, the case histories, as does Durkheim, and insists that the general, the recurring characteristics, abstracted from the particular cases, alone are valid.

This study emphasizes that case studies and official statistics are the complementary data of suicide: that while court records are indispensable in structuring theoretical models, case studies provide the necessary in-depth meaning and reveal the vitally important personal dimension.

Court records are the only source where suicides are found *en masse*. Thus they alone provide the information necessary for abstracting general patterns. But they are insufficient in themselves, in most instances, communicating the barest bones of the

suicide phenomenon . They do give important leads to
the real life problems but it is left to the researcher's
skill, insight, imagination, experience - call it what
you may - to fill in the missing links and make
plausible interpretations.

The use of case studies is problematic in the study
of suicide, since the suicides themselves are dead and
beyond recall. Suicide notes are important but, as the
Durban study indicates, few suicides leave notes.
Moreover, the notes generally explain little more than
the immediate 'cause' or act of suicide. Apart from
the notes, the Inquest Court records the probable motives
for suicide as seen by the investigating officer and
witnesses. The witnesses may also cast some light on
the personality of the suicide, but such information is
highly coloured by the motives of the witnesses themselves, who are also participants in the suicide,
having, from the suicide's point of view, provoked it.
None the less, such evidence points to the real life
situation, which will only come into focus when these
pointers are retraced to that situation and probed
through exhaustive interviews with the witnesses - with
those who constituted the problematic society of the
suicide.

Parts two and three of this study have analysed
court statistics and abstracted suicide patterns by
race and sex in South Africa's racist, sexist society.
Part four has attempted to reach out to the suicide in
person. Two broad generalizations are made: the
behaviour in suicide, contrary to the suggestions of
Durkheim and others, does not conform to certain universal principles but responds to particular social
conditions. Deprivation, material and emotional, is
a constant factor in suicide.

The variations in the patterns of suicide by race or
culture in Durban suggest that each society, by social
prescription, determines its areas of conflict and the
modes whereby such conflicts may be resolved. It
simultaneously determines the occasions for suicide
and the frequency with which it may be resorted to.
Component members, responding to social suggestion,
generally express their aggressions in directions and
manners prescribed by the group. While on the one
hand there is pressure to adjust, there is, on the
other, the recognition that friction can become irre-
concilable, and there is an element of condonation of
the deviant acts which may ensue, such acts being in
effect socially suggested, and extenuated by the common
remark, 'What could you expect under the circumstances?'

Underlining this is the issue of economic class which coincides with race.   The greatest difference in suicide behaviour in Durban is between Black and White and not between two distinct cultures.   Thus, though culturally Coloureds are Whites, and there are vast differences between the cultures of the Indians and Africans, African, Indian and Coloured suicide models share a number of common characteristics which distinguish them from the White model.

The typical Black suicide is accordingly young, impoverished and without hope of improving his life situation.   The typical White suicide has long passed his youth, is ill, infirm and lonely.   Both are deprived, but whereas the deprivation of the Black is economic, that of the White is emotional.   The common factor, however, is deprivation, albeit different kinds of deprivation and a deprived person is under-integrated, alienated, or close to these conditions.

Young Whites, born into privilege, move confidently on the escalator of success, and see only ever-growing opportunities ahead of them.   Aged Whites on the other hand have nothing more to move forward to.   They may in that situation suffer disillusion, a sense of powerlessness and, worst of all, of deprivation.

Poverty, insecurity and role integration are closely related to each other.   A secure person is also a well integrated person - in terms of his personality, and in relation to his society.   He is well integrated because he has the means to fulfil the expectations demanded of him and he has the means to extract the expectations due to him.   Such a person has power to infuse meaning into life and to extract meaning from life.   His security, material and emotional, is attendant on his power to give and to take.   It stands to reason that such a person is happy with life and, being happy, is well integrated.

The key factor in suicide as in all social relations is 'integration', or the prevailing state of accord between the needs, aspirations, attitudes and values of the person and that of his group.   The greater the community of interests between these two interacting parties, the greater the state of integration.   Common sense suggests that the suicide rate is related to status, since integration, social and personal, can only take place through role playing, or more simply, relating one's self to other selves.   Roles in turn are structured and thereby differentially and unequally rated.   The integration capacity of a role, and consequently status, is neither universal nor constant in

a particular society.   High status may well be less
integrative in some social situations than low status,
and produce greater stress and greater suicide, but
the reverse is also true, as is demonstrated by the
Durban data.

The theory that there is a positive correlation
between external critical restraint, high integration
and low suicide is dubious.   Although social restraint,
that is discipline and control, facilitate integration
of social norms, restraint and integration are in fact
contradictory.   Whereas integration in the context of
accord between self and society is self-operative,
restraint is external and imposed and there is resistance and resentment against it which, if blocked
expression, builds up great internal tension and
threatens explosion.   Restraint or repression is never
internalized.   What is internalized is the rationalization, often religious, which helps the victim to
cope with restraint/repression, and this is integrated
only because it helps to cope with restraint.   Restraint/
repression would thus aggravate suicide, integration
inhibit it.

The authority of the superordinate, far from having
an ameliorative effect on the subordinate and saving
them from anomie, as Durkheim suggests, (1) inhibits
and frustrates them.   The poor are hindered by the
social controls of those above them, by the regulations
and laws that protect the rights, privileges and
property of those who *have* rights, privileges and
property.   In the racist organization of South African
society, the Blacks as a generality - African, Indian
and Coloured - are repressed and kept repressed by the
laws that blatantly and unequivocally protect the
dominating role of Whites.   Not only do Blacks have
high suicide rates in Durban, but the Black suicide
rate increases with Black poverty.   Poverty in its
total context is a condition of both material and
emotional deprivation.   While the latter can occur
without the former, the former is often the cause of
the latter.

The Durban data, contrary to the observations of
Durkheim and other sociologists, establish a relation
between high suicide rates and poverty.   Durkheim
maintains that those of high social status in terms of
education, wealth and occupation, are more prone to
suicide than those of lower social status. (2)   The
emergent patterns in Durban in relation to race, sex,
age, religion, residential areas, income and occupation
point to the reverse.

Thus not Whites, but Indians, have the highest
suicide rate by race, and White women have the lowest
rate of all.   While White women as the 'inferior'
sex have a lower rate than White men, Black women,
despite their greater subordination to Black men,
have equal and at times higher rates than Black men;
Blacks in manual occupations have higher rates than
Blacks in non-manual occupations.

Suicide in Durban is concentrated in the slums,
the impoverished Black townships, and in the boarding
and rooming houses occupied by the old, infirm and
unattached Whites in the central business district.
When areas of mixed racial living existed in Durban,
the White rate was higher, since only the poorest
Whites were forced to continue living alongside Blacks,
but the Black rate was lower, since for them moving
into 'White' areas was an economic advance.

Suicide is a problem of integration, social and
personal.   The requirements of integration are complex,
its definition neither universal nor constant, yet
integration is closely related to power, and hence to
material and emotional well-being.   People who find
meaning in life are people who believe themselves to
be in control of life.   Such people are not likely
to commit suicide - life holds them.   But the powerless, the dispossessed, the discarded, those without
hope, these are the people who live in the shadow of
suicide.

Tables

TABLE 1   Annual suicide rate per 100,000 for Durban by race, 1924-60

Year	African Suicides	Rate	White Suicides	Rate	Coloured* Suicides	Rate	Indian Suicides	Rate
1924	3	6.0	21	30.7	–	–	12	19.2
1925	3	5.8	23	32.5	–	–	3	4.6
1926	1	1.8	16	21.9	–	–	15	22.5
1927	2	3.6	11	14.5	–	–	10	14.5
1928	1	1.7	11	14.1	–	–	7	9.8
1929	1	1.7	3	3.6	–	–	7	9.5
1930	5	8.4	17	20.6	–	–	11	14.6
1931	1	1.6	15	17.6	–	–	11	14.2
1932	2	3.2	12	13.7	–	–	12	15.0
1933	1	1.5	8	8.9	–	–	11	13.4
1934	1	1.5	17	18.4	–	–	3	3.5
1935	5	7.4	14	14.8	–	–	9	10.4
1936	2	2.9	15	15.4	–	–	18	20.4
1937	1	1.3	9	8.9	–	–	11	12.2
1938	5	6.5	13	12.4	–	–	15	16.3
1939	7	8.8	17	15.7	–	–	17	18.1
1940	2	3.4	10	8.9	1	10.9	3	31.3
1941	4	4.6	17	14.7	1	10.4	15	15.3
1942	3	3.3	15	12.6	5	50.4	9	9.0
1943	6	6.3	15	12.2	–	–	21	21.0
1944	9	9.2	9	7.1	5	46.9	30	29.1
1945	9	8.9	17	13.1	2	18.1	34	32.4

Year	African Suicides	African Rate	White Suicides	White Rate	Coloured* Suicides	Coloured* Rate	Indian Suicides	Indian Rate
1946	10	9.5	17	12.7	5	43.8	30	28.1
1947	10	8.8	24	17.5	2	15.8	24	20.5
1948	22	18.1	27	19.2	5	36.3	30	23.6
1949	7	5.4	19	13.2	5	33.4	27	19.6
1950	9	6.5	12	8.1	1	6.1	10	6.7
1951	12	8.2	26	17.2	3	17.3	22	13.9
1952	10	6.6	11	7.2	–	–	22	13.4
1953	12	7.8	20	13.0	1	5.2	29	17.1
1954	13	8.2	20	12.8	–	–	27	15.3
1955	10	6.1	21	13.4	1	4.8	36	19.8
1956	28	16.8	19	12.0	–	–	15	8.0
1957	16	9.4	26	16.3	1	4.4	23	11.9
1958	18	10.3	23	14.3	4	17.2	26	13.0
1959	23	12.9	26	16.0	–	–	21	10.2
1960	31	17.0	18	11.0	1	4.0	23	10.9
Mean rate 1940–60		8.91		13.02		15.51		17.70

* Coloured rates only available from 1940. Whites include Coloureds up to 1940.

TABLE 2   Annual suicide rate per 100,000 for Durban by race, 1962-71

Year	Suicides	Rates	Suicides	Rates
(a)	African		White	
1962	20	10.5	30	17.7
1963	22	11.4	38	22.1
1964	32	16.4	32	18.2
1965	27	13.6	35	19.6
1966	29	14.4	41	22.6
1967	35	17.2	35	19.0
1968	22	19.7	26	13.8
1969	16	14.9	36	18.9
1970	24	12.3	38	19.7
1971	17	17.5	33	17.1
Total	244		344	
Mean rate 1962-71		14.8		18.9
(b)	Coloured		Indian	
1962	4	15.1	16	6.9
1963	5	18.3	27	11.4
1964	8	28.4	27	11.1
1965	8	27.6	35	14.0
1966	5	16.8	58	22.6
1967	3	9.8	50	19.0
1968	7	22.2	48	17.8
1969	6	18.5	46	16.6
1970	3	7.0	49	16.9
1971	4	9.2	51	17.3
Total	53		407	
Mean rate 1962-71		17.3		15.4

TABLE 3   Annual executions in South Africa, 1966-9*

	African	Coloured	White	Indian
1966	98	35	5	–
1967	72	19	1	–
1968	81	14	2	–
1969	95	20	3	–

* Abstracted from Horrell, op. cit., vols 1966, 1967, 1968, 1969, 1970.

TABLE 4   Annual deaths in South Africa due to violence other than suicide, 1965-8*

	African	Coloured	White	Indian
1965-6	7,077	651	811	101
1966-7	7,405	744	656	101
1967-8	7,602	697	944	104

* Abstracted from Horrell, op. cit., vols 1966, 1967, 1968, 1969.

TABLE 5 Distribution of suicide by race and sex in Durban (1940-60, 1962-71) as abstracted from Court records

	1940-60						1962-71					
	Men		Women		Total per race		Men		Women		Total per race	
	No.	%	No.	%	No.	%	No.	%	No.	%	No.	%
African	181	68.6	83	31.4	264	100	145	22.3	95	24.1	240	23.0
White	310	79.1	82	20.9	392	100	243	37.4	101	25.6	344	32.9
Coloured	15	34.8	28	65.2	43	100	24	3.7	29	7.4	53	5.1
Indian	251	50.7	244	49.3	495	100	238	36.6	169	42.9	407	39.0
Total	757	63.4	437	36.6	1,194	100	650	100	394	100	1,044	100

TABLE 6 Mean annual suicide rate per 100,000 for Durban analysed into various time periods

	1924-60 (37 years)	1940-60 (21 years)	1941-50 (10 years)	1951-60 (10 years)	1962-70 (9 years)
Indian	15.95	17.70	20.65	13.38	15.4
White	14.54	13.02	13.09	13.35	18.9
African	6.80	8.91	8.10	10.37	14.8
Coloured	-*	15.51	26.17	5.31	17.3
All races	12.43	13.78	17.00	10.60	16.6

* Unobtainable

TABLE 7 Mean annual rate per 100,000 by race during depression and post-depression, war and post-war years in Durban

	1929-33 (depression)	1934-40 (post-depression)	1939-45 (Second World War)	1946-50 (post-war years)
Indian	13.38	16.06	22.47	19.74
White	12.92	13.57	12.10	14.18
African	3.31	4.43	6.23	9.70
Coloured	*	*	22.82	22.14
Total average	9.87	11.35	15.90	17.69

* Unobtainable

TABLE 8 Mean suicide rate per 100,000 in Durban by race and sex

	1940-60			1962-71		
	Men	Women	Total	Men	Women	Total
African	9.2	9.2	8.91	16.9	20.5	18.1
White	23.1	5.8	13.02	39.3	14.3	26.2
Coloured	9.2	15.2	15.51	30.0	36.9	33.8
Indian	16.0	16.2	17.70	36.7	26.4	31.7

TABLE 9   Distribution by religious affiliation in the
495 cases of Indian suicides, by sex

	Men No.	%	Women No.	%	Total No.	%	Durban Indian Population 1951*
Hindus	220	87.7	210	86.1	430	86.8	73.87
Muslims	12	4.8	21	8.7	33	6.6	16.03
Christians	7	2.7	7	2.8	14	2.8	6.68
Other	-	-	-	-	-	-	0.17
Unknown†	12	4.8	6	2.4	18	3.8	3.25
Total	251	100	244	100	495	100	100

* By major religions.   L. Kuper's reference - quasi-
  religious, no religion, unspecified.
† Kuper et al., op. cit., p. 83.

TABLE 10   Suicide, religion and income among Indians,
Durban, 1940-60

Religion	Proportion of suicide per group	Proportion of Indian population*	Mean income (£)†	Per capita income (£)†
Hindu	86.8	73.87	165.16	36.16
Muslims	6.6	16.03	281.72	56.61
Christians	2.8	6.68	188.11- 167.07	50.77- 48.44
Other	-	0.17	-	-
Other and unspecified	3.8	3.25	162.55- 150.89	37.69- 35.41
Total	100	100	£182.85	£40.02

* Kuper et al., op. cit., p. 83.
† Kuper et al., op. cit., p. 92.

TABLE 11   Suicide of Hindus in relation to language and income*

Language groups	Suicides	% of total no. of cases	Rate per 100,000	Mean income 1951†
Tamil-Telugu	327	76.1	21.42	£144-95– £146.09
Hindustani	98	22.7	12.38	£165.06
Gujerati	5	1.2	2.38	£458.42

* Rate per 100,000 of Indians by language and income calculated from figures of Kuper et al., op. cit., p. 86.
† Indian population of Durban.   Kuper et al., op. cit., p. 90.

TABLE 12   Percentage distribution of population by race (1951 census)*

	African	White	Coloured	Indian	Total
Old borough	45.05	68.66	21.21	36.81	43.84
New borough	54.95	31.34	78.79	63.19	56.16

* Leo Kuper, Hilstan Watts and Ronald Davies, 'Durban. A Study in Racial Ecology', Cape, London, 1958, p. 118.

TABLE 13 Suicide rate per 100,000 and percentage distribution of race groups in the sociographic zones*

Sociographic zone	Suicide rates		Percentage distribution of race groups				
	Average rate for 21 years 1940–60	Average rate for 5 years 1949–53	Africans	Whites	Coloured	Indians	Total Blacks
1 Central Berea Ridge	4.76	5.1	25.18	72.63	0.63	1.56	27.37
2 Seafront (excluding Tracts 5 and 17)	4.50	5.1	31.47	62.45	0.64	5.44	37.55
3 Seaward Transitional	6.23	7.0	18.28	59.45	6.61	15.66	40.55
4 Inland Transitional	14.38	16.9	15.77	22.08	6.91	55.24	77.92
5 Peripheral	9.76	8.6	48.13	12.48	2.65	37.49	88.27
6 Alluvial Flats	13.14	10.9	35.23	4.69	4.73	55.35	95.31
Total			31.68	30.51	3.83	33.98	69.49

* The six sociographic zones were compiled from the thirty-six census tracts into which Durban was divided during the 1951 population count.

TABLE 14 Distribution of suicide by per capita income
and race in high, medium, medium low, low and very low
suicide rate areas in Durban

Suicide rate areas	Average per capita income by race in residential areas (R)			Average suicide rates per 100,000 1940-60
	White	Coloured	Indian	
High	384.82	126.14	115.06	35.02
Medium	408.78	99.82	71.20	15.41
Medium low	513.06	134.58	169.28	9.35
Low	399.86	138.80	87.00	5.33
Very low	516.06	127.74	95.60	2.07

TABLE 15 Suicide by type of housing by race, Durban, 1940-60 and 1962-70 (%)

	African 1940-60	African 1962-70	White 1940-60	White 1962-70	Coloured 1940-60	Coloured 1962-70	Indian 1940-60	Indian 1962-70
Squatters' slum	22.0	3.1	-	-	2.3	8.2	4.3	2.4
Inadequate slum type (rented rooms)	23.4	7.9	2.5	0.3	48.8	38.8	58.0	27.6
Municipal sub-economic	5.6	30.1	0.2	-	-	4.1	0.4	22.0
Municipal economic	-	0.4	0.5	0.3	-	22.4	0.4	32.4
Adequate private dwelling	-	1.3	27.0	40.5	-	-	3.5	1.0
Flat	-	-	15.6	33.1	9.4	10.2	2.8	5.2
Boarding house	-	-	15.0	3.2	-	-	-	0.4
Hotel	-	-	2.5	12.9	-	-	-	-
Compound/single persons	9.0	31.4	1.0	1.0	-	6.1	0.2	0.7
Barracks/family	0.7	3.1	1.0	-	-	-	5.6	1.7
Other	14.3	-	3.4	3.2	2.3	-	2.0	0.4
Unknown	25.0	22.7	31.3	5.5	37.2	10.2	22.8	6.2
Total	100	100	100	100	100	100	100	100

TABLE 16   Suicide rate per 100,000 in 'mixed areas' by race and income

Census tract no.	Suicide rate per total population		African	White	Coloured	Indian
8	4.85	% population per race*	19.95	60.76	5.84	13.45
		Suicide rate by race	4.04	6.66	-	-
		Per capita income†	-	£177.56	£90.99	£81.81
9	12.28	% population per race	18.83	51.55	5.63	23.99
		Suicide rate by race	5.95	15.19	19.90	9.33
		Per capita income†	-	£213.65	£68.40	£128.69
13	10.85	% population per race	11.70	31.22	17.16	39.92
		Suicide rate by race	3.19	18.00	10.90	7.52
		Per capita income†	-	£204.05	£78.56	£74.86
18	8.71	% population per race	15.20	7.16	7.77	69.87
		Suicide rate by race	-	38.28	16.00	6.76
		Per capita income†	-	£238.84	£63.10	£70.80

* Kuper et al., op. cit., p. 237.
† Kuper et al., op. cit., p. 243.

TABLE 17 Suicide rate per 100,000 by population and density

Tract no.*	Population in census tracts 1951	Suicide rate	Density per square acre
1	6,602	2.19	0-12
3	10,648	2.66	50-100
4	8,431	1.09	6-12
5	2,705	29.90	3-6
10	7,035	6.04	6-12
11	8,897	3.19	25-50
12	18,509	7.95	25-50
15	14,328	1.61	25-100
16	14,833	0.28	0-6
17	17,538	22.52	100-1
21	10,158	38.90	0-3
27	3,809	22.52	6-12
30	8,625	1.61	12-50
31	12,727	2.95	12-50
32	4,784	3.95	0-3
33	6,252	46.33	0-3
36	9,759	1.90	0-3

* The enumeration of the physical areas in Durban has been changed since 1951.

TABLE 18   Mean suicide rate per 100,000 by age, race and sex in Durban, 1940-60*

Age	African			White			Coloured			Indian		
	Men	Women	Total	Men	Women	Total	Men	Women	Total	Men	Women	Total
10-14	1.0	-	0.5	-	-	-	-	-	-	2.9	9.0	5.9
15-19	1.9	13.8	7.6	2.0	2.9	2.45	6.2	33.3	19.8	11.0	57.6	34.3
20-24	5.7	24.3	15.0	15.7	4.8	10.25	5.9	10.5	8.1	33.8	38.6	36.2
25-29	42.9	22.9	32.9	18.1	3.3	10.7	35.2	38.1	36.7	33.3	20.5	26.9
30-34	13.3	20.5	16.9	21.0	5.2	13.1	19.5	15.2	17.6	23.3	13.8	18.6
35-39	14.3	5.7	12.4	26.7	9.2	17.9	12.4	46.2	29.3	21.9	27.6	24.8
40-44	16.7	5.2	14.3	27.6	7.6	17.6	76.2	48.1	40.5	18.1	13.3	15.7
45-49	18.7	1.8	6.7	33.3	16.2	24.6	-	15.5	10.1	43.4	18.3	30.5
50-59	26.7	19.5	23.1	40.0	7.6	23.8	-	15.2	7.6	40.0	16.2	28.1
60-69	18.6	21.0	19.8	56.7	5.7	28.6	-	-	-	44.3	15.2	29.8
70+	-	-	-	28.6	5.7	17.2	-	38.4	23.1	31.9	63.8	52.8

* The annual rate for Indians, Whites and Coloureds for the twenty-one year period has been calculated from the age distribution of the total Durban population by race and sex for the Magisterial area of Durban as estimated for 1950 from the 1951 census figures (U.G. 42/1958) and the 1946 census figures (U.G. 60/1950). The African rates have been calculated from the 1946 census figures (U.G. 60/1950) since these at the time of the study were the only published figures for Africans in 5-year age categories. There is no appreciable change in the age structure of the African population in the two periods, as a comparison of the figures, Kuper et al., 'Durban. A Study in Racial Ecology', p. 70 and 'The Durban Housing Survey', University of Natal Press, 1952, p. 39 shows. Thus the use of the 1946 figures does not in any marked way affect the validity of the estimated rate.

TABLE 19 Mean suicide rate per 100,000 by age, race and sex in Durban, 1962-70

Age	African			White			Coloured			Indian		
	Men	Women	Total	Men	Women	Total	Men	Women	Total	Men	Women	Total
15-19	7.3	21.6	11.8	3.2	3.0	3.1	9.1	23.2	16.7	4.9	23.7	14.4
20-24	15.8	22.5	18.6	25.6	5.9	15.7	17.7	31.4	24.9	22.8	25.0	24.0
25-29	13.5	19.8	16.2	24.6	15.7	20.3	20.9	62.7	41.8	31.5	17.3	24.3
30-34	13.1	13.1	13.1	39.0	6.7	23.1	26.6	81.0	55.7	25.4	15.3	20.6
35-39	15.1	10.8	13.7	38.2	14.4	26.1	89.9	47.9	64.7	32.8	28.4	30.7
40-44	30.7	6.8	22.1	50.4	13.7	31.9	75.2	14.4	36.6	33.1	24.8	29.3
45-49	17.9	7.1	14.5	41.5	21.7	31.4	98.1	18.4	52.5	55.4	14.6	36.0
50-59	15.3	9.3	13.3	51.9	19.0	35.0	-	-	-	48.7	7.9	31.0
60-69	16.8	23.2	19.5	40.8	16.6	26.5	48.9	30.4	37.5	43.8	6.0	26.8
70+	-	-	-	41.2	9.8	22.4	77.2	-	27.4	62.1	31.3	51.0
Total	15.1	16.0	15.4	36.0	13.0	24.0	33.7	35.7	35.0	28.0	20.5	24.4

TABLE 20   Mean suicide rate* per 100,000 by race and sex in the five age categories in Durban, 1940-60

Age	African			White			Coloured			Indian		
	Men	Women	Total	Men	Women	Total	Men	Women	Total	Men	Women	Total
10-14	1.3	6.2	4.1	-	-	-	-	-	-	2.8	6.7	4.8
10-19	-	-	-	-	-	-	-	-	-	-	-	-
15-39	-	-	-	16.9	5.0	11.0	14.5	24.8	20.2	23.3	29.0	26.2
20-39	8.3	13.5	10.7	-	-	-	-	-	-	-	-	-
40-59	13.3	6.7	12.2	33.1	9.1	20.8	25.1	20.0	20.4	31.9	13.8	24.0
60-69	16.0	13.3	15.1	56.9	5.8	28.0	-	-	-	42.7	14.5	32.3
70+	-	-	-	28.7	5.7	15.6	-	35.3	22.6	39.6	51.2	43.8

* The average annual rates are calculated from the distribution of age categories in the total population for the Magisterial area of Durban 1951 (U.G. 42/1958). In the age period 10-39 years the census figures use wider age groupings for Africans than they do for the other races, thus the difference in tabulation for the Africans.

TABLE 21 Mean suicide rate per 100,000 by race and sex in the five age categories in Durban, 1962-70

| Age | African | | | White | | | Coloured | | | Indian | | |
---	Men	Women	Total	Men	Women	Total	Men	Women	Total	Men	Women	Total
15-19	14.3	14.0	15.4	3.2	3.0	3.1				4.9	23.7	14.4
20-39	14.3	14.0	15.4	31.6	10.1	21.3	38.7	55.6	46.1	28.1	21.5	24.9
40-59	21.3	7.7	16.6	47.6	14.6	32.7	57.7	10.7	26.7	42.4	15.7	32.1
60-69	16.8	23.2	19.5	40.8	16.6	26.5	48.9	30.4	37.5	43.8	6.0	26.8
70+	-	-	-	41.2	9.8	22.4	77.2	-	27.4	62.1	31.3	51.0

TABLE 22   Relation of suicide to occupation, Tulsa County,
Oklahoma, 1937-46

Occupation	Rate per 100,000
1 Professional/managerial	35.4
2 Sales and clerical	11.6
3 Skilled	14.3
4 Semi-skilled	20.5
5 Unskilled	38.7

TABLE 23 Occupational distribution of suicides by race and sex by number and percentage, Durban, 1940-60

	Men No.	%	Women No.	%	Total No.	%	Men No.	%	Women No.	%	Total No.	%
(a)			African						White			
Professional	0	-	0	-	0	-	7	2.3	1	1.2	8	2.0
Semi-professional	1	0.6	8	9.6	9	3.4	10	3.2	5	6.1	15	3.8
Independent/managerial	0	-	0	-	0	-	10	3.2	0	-	10	2.6
Independent/urban	0	-	0	-	0	-	15	4.8	0	-	15	3.8
Independent/rural	2	1.1	0	-	2	0.8	2	0.6	0	-	2	0.5
Clerical & sales	2	1.1	0	-	2	0.8	27	8.7	2	2.4	29	7.4
Military & police	6	3.3	0	-	6	2.3	28	9.0	0	-	28	7.1
Skilled artisans	3	1.7	1	1.2	4	1.5	21	6.8	0	-	21	5.4
Semi-skilled	28	15.6	0	-	28	10.6	11	3.5	1	1.2	12	3.1
Unskilled	83	46.1	3	3.6	86	32.6	3	1.0	0	-	3	0.8
Domestic service	13	7.2	13	15.7	26	9.9	2	0.6	3	3.7	5	1.3
Housewife	0	-	53	63.9	53	20.2	0	-	44	53.7	44	11.2
Student/scholar	1	0.6	1	1.2	2	0.8	5	1.6	1	1.2	6	1.5
Retired	0	-	3	3.6	3	1.1	50	16.3	11	13.4	61	15.6
Retired/incapacitated	6	3.3	1	1.2	7	2.7	12	3.9	3	3.7	15	3.8
Unemployed	13	7.2	0	-	13	4.9	26	8.4	4	4.9	30	7.7
Never worked	0	-	0	-	0	-	1	0.3	0	-	1	0.3
Employee	0	-	0	-	0	-	18	5.8	0	-	18	4.6
Unknown	22	12.2	0	-	22	8.4	62	20.0	7	8.5	69	17.5
Total	180	100	83	100	263	100	310	100	82	100	392	100

(b)	Men No.	%	Women No.	%	Total No.	%	Men No.	%	Women No.	%	Total No.	%
			Coloured						Indian			
Professional	0	-	0	-	0	-	0	-	0	-	0	-
Semi-professional	0	-	2	7.1	2	4.7	5	2.0	2	0.8	7	1.4
Independent/ managerial	0	-	0	-	0	-	1	0.4	0	-	1	0.2
Independent/ urban	0	-	0	-	0	-	15	6.0	1	0.4	16	3.2
Independent/ rural	0	-	1	3.6	1	2.3	14	5.6	2	0.8	16	3.2
Clerical & sales	0	-	0	-	0	-	10	3.8	2	0.8	12	2.4
Military & police	1	6.7	0	-	1	2.3	0	-	0	-	0	-
Skilled artisans	3	20.0	1	3.6	4	9.3	16	6.4	0	-	16	3.2
Semi-skilled	4	26.6	1	3.6	5	11.6	54	21.5	2	0.8	56	11.3
Unskilled	0	-	0	-	0	-	22	8.8	1	0.4	23	4.6
Domestic service	1	6.7	1	3.6	2	4.7	8	3.2	9	3.7	17	3.4
Housewife	0	-	16	57.0	16	37.2	0	-	211	86.6	211	42.8
Student/ scholar	0	-	1	3.6	1	2.3	11	4.4	3	1.2	14	2.8
Retired	0	-	0	-	0	-	20	8.0	10	4.1	30	6.1
Retired/in-capacitated	0	-	0	-	0	-	6	2.4	0	-	6	1.2
Unemployed	1	6.7	3	10.7	4	9.3	35	13.9	0	-	35	7.1
Never worked	0	-	0	-	0	-	5	2.0	0	-	5	1.0
Employee	1	6.7	1	3.6	2	4.7	4	1.6	0	-	4	0.8
Unknown	4	26.6	1	3.6	5	11.6	25	10.0	1	0.4	26	5.3
Total	15	100	28	100	43	100	251	100	244	100	495	100

TABLE 24 Occupational distribution of suicides by race and sex by number and percentage, Durban, 1962-70

	Men No. %		Women No. %		Total No. %		Men No. %		Women No. %		Total No. %	
(a)		African						White				
Professional	0	-	0	-	0	-	6	2.7	1	1.1	7	2.3
Semi-professional	0	-	2	2.3	2	0.9	14	6.3	3	3.4	17	5.4
Independent/ managerial	1	0.7	0	-	1	0.4	26	11.7	0	-	26	8.3
Independent/ urban	0	-	0	-	0	-	7	3.1	0	-	7	2.3
Independent/ rural	0	-	0	-	0	-	0	-	0	-	0	-
Clerical & sales	1	0.7	1	1.1	2	0.9	39	17.5	17	19.4	56	18.0
Military & police	1	0.7	0	-	1	0.4	6	2.7	0	-	6	1.9
Skilled artisans	1	0.7	0	-	1	0.4	43	19.3	0	-	43	13.8
Semi-skilled	1	0.7	0	-	1	0.4	15	6.7	0	-	15	4.8
Unskilled	94	67.6	4	4.6	98	43.2	7	3.1	0	-	7	2.3
Domestic service	4	2.9	31	35.2	35	15.4	1	0.4	0	-	1	0.3
Housewife	0	-	28	31.8	28	12.4	0	-	54	61.4	54	17.4
Student/ scholar	1	0.7	1	1.1	2	0.9	2	0.9	1	1.1	3	1.0
Retired/in-capacitated	2	1.5	0	-	2	0.9	37	16.6	8	9.1	45	14.5
Unemployed	22	15.9	17	19.3	39	17.2	10	4.5	3	3.4	13	4.2
Never worked	0	-	0	-	0	-	0	-	1	1.1	1	0.3
Other	0	-	0	-	0	-	2	0.9	0	-	2	0.6
Unknown	11	7.9	4	4.6	15	6.6	8	3.6	0	-	8	2.6
Total	139	100	88	100	227	100	223	100	88	100	311	100

	Men		Women		Total		Men		Women		Total	
	No.	%	No.	%	No.	%	No.	%	No.	%	No.	%
(b)			Coloured						Indian			
Professional	0	-	0	-	0	-	1	0.6	0	-	1	0.3
Semi-professional	0	-	0	-	0	-	2	1.1	1	0.8	3	1.0
Independent/ managerial	0	-	0	-	0	-	3	1.7	0	-	3	1.0
Independent/ urban	0	-	0	-	0	-	6	3.5	0	-	6	2.1
Independent/ rural	0	-	0	-	0	-	1	0.6	0	-	1	0.3
Clerical & sales	0	-	0	-	0	-	13	7.5	1	0.8	14	4.8
Military & police	0	-	1	3.7	1	2.0	1	0.6	0	-	1	0.3
Skilled artisans	1	4.5	0	-	1	2.0	16	9.2	0	-	16	5.5
Semi-skilled	1	4.5	3	11.1	4	8.2	15	8.7	3	2.6	18	6.2
Unskilled	10	45.5	2	7.4	12	24.5	51	29.5	7	5.9	58	19.9
Domestic service	0	-	4	14.8	4	8.2	2	1.1	18	15.3	20	7.0
Housewife	0	-	11	40.8	11	22.5	0	-	62	52.5	62	21.3
Student/ scholar	0	-	0	-	0	-	5	2.9	8	6.8	13	4.5
Retired/in-capacitated	1	4.5	0	-	1	2.0	14	8.1	3	2.6	17	5.9
Unemployed	8	36.4	6	22.2	14	28.6	36	20.8	0	-	36	12.4
Never worked	0	-	0	-	0	-	1	0.6	0	-	1	0.3
Other	0	-	0	-	0	-	1	0.6	15	12.7	16	5.5
Unknown	1	4.5	0	-	1	2.0	5	2.9	0	-	5	1.7
Total	22	100	27	100	49	100	173	100	118	100	291	100

TABLE 25   Male suicide rate per 100,000 by occupational class, Durban, 1940-60

Occupational class	African	Per 100,000 White	Coloured	Indian
I	-	17.3	-	3.1
II	-	24.4	-	60.5
III	30.3	22.0	-	23.8
IV	12.1	16.8	21.6	23.6
V	8.9	8.0	29.7	33.6
VI	9.4	8.2	-	21.5

TABLE 26   Male suicide rates per 100,000 in manual and non-manual occupations, Durban, 1940-60 and 1961-70

	African	White	Coloured	Indian
(a)		1940-60		
Manual	15.9	8.2	18.5	28.7
Non-manual	8.9	26.3	-	25.2
(b)		1961-70		
Manual	18.0	28.8	30.2	23.7
Non-manual	1.6	56.4	-	21.8

TABLE 27 Suicide rate per 100,000 of retired,
unemployed and employed by race and sex, Durban, 1940-60

	African	White	Coloured	Indian
(a)		**Men**		
Retired	-	62.9	-	109.8
Unemployed	14.2	76.0	7.0	50.4
Employed (inclusive of house-wives)	9.2	16.5	18.6	27.9
(b)		**Women**		
Retired	185.3	28.1	1.8	89.5
Unemployed	-	31.6	126.4	-
Employed (inclusive of house-wives)	18.0	5.7	30.3	40.8

TABLE 28 Number and suicide rate per 100,000* by race
of housewives and gainfully employed women

	Housewives		Gainfully employed women	
	Total no. of suicides	Suicide rate	Total no. of suicides	Suicide rate
African	53	33.3	25	9.1
White	44	6.7	12	3.8
Coloured	16	37.0	6	19.6
Indian	211	39.0	19	75.4

* The rate is calculated from the Distribution of
Occupations of Women in Durban in 1946 (U.G. 41/1954).

TABLE 29   Percentage distribution of suicide by marital status by race and sex, Durban, 1940-60

(a)

| | African | | | | | | White | | | | | |
| | Men | | Women | | Total | | Men | | Women | | Total | |
	No.	%	No.	%	No.	%	No.	%	No.	%	No.	%
Married	39	21.6	26	31.4	65	24.6	126	40.7	37	45.2	163	41.6
Never married	27	14.9	11	13.3	38	14.4	49	15.8	9	10.9	58	14.9
Living together	36	19.9	37	44.5	73	27.6	2	0.7	6	7.3	8	2.1
Remarried	1	0.6	2	2.4	3	1.1	8	2.6	2	2.5	10	2.5
Widowed	2	1.1	2	2.4	4	1.6	20	6.5	9	10.9	29	7.4
Separated	3	1.6	0	–	3	1.1	22	7.1	1	1.2	23	5.8
Divorced	0	–	0	–	0	–	12	3.8	2	2.4	14	3.5
Deserted	3	1.6	0	–	3	1.1	4	1.3	0	–	4	1.1
No relative at time of death	9	4.9	0	–	9	3.4	22	7.0	1	1.3	23	5.8
Unattached in urban situation	23	13.4	0	–	23	9.1	0	–	0	–	0	–
Living in celibate conditions	12	6.6	0	–	12	4.5	11	3.5	0	–	11	2.7
Unknown	25	13.8	5	6.0	30	11.4	34	10.9	15	18.3	49	12.6
Total	181	100	83	100	264	100	310	100	82	100	392	100

(b)

| | Coloured | | | | | | Indian | | | | | |
| | Men | | Women | | Total | | Men | | Women | | Total | |
	No.	%	No.	%	No.	%	No.	%	No.	%	No.	%
Married	3	20.0	6	21.4	9	20.9	106	42.4	98	40.2	204	41.4
Never married	6	40.0	6	21.4	12	27.9	79	31.5	102	41.9	181	36.5
Living together	4	26.6	9	32.1	13	30.3	4	1.6	9	3.6	13	2.6
Remarried	0	-	0	-	0	-	8	3.2	0	-	8	1.6
Widowed	0	-	3	10.7	3	6.9	20	7.9	15	6.2	35	7.1
Separated	0	-	0	-	0	-	8	3.2	5	2.0	13	2.6
Divorced	0	-	2	7.2	2	4.6	2	0.8	0	-	2	0.4
Deserted	0	-	0	-	0	-	0	-	2	0.8	2	0.4
No relative at time of death	2	13.4	2	7.2	4	9.4	1	0.3	2	0.8	3	0.6
Unattached in urban situation	0	-	0	-	0	-	0	-	0	-	0	-
Living in celibate conditions	0	-	0	-	0	-	0	-	0	-	0	-
Unknown	0	-	0	-	0	-	23	9.1	11	4.5	34	6.8
Total	15	100	28	100	43	100	251	100	244	100	495	100

TABLE 30 Percentage distribution of suicide by marital status by race and sex, Durban, 1962-70

(a)

| | African | | | | | | White | | | | | |
| | Men | | Women | | Total | | Men | | Women | | Total | |
	No.	%	No.	%	No.	%	No.	%	No.	%	No.	%
Married	45	32.4	20	22.7	65	28.6	116	52.0	43	48.9	159	51.1
Never married	61	43.9	39	44.3	100	44.1	44	19.7	13	14.8	57	18.3
Living together	4	2.9	18	20.4	22	9.7	4	1.8	0	-	4	1.3
Remarried	0	-	0	-	0	-	0	-	0	-	0	-
Widowed	2	1.4	3	3.4	5	2.2	14	6.3	15	17.0	29	9.3
Separated	5	3.6	1	1.2	6	2.6	11	4.9	7	7.9	18	5.8
Divorced	0	-	1	1.2	1	0.5	20	9.0	10	11.4	30	9.7
Deserted	0	-	0	-	0	-	1	0.5	0	-	1	0.3
Unknown	22	15.8	6	6.8	28	12.3	13	5.8	0	-	13	4.2
Total	139	100	88	100	227	100	223	100	88	100	311	100

(b)

	Coloured						Indian					
	Men		Women		Total		Men		Women		Total	
	No.	%	No.	%	No.	%	No.	%	No.	%	No.	%
Married	10	45.5	10	37.1	20	40.8	99	57.2	57	48.7	156	53.8
Never married	9	40.9	5	18.5	14	28.6	48	27.7	41	35.0	89	30.7
Living together	0	–	6	22.2	6	12.3	4	2.3	7	6.0	11	3.8
Remarried	0	–	0	–	0	–	0	–	0	–	0	–
Widowed	0	–	1	3.7	1	2.0	11	6.4	10	8.5	21	7.3
Separated	0	–	3	11.1	3	6.1	6	3.5	0	–	6	2.1
Divorced	0	–	2	7.4	2	4.1	0	–	1	0.9	1	0.3
Deserted	1	4.5	0	–	1	2.0	0	–	1	0.9	1	0.3
Unknown	2	9.1	0	–	2	4.1	5	2.9	0	–	5	1.7
Total	22	100	27	100	49	100	173	100	117	100	290	100

TABLE 31 Suicide rate per 100,000 by marital status, race and sex, Durban

	African		White		Coloured		Indian	
	Men	Women	Men	Women	Men	Women	Men	Women
(a)				1940-60				
Married	3.6	7.9	17.6	5.3	6.7	11.2	20.2	17.7
Never married	3.0	4.8	22.3	4.3	14.8	8.3	47.4	36.3
Widowed	4.3	2.7	55.1	5.8	-	15.0	74.5	13.2
Divorced	-	-	48.0	3.3	-	70.5	57.7	-
(b)				1962-70				
Married	8.5	7.4	27.8	10.4	38.0	18.7	31.7	16.5
Never married	60.1	12.7	48.9	14.8	51.9	11.4	41.1	22.5

TABLE 32   Suicide rate per 100,000 by marital status, age, race and sex, Durban 1940-60

	Married		Never married		Widowed		Divorced	
	Male	Female	Male	Female	Male	Female	Male	Female
African								
0-14	-	-	0.1	-	-	-	-	-
15-19	-	16.1	2.2	4.4	-	-	-	-
20-24	3.3	19.9	2.3	3.6	-	-	-	-
25-29	3.5	7.2	2.5	2.8	78.0	-	-	-
30-34	4.1	8.0	2.9	4.5	-	-	-	-
35-39	2.9	2.9	3.2	22.6	-	-	-	-
40-44	2.6	-	7.3	-	-	-	-	-
45-49	3.0	9.4	-	-	-	-	-	-
50-59	6.5	-	14.8	-	-	13.5	-	-
60-69	4.2	-	44.5	-	-	-	-	-
70+	24.2	-	-	-	-	-	-	-
White								
0-14	-	-	-	-	-	-	-	-
15-19	-	13.1	1.0	2.3	-	-	-	-
20-24	38.6	2.0	8.3	6.9	-	-	-	-
25-29	6.6	3.5	61.7	8.0	226.7	-	-	-
30-34	11.8	4.0	61.4	9.5	103.6	-	58.7	-
35-39	15.3	4.5	31.1	8.4	116.1	16.7	27.6	-
40-44	19.3	5.9	16.5	-	-	-	85.0	-
45-49	24.2	16.7	21.3	-	-	7.4	116.1	31.3
50-59	30.6	7.0	28.0	13.8	82.3	2.4	29.7	-
60-69	34.4	28.7	32.5	30.9	36.6	8.4	61.8	-
70+	33.4	12.2	-	-	62.3	6.4	-	-
Coloured								
0-14	-	-	-	-	-	-	-	-
15-19	-	-	6.0	26.4	-	-	-	-
20-24	-	-	7.4	9.4	-	-	-	-
25-29	-	19.3	34.3	-	-	226.7	-	-
30-34	-	10.8	38.1	-	-	136.3	-	-
35-39	-	24.6	-	-	-	-	-	
40-44	5.6	18.7	-	-	-	-	-	472.1
45-49	-	-	-	-	-	-	-	-
50-59	-	-	-	-	-	-	-	-
60-69	-	-	-	-	-	-	-	-
70+	-	-	-	-	-	-	-	-
Indian								
0-14	-	-	0.5	0.2	-	-	-	-
15-19	-	39.7	10.7	43.0	-	-	-	-
20-24	27.9	26.2	30.4	27.2	-	-	-	-
25-29	24.9	12.4	32.6	22.5	-	-	-	-
30-34	13.7	11.2	8.1	-	386.1	17.6	198.4	-
35-39	10.1	18.5	7.7	-	70.0	12.6	-	-
40-44	14.0	14.0	-	-	-	-	432.9	
45-49	37.6	13.9	-	-	45.7	8.5	-	-
50-59	23.8	19.2	-	-	120.0	13.5	-	-
60-69	15.4	-	77.6	-	88.3	17.4	-	-
70+	28.1	153.6	-	-	44.1	34.6	-	-

TABLE 33   Suicide rate per 100,000 by marital status, age, race and sex, Durban 1962-70

	15 - 24			25 - 34			35 - 64			65+			Total
	Never married	Mar-ried	Other	Never married	Mar-ried	Other	Never married	Mar-ried	Other	Never married	Mar-ried	Other	
African													
Male	12.8	3.5	59.1	24.8	6.1	69.3	62.4	12.4	68.1	140.6	12.3	–	14.8
Female	23.1	11.2	478.5	26.7	8.8	63.0	5.1	9.6	8.7	–	–	58.0	18.0
Total	16.0	7.8	279.9	25.6	7.0	64.8	35.6	11.7	19.5	76.6	10.2	46.4	15.9
White													
Male	14.1	21.6	158.7	38.8	21.8	352.7	84.4	32.9	165.2	58.3	35.2	77.7	36.3
Female	4.8	2.7	123.5	41.5	8.5	–	12.9	12.6	42.2	–	19.9	14.0	13.8
Total	10.0	7.8	138.9	39.6	14.7	138.4	44.9	23.1	70.5	18.0	29.5	25.6	24.5
Coloured													
Male	11.4	–	–	39.5	17.0	–	157.0	41.9	–	–	97.5	–	30.0
Female	23.9	14.7	925.9	21.8	55.3	376.6	–	6.1	91.3	–	–	–	36.9
Total	17.5	10.4	435.7	31.1	38.2	248.3	70.3	24.2	76.9	–	60.7	–	33.8
Indian													
Male	12.7	16.9	97.0	36.1	24.0	150.8	115.7	35.7	152.0	–	55.2	90.5	29.3
Female	22.6	24.9	341.1	28.8	14.7	15.8	39.8	18.5	16.1	–	–	31.2	21.3
Total	17.0	23.2	218.8	33.5	19.1	48.2	83.7	28.6	35.5	–	46.1	52.8	25.4

TABLE   34   Availability of information on family density (%)

	African	White	Coloured	Indian
Parental status	43.1	53.8	59.1	79.6
Family type	56.8	72.1	67.5	78.5
Family density	37.3	37.1	34.9	52.0

TABLE 35   Suicide by family type and density, 1940–60

Family type

(a)

| | African | | | | | | White | | | | | |
| | Male | | Female | | Total | | Male | | Female | | Total | |
	No.	%	No.	%	No.	%	No.	%	No.	%	No.	%
Nuclear	46	25.5	39	47.1	85	32.2	114	36.7	35	42.6	149	38.4
Extended	2	1.1	7	8.0	9	3.4	19	6.2	7	8.5	26	6.3
Joint	6	3.3	4	4.5	10	3.8	3	1.3	2	2.5	5	1.2
Fragmentary	2	1.1	3	3.4	5	1.9	5	1.7	3	3.6	8	2.0
Living alone	34	18.8	7	8.0	41	15.5	76	24.5	19	23.2	95	24.2
Unknown	91	50.2	23	29.0	114	43.2	93	29.6	16	19.6	109	27.9
Total	181	100	83	100	264	100	310	100	82	100	392	100

(b)

| | Coloured | | | | | | Indian | | | | | |
| | Male | | Female | | Total | | Male | | Female | | Total | |
	No.	%	No.	%	No.	%	No.	%	No.	%	No.	%
Nuclear	8	53.3	4	14.3	13	30.3	86	34.2	99	40.6	185	37.3
Extended	2	13.3	6	21.4	8	18.6	27	10.7	34	13.9	61	12.3
Joint	0	-	0	-	0	-	52	20.7	56	22.9	108	21.8
Fragmentary	1	6.7	3	10.7	4	9.3	6	2.5	13	5.4	19	3.8
Living alone	1	6.7	3	10.7	4	9.3	10	3.9	6	2.5	16	3.3
Unknown	3	20.0	12	42.9	14	32.5	70	28.0	36	14.7	106	21.5
Total	15	100	28	100	43	100	251	100	244	100	495	100

A *nuclear family* is considered to be a family of parents and immediate children. An *extended family* is a unit of parents, children and other relatives who live together as one social and economic unit. A *joint family* is two or more conjugal families, related by blood, sharing a common residence, and to a certain extent a common social life, but not necessarily constituting a single economic whole. A *fragmentary family* is one in which a spouse is missing either through death, separation, desertion or divorce.

TABLE 36 Suicide by family type and density, 1962-70

	African No.	%	White No.	%	Coloured No.	%	Indian No.	%	Total No.	%
Nuclear	58	25.3	152	48.9	18	36.7	141	48.6	369	42.0
Extended	15	6.6	20	6.4	9	18.4	43	14.8	87	9.9
Joint	4	1.7	1	0.3	1	2.0	40	13.8	46	5.2
Fragmentary	10	4.4	12	3.9	5	10.2	8	2.8	35	4.0
Living alone	73	31.9	100	32.1	7	14.3	15	5.2	195	22.2
Unknown	69	30.1	26	8.4	9	18.4	43	14.8	147	16.7
Total	229	100	311	100	49	100	290	100	879	100
Persons										
2-3	96	41.9	163	52.4	16	32.6	31	10.7	306	34.8
3-4	14	6.1	56	18.0	4	8.2	32	11.0	106	12.1
5-7	10	4.4	10	3.2	5	10.2	57	19.6	82	9.3
8-10	4	1.7	0	-	3	6.1	15	5.2	22	2.5
10+	0	-	0	-	0	-	8	2.8	8	0.9
Unknown	105	45.9	82	26.4	21	42.9	147	50.7	355	40.4
Total	229	100	311	100	49	100	290	100	879	100

TABLE 37   Suicide rate by family density, Durban, 1940-60

| Density (persons) | African | | | | | | White | | | | | |
| | Men | | Women | | Total | | Men | | Women | | Total | |
	No.	%	No.	%	No.	%	No.	%	No.	%	No.	%
(a)												
2	26	14.3	29	34.4	55	20.7	42	13.6	20	24.1	62	15.8
3-4	11	6.1	13	15.3	24	9.0	39	12.6	15	18.1	54	13.8
5-7	9	4.9	6	7.1	15	5.7	19	6.1	7	8.5	26	6.6
8-10	1	0.6	1	1.1	2	0.7	3	0.9	0	-	3	0.7
10+	3	1.6	0	-	3	1.2	1	0.3	0	-	1	0.2
Unknown	131	72.5	34	42.1	165	62.7	206	66.5	40	49.3	246	62.9
Total	181	100	83	100	264	100	310	100	82	100	392	100

(b)

	Coloured						Indian					
2	2	13.4	2	7.1	4	9.4	1	0.4	9	3.6	10	2.0
3-4	1	6.6	2	7.2	3	6.9	12	4.8	11	4.6	24	4.7
5-7	2	13.6	6	21.3	8	18.6	64	25.5	91	37.3	164	31.6
8-10	0	-	0	-	0	-	20	7.9	30	12.3	52	10.1
10+	0	-	0	-	0	-	10	4.0	9	3.7	19	3.6
Unknown	10	66.4	18	64.4	28	65.1	144	57.4	94	38.5	226	48.0
Total	15	100	28	100	43	100	251	100	244	100	495	100

TABLE 38 Suicide rate by number of children, Durban, 1940-60

No. of children	African						White					
	Men		Women		Total		Men		Women		Total	
	No.	%	No.	%	No.	%	No.	%	No.	%	No.	%
(a)												
None	12	6.6	21	25.4	33	12.6	18	5.9	13	15.9	31	7.9
1	13	7.1	9	10.8	22	8.2	35	12.0	10	12.1	46	12.5
2-3	12	6.6	11	13.2	23	8.8	45	15.0	21	25.7	66	16.8
4-6	4	2.2	0	-	4	1.5	11	3.5	2	2.4	13	3.3
7-10	2	1.1	0	-	2	0.7	0	-	0	-	0	-
10+	0	-	0	-	0	-	0	-	0	-	0	-
Unknown	117	64.7	33	39.8	150	56.9	153	49.5	28	34.2	181	46.2
Not applicable	21	11.7	9	10.8	30	11.3	47	14.2	8	9.7	55	13.3
Total	181	100	83	100	264	100	310	100	82	100	392	100

(b)	Coloured						Indian					
None	1	6.6	6	20.6	7	15.9	14	5.6	32	13.2	46	9.3
1	0	-	5	17.3	5	11.4	13	5.2	19	7.7	32	6.4
2–3	1	6.6	1	3.4	2	4.5	30	11.9	36	14.8	66	13.3
4–6	0	-	3	10.3	3	6.8	45	17.9	26	10.6	71	14.3
7–10	0	-	0	-	0	-	8	3.2	5	2.0	13	2.6
10+	0	-	0	-	0	-	1	0.4	1	0.4	0	-
Unknown	9	60.1	9	31.1	18	40.9	68	28.1	33	13.6	102	21.0
Not applicable	4	26.7	4	17.3	8	20.5	72	27.7	92	37.7	165	33.1
Total	15	100	28	100	43	100	251	100	244	100	495	100

TABLE 39   Suicide by race by number of children, Durban, 1962-70

No. of children	African Men No.	%	African Women No.	%	African Total No.	%	White Men No.	%	White Women No.	%	White Total No.	%
(a)	African						White					
None	8	5.8	14	15.9	22	9.7	21	9.4	25	28.4	46	14.8
1	3	2.2	9	10.2	12	5.3	19	8.5	16	18.2	35	11.3
2-3	5	3.6	3	3.4	8	3.5	28	12.6	9	10.2	37	11.9
4-6	7	5.0	3	3.4	10	4.4	1	0.5	0	-	1	0.3
7-10	1	0.7	0	-	1	0.4	0	-	0	-	0	-
10+	0	-	0	-	0	-	0	-	0	-	0	-
Unknown	56	40.3	20	22.7	76	33.5	110	49.3	25	28.4	135	43.4
Not applicable	59	42.4	39	44.3	98	43.2	44	19.7	13	14.8	57	18.3
Total	139	100	88	100	227	100	223	100	88	100	311	100

(b)

	Coloured								Indian			
None	1	4.5	8	29.6	9	18.4	8	4.6	20	17.1	28	9.7
1	2	9.1	3	11.1	5	10.2	6	3.5	7	6.0	13	4.5
2-3	0	-	3	11.1	3	6.1	17	9.8	18	15.4	35	12.1
4-6	1	4.5	5	18.5	6	12.3	31	17.9	12	10.2	43	14.8
7-10	0	-	1	3.7	1	2.0	6	3.5	5	4.3	11	3.8
10+	0	-	0	-	0	-	2	1.2	0	-	2	0.7
Unknown	9	40.9	4	14.8	13	26.5	55	31.8	15	12.8	70	24.1
Not applicable	9	40.9	3	11.1	12	24.5	48	27.7	40	34.2	88	30.3
Total	22	100	27	100	49	100	173	100	117	100	290	100

TABLE 40   Percentage distribution of suicide by time of day, race and sex, Durban 1940–60

Time	Men				Women				Total		
	African	White	Coloured	Indian	African	White	Coloured	Indian	Men	Women	Total
1– 4 a.m.	3.9	5.8	–	3.6	4.8	–	–	2.9	4.5	2.5	3.6
4– 7 a.m.	12.8	9.4	13.3	9.2	10.8	3.8	3.6	9.8	10.2	8.1	9.5
7–10 a.m.	8.9	11.6	–	11.9	2.4	4.9	7.1	16.5	10.8	11.0	10.7
10 a.m.–1 p.m.	9.9	7.7	6.7	9.2	8.5	13.4	10.7	13.9	8.7	11.6	10.2
1– 4 p.m.	8.8	9.4	6.7	11.2	9.6	13.4	21.4	9.0	9.8	10.8	10.1
4– 7 p.m.	8.3	9.7	13.3	13.5	12.0	13.4	14.4	14.8	10.7	13.9	10.5
7–10 p.m.	8.8	10.0	26.6	11.5	25.4	9.7	10.7	13.5	10.5	14.9	11.0
10 p.m.–1 a.m.	7.7	11.6	6.7	7.2	12.0	9.7	10.7	5.3	9.1	7.8	9.4
Unknown	30.9	24.8	26.7	22.7	14.5	31.7	21.4	14.3	25.7	19.4	25.0
Total	100	100	100	100	100	100	100	100	100	100	100

TABLE 41 Percentage distribution of suicide by day of week, race and sex,* Durban 1940-60

Day	Men		Women		Total (Both sexes)		Men		Women		Total (both sexes)		Men		Women		Total	
	In-dian	White	In-dian	White	In-dian	White	Afri-can	Col-oured	Afri-can	Col-oured	Afri-can	Col-oured	No.	%	No.	%	No.	%
Mon.	13.5	12.5	11.5	8.6	12.5	10.5	17.2	-	4.8	21.4	11.0	10.7	104	13.7	45	10.3	149	12.4
Tues.	14.3	12.5	11.1	9.8	12.7	11.0	11.1	13.3	10.9	7.2	11.0	10.2	97	12.8	46	10.5	143	12.0
Wed.	11.2	15.2	14.4	12.2	12.8	13.7	12.7	13.3	7.3	3.6	10.0	8.4	100	13.2	52	11.9	152	12.7
Thur.	13.5	13.6	12.1	13.4	12.8	13.5	9.3	13.3	12.1	10.7	10.7	12.0	95	12.6	54	12.4	149	12.5
Fri.	11.2	13.8	16.9	10.9	14.1	12.4	11.1	13.3	14.4	3.6	12.8	8.4	93	12.3	63	14.4	156	13.1
Sat.	14.7	8.1	13.9	12.2	14.3	10.2	12.7	13.3	15.6	17.8	14.1	15.6	87	11.5	62	14.2	149	12.5
Sun.	10.4	9.1	12.3	12.2	11.3	10.7	13.8	20.2	22.8	28.5	18.3	24.4	82	10.9	67	15.3	149	12.5
Un-known	11.2	15.2	7.8	20.7	9.5	18.0	12.1	13.3	12.1	7.2	12.1	10.3	99	13.0	48	11.0	147	12.3
Total	100	100	100	100	100	100	100	100	100	100	100	100	757	100	437	100	1,194	100

* Indian and White, African and Coloured, have been grouped together for the purpose of comparison.

TABLE 42   Percentage distribution of suicide by week of month, race and sex, Durban 1940-60

| Week | Men | | | | | Women | | | | |
	African	White	Col-oured	Indian	Total All races	African	White	Col-oured	Indian	Total All races
1st	25.3	19.3	6.6	23.5	21.0	25.4	20.7	10.7	21.4	21.3
2nd	19.3	30.4	53.4	25.1	25.6	19.3	23.2	28.6	24.2	23.3
3rd	21.7	17.4	20.0	21.2	19.0	21.6	17.1	17.9	20.4	19.9
4th	28.9	20.3	13.4	21.9	24.2	28.9	24.4	35.7	27.5	27.7
Unknown	4.8	12.6	6.6	8.3	10.2	4.8	14.6	7.1	6.5	7.8
Total	100	100	100	100	100	100	100	100	100	100

TABLE 43 Percentage distribution of suicide by month of year, race, sex and total population

Month	African			White			Coloured			Indian			All races		
	Men	Women	Total	Men	Women	Total	Men	Women	Total	Men	Women	Total	Men	Women	Total
Jan.	6.6	14.5	9.1	8.7	3.7	7.7	6.6	–	2.3	11.6	9.0	10.3	9.2	8.7	9.0
Feb.	7.2	15.7	9.9	5.2	4.9	5.2	20.0	17.9	18.6	9.1	10.3	9.6	7.1	10.8	8.5
March	8.3	8.4	8.3	9.7	7.3	9.1	–	7.1	4.7	7.6	12.3	9.9	8.5	10.3	9.1
April	7.1	4.8	6.4	8.0	18.2	10.2	6.6	14.3	11.6	6.4	4.1	5.3	7.1	7.6	7.4
May	8.3	4.8	7.2	9.7	15.8	11.0	6.6	7.1	6.9	6.8	9.8	8.3	8.0	9.8	8.9
June	3.8	1.2	3.0	7.4	9.8	7.9	–	14.3	9.4	4.8	8.2	6.5	5.5	7.6	6.3
July	5.0	9.6	6.4	5.8	4.9	5.6	–	10.7	6.9	8.8	4.9	6.9	6.4	6.2	6.4
Aug.	10.5	9.6	10.3	7.7	6.1	7.4	6.6	10.7	9.4	8.0	7.0	7.5	8.4	7.6	8.1
Sept.	6.1	6.0	6.1	8.4	3.7	9.1	20.0	3.6	9.4	9.2	7.4	8.3	9.1	6.2	8.1
Oct.	14.3	15.8	14.8	9.4	8.5	8.4	13.8	3.6	6.9	8.0	9.0	8.5	9.5	6.2	9.8
Nov.	12.7	3.6	9.8	9.4	4.9	8.4	6.6	–	12.3	11.3	7.4	9.0	10.2	5.7	9.0
Dec.	8.2	6.0	6.8	6.8	7.3	6.9	6.6	7.1	6.9	8.0	9.0	8.5	7.0	8.0	7.5
Un-known	2.8	–	1.9	2.6	4.9	3.1	6.6	3.6	4.7	0.4	1.6	1.4	14.0	1.7	1.9
Total	100	100	100	100	100	100	100	100	100	100	100	100	100	100	100

TABLE 44 Percentage distribution of suicide over the three periods of the year by race and sex, Durban 1940-60

Period	Men				Women				Men	Women	Total
	African	White	Coloured	Indian	African	White	Coloured	Indian			
Jan./ April	29.4	31.6	33.2	34.7	43.4	34.1	42.2	35.7	32.1	38.2	35.1
May/ Aug.	27.6	30.6	13.2	28.4	25.2	36.6	33.6	29.9	25.0	33.6	29.3
Sept./ Dec.	40.2	35.2	47.0	36.5	31.4	24.4	19.3	32.8	39.8	25.7	32.8
Unknown	2.8	2.6	6.6	0.4	—	4.9	4.9	1.6	3.1	2.5	2.8
	100	100	100	100	100	100	100	100	100	100	100

TABLE 45   Distribution of suicides by method used, race and sex, Durban, 1940-60

Method	African						White					
	Men		Women		Total		Men		Women		Total	
	No.	%	No.	%	No.	%	No.	%	No.	%	No.	%
(a)												
Poison	12	6.2	5	6.0	17	6.4	60	19.3	38	46.4	98	25.1
Hanging	108	59.8	9	10.9	117	42.0	46	14.9	8	9.8	54	13.6
Burning	13	7.2	61	73.4	74	28.4	1	0.3	3	3.6	4	1.1
Shooting	0	–	1	1.2	1	0.4	113	37.0	11	13.5	123	31.5
Laceration	4	2.1	0	–	4	1.5	20	6.2	1	1.2	21	5.4
Drowning	7	3.8	0	–	7	2.6	11	3.5	9	11.0	20	5.3
Jumping from heights	10	5.6	3	3.7	13	4.9	19	6.1	10	12.0	29	7.4
Electrocution	0	–	0	–	0	–	5	1.6	0	–	5	1.3
Gassing	0	–	0	–	0	–	18	5.7	0	–	18	4.5
Moving vehicles	23	12.5	4	4.8	27	10.2	11	3.5	2	2.5	13	3.3
Unknown	4	2.2	0	–	4	1.6	6	1.9	0	–	6	1.5
Total	181	100	83	100	264	100	310	100	82	100	391	100

(b)

	Coloured						Indian					
	Men		Women		Total		Men		Women		Total	
	No.	%	No.	%	No.	%	No.	%	No.	%	No.	%
Poison	6	40.0	7	25.1	13	30.9	85	33.7	38	15.6	123	24.9
Hanging	5	33.3	1	3.5	6	14.3	94	37.3	15	6.2	109	22.0
Burning	3	20.0	19	67.9	21	50.0	19	8.5	170	69.7	189	38.1
Shooting	1	6.7	0	-	1	2.4	4	1.5	1	0.4	5	1.1
Laceration	0	-	0	-	0	-	3	1.1	0	-	3	0.6
Drowning	0	-	1	3.5	1	2.4	30	11.8	14	5.7	44	8.9
Jumping from heights	0	-	0	-	0	-	4	1.5	4	1.6	8	1.6
Electrocution	0	-	0	-	0	-	0	-	0	-	0	-
Gassing	0	-	0	-	0	-	0	-	0	-	0	-
Moving vehicles	0	-	0	-	0	-	12	4.6	2	0.8	14	2.8
Unknown	0	-	0	-	0	-	0	-	0	-	0	-
Total	15	100	28	100	42	100	251	100	244	100	495	100

TABLE 46 Distribution of suicides by method used, race and sex, Durban, 1962-70

(a)

Method	African						White					
	Men		Women		Total		Men		Women		Total	
	No.	%	No.	%	No.	%	No.	%	No.	%	No.	%
Poison	5	3.7	1	1.1	6	2.7	37	16.7	41	46.6	78	25.1
Hanging	71	52.6	10	11.5	81	36.5	28	12.6	3	3.4	31	10.0
Burning	10	7.4	62	71.3	72	32.4	2	0.9	1	1.1	3	1.0
Shooting	0	-	0	-	0	-	78	35.1	20	22.7	98	31.6
Laceration	1	0.7	0	-	1	0.4	4	1.8	2	2.3	6	1.9
Drowning	14	10.4	6	6.9	20	9.0	6	2.7	1	1.1	7	2.3
Jumping from heights	8	5.9	1	1.1	9	4.1	19	8.5	17	19.4	36	11.6
Electrocution	0	-	0	-	0	-	3	1.4	0	-	3	1.0
Gassing	0	-	0	-	0	-	45	20.3	2	2.3	47	15.2
Moving vehicles	26	19.3	7	8.1	33	14.9	0	-	1	1.1	1	0.3
Total	135	100	87	100	222	100	222	100	88	100	310	100

(b)

	Coloured						Indian					
	Men		Women		Total		Men		Women		Total	
	No.	%	No.	%	No.	%	No.	%	No.	%	No.	%
Poison	3	13.6	3	11.1	6	12.2	33	19.3	26	22.2	59	20.5
Hanging	7	31.8	2	7.4	9	18.4	85	49.7	22	18.8	107	37.2
Burning	3	13.6	21	77.8	24	49.0	8	4.7	55	47.0	63	21.9
Shooting	2	9.1	0	-	2	4.1	2	1.2	1	0.9	3	1.0
Laceration	0	-	0	-	0	-	1	0.6	0	-	1	0.4
Drowning	5	22.8	1	3.7	6	12.2	30	17.5	8	6.8	38	13.2
Jumping from heights	0	-	0	-	0	-	1	0.6	2	1.7	3	1.0
Electrocution	0	-	0	-	0	-	0	-	0	-	0	-
Gassing	0	-	0	-	0	-	6	3.5	1	0.9	7	2.4
Moving vehicles	2	9.1	0	-	2	4.1	5	2.9	2	1.7	7	2.4
Total	22	100	27	100	49	100	171	100	117	100	288	100

TABLE 47 Distribution of active/aggressive and passive/receptive suicide means by race and sex, Durban, 1940-60 (%)

| | Men | | | | Women | | | |
	African	White	Coloured	Indian	Total	African	White	Coloured	Indian	Total
Active/aggressive	88.6	68.8	60.0	54.5	69.3	94.0	42.6	71.4	78.7	74.4
Passive/receptive	11.4	31.2	40.0	45.5	30.7	6.0	57.4	28.6	21.3	25.6
Total	100	100	100	100	100	100	100	100	100	100

TABLE 48   Cases in which Inquest Court records information was available, 1940-70 (%)

Year	African			White			Coloured			Indian			Total
	Men	Women	Total	Men	Women	Total	Men	Women	Total	Men	Women	Total	
1940-60	51	68	66	82	90	85	68	75	72	82	68	75	73
1962-70	56	76	60	77	94	85	62	72	70	82	66	74	73

TABLE 49 Probable reasons responsible for suicides in Durban, 1940-71 (%)

	Men				Women				Total (Both sexes)
	African	White	Coloured	Indian	African	White	Coloured	Indian	
Rupture of intimate relationship/divorce	10.7	8.5	18.2	8.1	30.7	12.4	37.0	26.3	14.9
Accusation or discovery by respected person(s) of shameful act, bigamy	0.7	1.2	–	1.7	3.4	1.2	3.7	5.1	2.1
Unmarried pregnancy	–	0.4	–	0.6	5.7	1.2	–	1.7	1.1
Bereavement	–	1.2	–	1.2	1.1	10.2	–	5.1	2.4
Arrest or pending case	7.1	2.2	4.6	3.4	1.1	1.0	3.7	–	2.7
Mental incapacity or illness	16.6	18.8	22.7	16.2	19.3	21.4	14.8	12.7	17.4
Physical incapacity or illness/incurable complaint	10.8	25.5	13.6	15.0	4.6	28.4	7.4	8.5	16.0
Loss or fear of loss of job; transfer	4.3	2.6	–	2.3	–	1.1	–	–	1.9
Financial trouble	3.6	9.1	–	4.6	2.3	1.2	3.7	2.5	4.1
Step-parents	–	0.4	–	–	–	–	–	–	0.1
Other: relatives, parents	1.4	0.9	–	4.6	3.4	2.5	3.7	6.8	3.0
Rupture of intimate relationship plus accusation or discovery of shameful act	0.7	0.0	0.3	0.0	0.0	0.0	3.7	1.6	0.5

	Men				Women				Total (both sexes)
	African	White	Coloured	Indian	African	White	Coloured	Indian	
Rupture of intimate relationship plus bereavement	0.0	0.5	0.0	0.0	0.0	0.0	0.0	0.0	0.1
Rupture of intimate relationship plus physical incapacity	0.0	0.5	0.0	0.6	0.0	1.1	0.0	0.0	0.2
Rupture of intimate relationship plus financial trouble	0.7	0.5	0.0	1.2	1.1	0.0	3.7	2.5	1.0
Accusation or discovery of shameful act plus arrest or pending arrest	0.7	2.2	0.0	0.0	1.1	1.1	0.0	0.0	0.9
Accusation or discovery of shameful act plus financial trouble	0.7	0.5	0.0	1.2	1.1	0.0	0.0	0.0	0.7
Unmarried plus loss or fear of loss of job	0.0	0.0	0.0	0.0	1.1	0.0	0.0	0.0	0.1
Bereavement plus arrest or pending case	0.0	0.9	0.0	0.0	0.0	0.0	0.0	0.0	0.3
Bereavement plus physical incapacity plus financial trouble	0.0	0.5	0.0	0.0	0.0	0.0	0.0	0.0	0.4
Arrest or pending case plus physical incapacity plus financial trouble	0.7	0.5	0.0	0.6	0.0	0.0	0.0	0.0	0.2

Mental incapacity or illness plus financial trouble	0.0	2.2	4.5	0.6	0.0	4.5	0.0	0.0	1.3
Physical incapacity plus [1] loss or fear of loss of job	0.7	0.5	0.0	0.6	0.0	0.0	0.0	0.0	0.4
Loss or fear of loss of job plus financial trouble	0.0	0.5	4.5	4.0	0.0	0.0	0.0	0.85	1.1
No known trouble	9.0	5.4	0.0	15.6	1.1	1.4	1.5	9.4	7.4
Unknown	31.6	16.5	31.7	17.9	22.9	11.3	11.4	17.0	19.7
Total	100	100	100	100	100	100	100	100	100

TABLE 50 Suicide by type of statements, 1940-71 (%)

Statement	Men					Women					Grand total
	African	White	Coloured	Indian	Total	African	White	Coloured	Indian	Total	
Abusive, blaming others	5.0	5.8	4.5	10.4	7.0	20.4	6.8	22.2	11.9	13.7	9.5
Generalized complaint of 'raw deal'	1.4	–	–	–	0.4	1.1	–	–	–	0.3	0.3
Self-blame	4.3	11.2	–	4.6	7.0	6.8	5.7	7.4	7.6	6.9	6.9
Relief	2.2	12.5	4.5	5.8	7.5	2.3	17.1	–	4.2	6.9	7.3
Confused	9.4	11.7	–	8.7	9.7	6.8	19.3	7.4	8.5	10.9	10.1
Neutral	7.2	13.5	31.8	19.7	14.5	5.7	17.1	14.8	19.5	14.6	14.6
Other	5.8	11.7	27.3	23.1	14.4	11.4	6.8	11.1	5.1	7.8	12.0
Disappointment in love	3.6	1.8	4.5	–	1.8	8.0	3.4	3.7	2.5	4.3	2.7
Unknown	61.1	31.8	27.4	27.7	37.7	37.5	23.8	33.3	40.7	34.6	36.6
	100	100	100	100	100	100	100	100	100	100	100

TABLE 51 Suicide by behaviour after act, 1940-71 (%)

Behaviour	Men					Women					Grand total
	African	White	Coloured	Indian	Total	African	White	Coloured	Indian	Total	
No conscious attempt to draw attention	72.7	80.3	54.5	73.4	75.2	30.7	72.7	33.3	39.8	45.8	64.5
Conscious attempt to draw attention	5.7	12.5	27.3	16.2	12.6	54.5	18.2	59.3	45.8	41.8	23.2
Resist attempt at saving	10.1	3.6	18.2	4.6	6.1	8.0	5.7	7.4	5.9	6.5	6.3
Asked for assistance	2.9	-	-	4.1	2.0	2.3	2.3	-	5.9	3.4	2.5
Other	0.7	-	-	-	0.2	-	-	-	-	-	0.1
Unknown	7.9	3.6	-	1.7	3.9	4.5	1.1	-	2.6	2.5	3.4
Total	100	100	100	100	100	100	100	100	100	100	100

TABLE 52 Suicide by reaction to external situation, 1940-71 (%)

Reaction	Men					Women					Grand total
	African	White	Coloured	Indian	Total	African	White	Coloured	Indian	Total	
Excessive drinking	5.8	13.0	36.3	18.5	13.8	11.4	3.4	22.2	3.4	7.2	11.4
Insomnia	–	0.9	–	0.6	0.5	–	–	–	–	–	0.4
Restless/nervous	4.3	5.4	–	4.6	4.7	8.0	2.3	3.7	7.6	5.9	5.1
Sexually loose	0.7	1.8	–	0.6	1.1	2.3	–	–	1.7	1.3	1.1
Abusive/violent	4.3	0.9	4.6	0.6	1.8	–	–	–	0.9	0.3	1.3
In bouts (verbal or physical)	4.3	1.4	–	2.3	2.3	3.4	–	7.4	4.2	3.1	2.6
Depression	4.3	22.4	–	11.0	13.5	6.8	40.9	11.1	9.3	17.4	14.9
Avoided company	0.7	3.1	–	2.3	2.1	–	3.4	3.7	0.9	1.6	1.9
Sociable	2.2	3.6	4.6	7.5	4.5	4.5	1.1	11.1	10.1	6.2	5.1
Leaving home	1.4	0.4	–	0.6	0.7	1.1	1.1	–	3.4	1.9	1.1
Illness	17.3	17.0	–	13.8	15.4	5.7	19.3	3.7	11.9	11.5	14.0
Excessive drinking & abusive/violent	1.4	1.8	–	10.4	4.3	2.3	1.1	7.4	2.5	2.5	3.7
Drug addict & alcoholic	0.7	1.4	–	0.6	0.9	–	6.8	–	–	1.9	1.3
Jealous & possessive	2.2	1.4	–	0.6	1.3	11.4	1.1	11.1	2.5	5.3	2.7
Excessive drinking & depression	–	3.1	–	–	1.3	–	1.1	–	0.9	0.6	1.0
Insomnia & rest-less/nervous & depression	–	0.4	–	–	0.2	1.1	2.3	–	–	0.9	0.5

Excessive drinking & sexually loose	–	–	–	–	–	–	–	–	0.9	0.3	0.1
Excessive drinking & avoided company	–	–	–	–	–	–	–	3.7	–	0.3	0.1
Unknown	50.4	22.0	54.5	26.0	31.6	42.0	16.1	14.9	39.8	31.8	31.7
Total	100	100	100	100	100	100	100	100	100	100	100

TABLE 53   Suicide by location of act, 1940-71 (%)

Location	Men					Women					Grand total
	African	White	Coloured	Indian	Total	African	White	Coloured	Indian	Total	
Having sought privacy at residence	21.6	46.2	27.3	31.8	34.8	19.3	57.9	29.6	30.5	34.9	34.8
Not having sought privacy at residence	3.6	8.0	9.1	17.9	10.1	44.3	22.7	48.2	52.5	41.7	21.6
Near place of residence - privacy	11.5	3.6	13.6	7.5	7.2	1.1	–	3.7	1.7	1.3	5.0
Near place of residence - no privacy	2.1	0.5	–	–	0.7	8.0	2.3	–	–	2.8	1.5
Removed from place of residence - privacy	39.6	29.2	22.7	34.1	33.0	17.1	10.2	11.1	8.5	11.5	25.2
Removed from place of residence - no privacy	12.9	4.0	27.3	6.9	8.1	5.7	2.3	7.4	3.4	4.0	6.6
Other - privacy	6.5	5.8	–	0.6	4.1	1.1	2.3	–	1.7	1.6	3.2
Other - no privacy	–	0.5	–	0.6	0.4	–	2.3	–	1.7	1.3	0.7
Unknown	2.2	2.2	–	0.6	1.6	3.4	–	–	–	0.9	1.4
Total	100	100	100	100	100	100	100	100	100	100	100

TABLE 54   Suicide by events immediately before act, 1940-71 (%)

Cause	Men					Women					Grand total
	African	White	Coloured	Indian	Total	African	White	Coloured	Indian	Total	
Involved in quarrel	7.9	8.5	13.7	7.5	8.3	38.7	15.9	25.9	32.2	29.0	15.8
Verbal aggression	1.4	0.5	–	2.9	1.4	1.1	–	3.7	3.4	1.9	1.6
Physical aggression	5.8	3.1	–	10.4	5.9	–	–	3.7	0.8	0.6	4.0
Physical aggression leading to murder	2.9	0.9	–	–	1.1	1.1	–	3.7	0.8	0.9	1.0
Violence, running amok & leading to murder	2.2	2.2	4.5	–	1.6	–	–	–	–	–	1.0
Reprimanded by person in authority	7.9	5.4	–	7.0	6.3	2.3	2.3	–	4.2	2.8	5.0
Physically assaulted by person in authority	0.7	–	–	–	0.2	–	–	–	0.8	1.9	0.8
Belittled and felt challenged into act	1.4	0.5	–	–	0.5	5.7	–	7.4	2.6	1.6	0.9
Other	25.9	55.1	50.0	43.9	44.2	25.0	68.2	37.1	22.1	36.7	41.5
Unknown	43.9	23.8	31.8	28.3	30.5	26.1	13.6	18.5	33.1	24.6	28.4
Total	100	100	100	100	100	100	100	100	100	100	100

292   Tables

TABLE 55 Suicidal tendency, 1940-71 (%)

Tendency	Men					Women					Grand total
	African	White	Coloured	Indian	Total	African	White	Coloured	Indian	Total	
Threatened before	7.2	15.7	–	11.0	11.5	1.2	10.2	3.7	4.3	5.0	9.1
Attempted before	2.2	8.5	–	4.0	5.2	3.4	21.6	7.4	3.4	8.7	6.5
Never attempted before	76.3	66.8	86.4	82.1	74.7	88.6	62.5	88.9	89.8	81.9	77.3
Never threatened before	–	0.5	–	–	0.2	–	–	–	–	–	0.1
Expressed 'death wish'	1.4	3.1	4.5	0.6	2.0	–	3.4	–	1.7	1.6	1.8
Unknown	12.9	5.4	9.1	2.3	6.4	6.8	2.3	–	0.8	2.8	5.2
Total	100	100	100	100	100	100	100	100	100	100	100

TABLE 56   Suicides who left notes by race and sex, 1940–71 (%)

Note	Men					Women					Grand total
	African	White	Coloured	Indian	Total	African	White	Coloured	Indian	Total	
Left note	5.0	25.6	-	10.4	14.7	6.8	15.9	3.7	2.5	7.5	12.1
Left no note	89.2	72.2	95.5	88.4	82.4	90.9	81.8	96.3	97.5	91.3	85.6
Unknown	5.8	2.2	4.5	1.2	2.9	2.3	2.3	-	-	1.2	2.3
Total	100	100	100	100	100	100	100	100	100	100	100

TABLE 57   Incidence of psychoneurotic tendencies among suicides in Durban (%)

	African	White	Coloured	Indian
1940–60	17	14	23	9
1962–70	7	20	2	8

TABLE 58   Suicide notes, by race and sex, 1940–70

	Men	Women	Total
White	78	71	149
Indian	27	21	48
African	23	13	36
Coloured	6	2	8
Total			241

Notes

CHAPTER 1   METHODOLOGICAL PROBLEMS IN THE STUDY OF
SUICIDE

1   Emile Durkheim, 'Suicide. A Study in Sociology',
    Routledge & Kegan Paul, London, 1952.
2   Jack D. Douglas, 'The Social Meaning of Suicide',
    Princeton University Press, 1967.
3   Karl A. Menninger, 'Man Against Himself', Harcourt,
    Brace & World, New York, 1963.
4   Durkheim, op. cit., p. 43.
5   Douglas, op. cit., pp. 247-9.
6   Durkheim, op. cit., p. 43.
7   Douglas, op. cit., p. 231.
8   Menninger, op. cit., p. 23.
9   Erwin Stengel, basing his observation on a study in
    London, states that upper and middle class families
    hush up suicide, and even oppose hospital admis-
    sions (Erwin Stengel, 'Suicide and Attempted
    Suicide', Penguin, Harmondsworth, 1971, pp. 14-15).
10 K.G. Dahlgrew, 'On Suicide and Attempted Suicide',
    Lindstedts, Lund, 1945; P.B. Schneider, 'La
    Tentative de Suicide', Dela Chaux & Niestlé, Paris,
    Neuchatel; E. Stengel and N.G. Cook, 'Attempted
    Suicide', Oxford University Press, 1958.
11 Stengel, op. cit., pp. 14-15.
12 Ibid., p. 80.
13 Stengel's study of 167 cases of attempted and 127
    cases of completed suicide shows that 57 per cent
    of the attempts were made in the company of others
    (as against 25 per cent of the completed) and
    18 per cent of the attempts were made in public
    places (as against 4 per cent of the completed)
    (ibid., p. 82).
14 Menninger, op. cit., p. 17.

15   Ibid., p. 18.
16   Ibid., p. 19.
17   Durkheim, op. cit., p. 148.
18   Emile Durkheim, 'The Rules of Sociological Method',
      ed. G. Catlin, Free Press, New York, 1964, pp. 44-5.
19   Ibid., p. 151.
20   Douglas, op. cit., p. 242.
21   Durkheim, 'Suicide. A Study in Sociology', p. 277.
      See also below,
22   Durkheim, 'The Rules of Sociological Method', p. 45.
23   Durkheim saw all general ideas as flowing from
      sensation but held that 'sensation may easily be
      subjective and that it is the rule of the natural
      science to discard these data of sensation that are
      too subjective.... Thus the physicist substitutes
      for the value impressions of temperature and elec-
      tricity the visual registrations of the thermometer
      or the electrometer' (ibid., p. 44).   The natural
      scientist of course does not discard subjective
      data and he continues to use his 'senses' as he
      must.   He simply 'sharpens' them through aids,
      whenever he can.
24   George H. Mead, 'Mind, Self and Society', University
      of Chicago Press, 1934.
25   Durkheim, 'The Rules of Sociological Method', pp.
      44, 45.
26   Douglas, op. cit., p. 25.
27   Durkheim, 'Suicide. A Study in Sociology', p. 149.
28   Douglas, op. cit., pp. 228-9.

CHAPTER 2   SOCIOLOGICAL AND PSYCHOLOGICAL CAUSES OF
SUICIDE

 1   Durkheim, 'Suicide. A Study in Sociology', Routledge
      & Kegan Paul, London, 1952, p. 319.
 2   Karl A. Benninger, 'Man Against Himself', Harcourt,
      Brace & World, New York, 1963, p. 5.
 3   Durkheim, op. cit., p. 299.
 4   Ibid., p. 309.
 5   Ibid., pp. 323-4.
 6   Ibid., pp. 225-6.
 7   Ibid., pp. 209-14.
 8   Ibid., pp. 254-8.
 9   Menninger, op. cit., p. 6.
10   Ibid., pp. 23-4.
11   Ibid., p. 23.
12   Durkheim, op. cit., p. 321.
13   Ibid., p. 321.

CHAPTER 3   THE DURBAN RECORDS

1   A.E. Bennet maintains that the suicide rate in the
    USA is nearer 50,000 than the reputed 16,000 to
    20,000 per annum ('Clues to Suicide', ed. E.S.
    Schneidman and Norman L. Farberow, McGraw-Hill,
    New York, 1957, p. 157).   Stengel suggests that
    the very low suicide rates of Egypt and the Republic
    of Ireland (according to 'World Health Statistics
    Report No. 21', 1968) is suspect in view of the
    strong Muslim and Roman Catholic prejudices against
    suicide.
2   The doctrine of St Augustine equated suicide with
    murder.   St Thomas Aquinas denounced suicide as
    usurpation of God's power to kill and make alive
    (Edward Alexander Westermarck, 'The Origin and
    Development of Moral Ideas', Macmillan, London,
    1912-17, pp. 251-4).   This attitude constituted
    the basis of the common law which influenced part
    of Europe and England until the eighteenth century
    and led to acts of revenge against the body of the
    suicide and his possessions.

CHAPTER 4   THE INCIDENCE OF SUICIDE

1   Calculated from the annual suicide and homicide
    figures reported for Europeans, Indians and
    Coloureds for the Republic ('Death. South Africa,
    South West Africa', 1958, vol. 2, 'Causes', G.
    328, 6805 U.5).
2   S.R. Steinmetz, Suicide among primitive peoples,
    'American Anthropologist', vol. VII, 1894, pp. 53-
    60; G. Zilboorg, Suicide among civilized and
    primitive races, 'Americal Journal of Psychiatry,
    vol. 92, 1935-6.
3   E.S. Schneidman and Norman L. Farberow (eds),
    'Clues to Suicide', McGraw-Hill, New York, 1957,
    p. 61.
4   Daily average prison population for South Africa
    for the year July 1969-June 1970 was: White, 80
    per 100,000; African, 476 per 100,000; Coloured,
    191 per 100,000; Indian, 80 per 100,000.   The
    prison population is estimated to be five times
    that of Britain and six times that of France.
    There were ninety-eight murders in Wynburg in 1963
    with an African and Coloured population of
    388,500; it is estimated that a thousand murders
    occur each year in Soweto - population 520,000 and

each year 80 to 100 Africans are executed for
murder, rape and theft, and 7,000 die violently
(M. Horrell, 'A Survey of Race Relations in South
Africa 1974', South African Institute of Race
Relations, Johannesburg, pp. 48, 74).   See Tables
3 and 4.

5   Hugh Graham and Ted Robert Gurr, 'The History of
Violence in America - A Report to the National
Commission on the Causes and Prevention of Violence'
Bantam Books, New York, 1969.

6   In terms of the (Natives) Urban Areas Act of 1923,
amended in 1936, the status of the Urban African
as a migrant labourer became clearly fixed.   It
decreed that African residence in urban areas was
strictly defined and wives were allowed to join
husbands on permit only on proof that the husbands
had been in continuous employment for 12 years with
one employer, and for 15 years with changes in
employers.   This restriction together with the
non-provision of housing and inadequate wages has
created the situation in which there has always
been a great disparity between the urban male and
female African population.   The male/female sex
ratio was 6.28 in 1920 and 2.6 in 1951 in Durban
according to Census Report U.G. 51 - 1949, p. 78.

7   In the urban areas, the custom of *kipita* or living
together has become normative and the traditional
sanctions against illegitimacy have tended to break
down so that in Durban the greater proportion of
African births registered each year are 'illegitimate'.   The law has thus led to considerable
weakening in the ethical foundations of the
married state in urban African life.

The Durban Municipal Department of Bantu Administration in its report to the South African Institute of Race Relations, Natal Conference on
'Homes and Community' (1960) analysed the housing
of 215,000 Africans in Durban and reported that
municipal family accommodation was provided for
113,000 people (73,000 permanent houses of which
43,000 came into being since 1960 after the
opening of Kwa Mashu and 40,000 temporary in the
Cato Manor Emergency Group).   Of an African population of 297,000 in 1967, family housing was
available for 201,000 in Durban (M. Horrell, 'A
Survey of Race Relations in South Africa 1967',
South African Institute of Race Relations, PO Box
97, Johannesburg, p. 211).

8   The Thembus were divided into two, under Paramount

Chief Sabata Dalindyebo and Kaiser Matanzima, later
appointed Paramount Chief by the Government.
Thirty of the charged were sentenced to death, of
whom nine lodged successful appeals (M. Horrell,
'Action, Reaction, and Counter-action', South
African Institute of Race Relations, Johannesburg,
1963).

9 According to figures abstracted from M. Horrell,
'Action, Reaction, and Counter-action', 192
Africans died in civil strife between 1950 and 1962.

1950 - Violence broke out in the Western areas of
Johannesburg when police escorted home those
who had not responded to the National stay-
away from work - called by the African,
Indian and Coloured Congresses. Police
opened fire on the demonstrators (18 dead
and 30 wounded; Horrell, op. cit., p. 21).

1952 - Coinciding with the call for defiance
(Defiance of Unjust Laws Campaign) by the
African, Indian and Coloured National Congresses, riots broke out in Port Elizabeth,
Kimberley, East London and Johannesburg
with the arrests of thousands of Black
passive resisters and their leaders (Port
Elizabeth: 9 Blacks and 4 Whites killed, 7
injured; Kimberley: 13 killed, 78
injured; East London: 8 Blacks and 2
Whites killed, many injured; Johannesburg:
3 killed, 4 injured; ibid., p. 23).

1957 - Friction developed between Zulu and Sotho
in the Men's Hostel at Dube in Johannesburg. Police moved in and opened fire
(40 dead, many injured; ibid., p. 35).

1960 - 3 Blacks and 9 police were killed and 6
injured in Cato Manor following the provocation of beer raids (ibid., p. 35).

1960 - In Sharpeville Africans who in a demonstration of passive resistance had assembled at
the police station to protest against
passes were shot by the police, in many
cases from the back while fleeing their
fire (83 Blacks and 3 police killed, 178
injured; ibid., p. 40).

1962 - The violence which erupted in the streets
of Paarl when Africans who had marched to
the police station to free their arrested
comrades were repelled by the police,
followed a long history of worker provocations by police and officials. The

repelled Africans set fire to two shops,
a post office and some petrol pumps and
broke into two private houses, killing two
Whites, an escaping woman and her helper.
5 Africans were killed (ibid., p. 60).

1962 - Matanzima. Police attacked tribesmen who
had collected, it was reported, with home-
made weapons on Ntlonze Hill in the
Transkei. A scuffle took place, the
police were repelled, but later 7 Africans
were arrested. The police on reports of
more militant tribesmen travelling to the
area, boarded a train. In the scuffle, a
White policeman and three Africans were
killed, and 9 Africans were admitted to
hospital. It was alleged that the tribesmen were members of Poqo and were plotting
to kill Chief Kaiser Matanzima.
Police arrested 155 Africans in other parts
of the Transkei on information that there
was a plot to murder local Whites - subsequently 5 Whites were found dead in the
same region (ibid., p. 62).

During the same period, about 30,000 Blacks were
imprisoned for political reasons.

1952	Defiance of Unjust Laws Campaign	
		8,000
1957	Women protesting against passes arrested in Zeerust	2,200
1958	Women protesting against passes arrested in Johannesburg	2,000
1960	Arrests under the Emergency Laws and Detention without Trial	11,279 Africans
		98 Whites
		90 Indians
		36 Coloureds

10 'The Durban Housing Survey', University of Natal
     Press, 1952, p. 19.
11 Leo Kuper, Hilstan Watts and Ronald Davies, 'Durban.
     A Study in Racial Ecology', Cape, London, 1958,
     pp. 44-6.
12 Ibid., p. 51.
13 Mayor's Minute 1970-1, Durban.
14 Since the implementation of the Group Areas Act
     they have been forced to the peripheries of the
     city. Indians still retain a downtown commercial
     area.
15 Kuper et al., op. cit., chapter III.
16 Ibid., p. 71.

17 A.D. Frenay, 'The Suicide Problem in the United
    States', Richard G. Badger, Boston, 1927, p. 44.
18 The annual mean rates for South Africa are calcu-
    lated from the report of the Bureau of Census and
    Statistics, G. 328.6804 U.5 ('Death. South Africa
    and South West Africa, 1958', vol. 2, 'Causes').
19 Ibid., pp. 24-5.
20 'United Nations Demographic Year Book 1957', Table
    17; 'World Health Statistics Report 21, No. 6,
    WHO, Geneva, 1968.
21 Ruth Shonle Cavan, 'Suicide', University of Chicago
    Press, 1923, p. 6.
22 He reports the decline accordingly: Austria by 50
    per cent, France and Italy by 40 per cent, Nether-
    lands by 36 per cent, England and Wales by 25 per
    cent (men only), Sweden by 18 per cent and Japan
    by 11 per cent (Louis J. Dublin and Bessie Bunzel,
    '"To be or Not to Be", A Study of Suicide', New
    York University Press, 1963, pp. 68-9).
23 Emile Durkheim, 'Suicide. A Study in Sociology',
    Routledge & Kegan Paul, London, 1952, p. 352.
24 Cavan, op. cit., pp. 273-5; Frenay, op. cit., p. 22.
25 Jack P. Gibbs, 'Suicide', in 'Contemporary Social
    Problems', ed. R.K. Merton and A.R. Nisbet, Harcourt,
    Brace & World, New York, 1961.
26 Dublin and Bunzel, op. cit., pp. 72-3.
27 Durkheim, op. cit., pp. 203-5.
28 Andrew F. Henry and James F. Short, 'Suicide and
    Homicide', Free Press, Chicago, 1954, p. 163.
29 'Metropolitan Life Assurance Company Statistical
    Bulletin May 1925', New York. The investigation
    showed a close correlation between business condi-
    tions and male suicides, but none between business
    conditions and female suicides.
30 See chapter 14.
31 In Durban, in one area alone, the African popula-
    tion rose from 500 to 17,000 ('The Durban Housing
    Survey', University of Natal Press, 1952, p. 344).

CHAPTER 5 THE RELATION BETWEEN SUICIDE, SOCIAL
INTEGRATION AND SOCIAL STATUS

1 Emile Durkheim, 'Suicide. A Study in Sociology',
   Routledge & Kegan Paul, London, 1952, p. 209.
2 R.K. Merton, 'Social Theory and Social Structure',
   Free Press, Chicago, 1951, Chapter II.
3 Andrew F. Henry and James F. Short, Jr, 'Suicide
   and Homicide', Free Press, Chicago, 1954, pp. 23-53.

Their extension of Durkheim's theory that suicide
is a function of social integration and the combination of this with Menninger's postulates of inner-
and outer-directed aggressions is discussed more
fully in chapter 11.

4   Ruth Shonle Cavan, 'Suicide', University of Chicago
    Press, 1923.
5   Jacqueline H. and Murray A. Strauss, Suicide, homi-
    cide and social structure in Ceylon, 'American
    Journal of Sociology', vol. 5, no. 5, 1953.
6   Jack P. Gibbs and Walter T. Martin, A theory of
    status integration and its relationship to suicide,
    'American Sociological Review', vol. 23, no. 2,
    1958.
7   Merton, op. cit., chapter ii.
8   Elwin M. Powell, Occupation, status and suicide:
    toward a redefinition of anomie, 'American Sociolo-
    gical Review', vol. 23, no. 2, 1958.   His hypo-
    thesis of suicide as a function of occupational
    status integrations is discussed more fully in
    chapter 10.
9   Durkheim, op. cit., pp. 252-4.
10 Ibid., p. 215.
11 Durkheim, op. cit., p. 102.
12 Henry and Short, op. cit., p. 70.
13 Ibid., p. 73.
14 Merton, op. cit.,
15 George C. Homans, 'The Human Group', Routledge &
    Kegan Paul, London, 1951.
16 Durkheim, op. cit.

CHAPTER 6   RACE, SEX AND SOCIAL INTEGRATION

1   Durkheim, 'Suicide. A Study in Sociology', Routledge
    & Kegan Paul, London, 1952;   Ruth Shonle Cavan,
    'Suicide', University of Chicago Press, 1923;   A.D.
    Frenay, 'The Suicide Problem in the United States',
    Richard G. Badger, Boston, 1927.
2   Jack P. Gibbs, Suicide, in 'Contemporary Social
    Problems', ed. R.K. Merton and A.R. Nisbet, Har-
    court, Brace & World, New York, 1961, p. 242.
3   'United Nations World Health Organization, Epidemio-
    logical and Vital Statistics Report', vol. 9, no. 4,
    1956, Table 2.   Also 'United Nations Demographic
    Year Book 1957', Table 17.
4   Frenay, op. cit., chapter IV reports the following
    rates per 100,000:   California - White, 28.2,
    Coloured, 36.9;   San Francisco - White, 43.1,

Coloured, 53.7;   Los Angeles - White, 29.8,
Coloured, 27.4.

5 Cavan, op. cit., p. 309.

6 Andrew F. Henry and James F. Short, Jr, 'Suicide
and Homicide', Free Press, Chicago, 1954, assert
that suicide is the reaction of a highly developed
superego, which strongly integrates social restraints.   The Indian personality tends to be
restrained and introverted.

7 M.K. Gandhi, 'Satyagraha in South Africa', Nava
Jivan Publishing House, 1928, Chapter 13.   The
case of the Buddhist monks who resorted to acts of
public burning to attract attention to their political grievances in Vietnam falls in this same
category.

8 'Death - South Africa and South West Africa, 1958',
vol. 2, 'Causes', G. 328-6804, U.5.

9 In the myth, the wicked Ravana abducts Sita.   Sus-
pecting violation of her chastity, she is set
alight.   The gods attest her purity and she
emerges unscathed from the flames.   However,
despite such supernatural defence, when gossip continues to challenge her virtue, Rama whom she has
faithfully followed in his fourteen years of
banishment, banishes her to the wilderness.   Her
end comes when she is finally absorbed by Mother
Earth - Jamuna Bhoomi, which cracks open and swallows
her.   Sita bears her calamities without a murmur
of protest.

10 The information on the recreational and integrative
factors in the life of African women near Durban
was provided by Dr M.V. Gumede, District Surgeon,
Magisterial Area of Maphumulo.

CHAPTER 7   RELIGION AND LANGUAGE AS INDICES OF SOCIAL
STATUS AMONG INDIANS AND THEIR RELATION TO THE SUICIDE
RATE

1 Leo Kuper, Ronald Watts and Hilstan Davies, 'Durban.
A Study in Racial Ecology', Cape, London, 1958.

CHAPTER 8   RESIDENTIAL AREAS, STATUS AND INTEGRATION

1 Emile Durkheim, 'Suicide. A Study in Sociology',
Routledge & Kegan Paul, London, 1952, p. 254.
Durkheim also attributed the low suicide rates in
Spain and France as due to poverty (p. 254).

Stengel, however, explains this as due to the effects of catholicism (Erwin Stengel, 'Suicide and Attempted Suicide', Penguin, Harmondsworth, 1971).

2   Andrew F. Henry and James F. Short, Jr, 'Suicide and Homicide', Free Press, Chicago, 1954, p. 60.

3   Ruth Shonle Cavan, 'Suicide', University of Chicago Press, 1923, pp. 73-105.

4   Leo Kuper, Hilstan Watts and Ronald Davies, 'Durban. A Study in Racial Ecology', Cape, London, 1958, p. 118.

CHAPTER 9   SUICIDE, AGE, STATUS AND INTEGRATION

1   Emile Durkheim, 'Suicide. A Study in Sociology', Routledge & Kegan Paul, London, 1952, p. 102.

2   Andrew F. Henry and James F. Short, Jr, 'Suicide and Homicide', Free Press, Chicago, 1954, p. 41.

3   Ruth Cavan, analysing the suicide rates of Massachusetts (1881-5) and Chicago (1919-21), found a rapidly increasing rate during adolescence, a gradual increase until middle age, a stationary rate during old age and an incline in extreme old age (Ruth Shonle Cavan, 'Suicide', University of Chicago Press, 1923, p. 310).   (Miner and Frenay found similar trends - Miner, Suicide and its relation to climate and other factors, 'American Journal of Hygiene', Monographic Series, no. 2, pp. 33-9; A.D. Frenay, 'The Suicide Problem in the United States', Richard G. Badger, Boston, 1927, pp. 78-9.)   Gibbs identifies increase with age, decline beyond a certain age, low rates between 30 and 50 years with high rates in the preceding and succeeding age categories (Jack P. Gibbs, 'Suicide', in 'Contemporary Social Problems', ed. R.K. Merton and A.R. Nisbet, Harcourt, Brace & World, New York, 1961, p. 241).

CHAPTER 10   OCCUPATION, STATUS AND INTEGRATION

1   Elwin M. Powell, Occupation, status and suicide: toward a redefinition of anomie, 'American Sociological Review', vol. 23, no. 2, 1958.

2   Ruth Shonle Cavan, 'Suicide', University of Chicago Press, 1923, p. 231.

3   Jack P. Gibbs and Walter I. Martin, A theory of status integration and its relationship to

suicide, 'American Sociological Review', vol. 23,
no. 2, 1958.

4 Durkheim, 'Suicide. A Study in Sociology', Routledge
& Kegan Paul, London, 1952.

5 Powell, op. cit.

6 Ibid.

7 Though Durkheim interprets anomie as a transitory
crisis situation, he clearly foresaw the advent of a
permanent state of anomie in modern industrial
society in terms of which Merton's theory is
developed (Durkheim, op. cit., p. 209).

8 Ibid., p. 249.

9 Powell, op. cit.

10 George H. Mead, 'Mind, Self and Society', University
of Chicago Press, 1934, pp. 133-226.

11 Durkheim, op. cit., p. 212.

12 Durkheim, op. cit., p. 257-8.

13 Louis J. Dublin, 'Statistical Bulletin Metropolitan
Life Insurance Company'

14 Andrew F. Henry and James F. Short, 'Suicide and
Homicide', Free Press, Chicago, 1954, p. 60.

15 Austin L. Porterfield and Jack P. Gibbs, Occupational
prestige and social mobility of suicides in New
Zealand, 'American Sociological Review', vol. 25,
no. 2, 1960.

16 R.K. Merton, 'Social Theory and Social Structure',
Free Press, Chicago, 1951.

17 Doric M. Jean, 'The development of mortality by
suicide in France', 'Population', Oct./Dec., 1956.

18 (a) Gibbs states that official statistics on
suicide by occupation are reported in only a few
countries and the occupations considered are seldom
strictly comparative. Consequently, observation
on the subject is sketchy and uncertain (Jack P.
Gibbs, Suicide, 'Contemporary Social Problems', ed.
R.K. Merton and A.R. Nisbet, Harcourt, Brace &
World, New York, 1961.
(b) Powell found data on death certificates scanty
and often inaccurate. He used newspaper reports
as checks and corrected discrepancies between the
two through police files and city directory. He
maintained that he obtained reasonably correct
estimates of occupations for all but 6 per cent of
his cases between 1937 and 1956 (Powell, op. cit.,
p. 131).
(c) Henry and Short, op. cit., p. 39, estimated
incomes of suicides in Chicago through residential
areas.

19 The occupational breakdown used by the Census

Department is 'industrially' motivated and this has little relevance to social status. This, together with the fact that the occupational categories used by the Department do not remain constant, have posed several difficulties in constructing a sociologically meaningful classification of occupations. Since a detailed breakdown by occupation was available by race and sex for 1946 alone, these figures were used to construct a sociologically meaningful occupational scale. A comparison between the 1946 and 1951 census figures indicated no significant change in the proportionate distribution of occupations by race and sex.

20 This is an extension of the Powell postulate that occupation constitutes the main index of status integration for American men (Powell, op. cit.).

21 It is interesting to note that 'freedom to work' is often specified as a fundamental right in human rights declarations. This is an acknowledgment of the vital importance of occupation in social life. Unemployment, in terms of both Merton and Durkheim, exposes the individual to a state of anomie. Durkheim contends that the class regimen based on division of labour is valid only if considered just by those involved in it; when it is forced on a group, it leads to social upheavals, i.e. disintegration and thus anomie (Durkheim, op. cit., p. 250).

22 Powell, op. cit., p. 131.

23 Official statistics of Indian unemployment, estimated at 3,587 by the Department of Labour in 1961, were seriously challenged by Margo Russell and I.K. Allan, who found it to be 15,000 ('Unemployment Among Indians in Durban, 1962', Institute for Social Research, University of Natal, 1962).

24 Gibbs and Martin, op. cit.

25 Henry and Short, op. cit.

26 George C. Homans, 'The Human Group', Routledge & Kegan Paul, London, 1951, p. 149.

27 Durkheim, op. cit., p. 167.

28 This is the term used by Elwin Powell.

29 Egoism and 'anomie' as used by Durkheim.

30 Durkheim, op. cit., p. 258

31 Ibid., pp. 378-9.

CHAPTER 11   MARITAL STATUS, FAMILY AND SUICIDE

1   Bertillon, Marriage, in 'Dictionnaire encyclo-
     pédique des sciences médicales', 2nd series,
     cited by Emile Durkheim, 'Suicide. A Study in
     Sociology', Routledge & Kegan Paul, London, 1952.
2   Henrico A. Morselli, 'Suicide. An Essay on Com-
     parative Moral Statistics', in 'International
     Scientific Series', vol. XXXVI, New York, 1822.
3   J. Bertillon, Jr, and M. Lebourmeau, cited by
     Durkheim, op. cit., p. 181.
4   Durkheim, op. cit., p. 179
5   Ibid., p. 201.
6   Ibid., p. 179.
7   Ibid., p. 262
8   Ibid., p. 172.
9   Ibid., p. 202.
10 Morselli, op. cit., pp. 231-320, using data for the
     1860s and 1870s for some European countries, main-
     tained that the suicide rate of the widowed was
     higher than that of the single and that of the
     divorced highest of all.   Ruth Shonle Cavan
     ('Suicide', University of Chicago Press, 1923,
     p. 319) gives the following distribution of suicide
     per 100,000: single 21.5; married 77.5; divorced
     146.5; unknown 15.3.   Andrew F. Henry and James
     F. Short, Jr, ('Suicide and Homicide', Free Press,
     Chicago, 1954, p. 116) and Jack P. Gibbs (Suicide,
     in 'Contemporary Social Problems', ed. R.K. Merton
     and A.R. Nisbet, Harcourt, Brace & World, New York,
     1961, p. 1, 246) also confirm the high suicide rates
     of the widowed and divorced.   A.D. Frenay ('The
     Suicide Problem in the United States', Richard G.
     Badger, Boston, 1927, p. 84), analysing American
     data for 1911-23, states: 'The widowed commit
     suicide more frequently than do the married or un-
     married.'   He observes the same pattern in Italy.
11 Durkheim, op. cit., p. 180.
12 Ibid., p. 191, refuting Morselli, contends that
     men suffer more when deprived of marriage since
     their loss is twofold, in terms of both conjugal
     and domestic association; and their disturbance is
     due to their difficulty in adjustment to the new
     situation.   He supports this contention by the
     observations that women commit three to four times
     less suicide in the divorced and widowed states
     than men; that women are reluctant to remarry,
     whereas men are eager; that wives without children
     commit suicide more often than single women and

widows with children; and that the existence of
divorce has a beneficial effect on women. With
reference to the last, he states: 'the more easily
the conjugal bond is broken, the more the wife is
favoured in comparison to the husband.' He found
that 60 per cent of divorce and 80 per cent of
separation proceedings were instituted by women in
France in the 1820s.

13 This is also confirmed by Bertillon, op. cit.;
Morselli, op. cit.; Henry and Short, op. cit.;
Frenay, op. cit.; Gibbs in Merton and Nisbet, op.
cit.

14 Durkheim, op. cit., p. 188.

15 Gibbs in Merton and Nisbet, op. cit., p. 246.

16 Postulate (b) is confirmed by Cavan, op. cit., p.
320; Henry and Short, op. cit., p. 116; Gibbs in
Merton and Nisbet, op. cit., p. 246; Frenay, op.
cit., p. 84.
Postulate (c) is confirmed by Bertillon, op. cit.;
Morselli, op. cit.; Henry and Short, op. cit.;
Frenay, op. cit.; and Gibbs in Merton and Nisbet,
op. cit.

17 Cavan, Frenay and Gibbs all confirm this, the latter
showing that the American figures for 1949-50 reflect a high rate for widows and lower rate for
divorced in the 20-24 age group.

18 Durkheim, op. cit., pp. 185-9, 271-3.

19 Ibid., pp. 270-1.

20 Ibid., p. 178. Durkheim contends that this is in
keeping with the generally higher mortality rate of
young married persons, especially men. He observed
the mortality rate of young married men to be 473
per cent higher than that of unmarried men in the
same age category.

21 Ibid., p. 179. These are observations made in the
latter part of the nineteenth century.

22 Ibid., pp. 178-9.

23 Henry and Short, op. cit., p. 70.

24 Gibbs, op. cit.

25 Durkheim, op. cit., p. 201.

26 Ibid., p. 202.

27 Ibid.

28 Parental status here means whether the married
suicides have children and, if so, how many.

29 Hilda Kuper investigating Indian families in Merebank and Springfield areas in 1953 found that 43
per cent of the families were joint and extended
and 50 per cent were nuclear (H. Kuper, 'The
Indian People of Natal', Natal University Press,

1960). V. Sirkari Naidoo in a survey of 1,000 households in the Municipal Barracks (Additional Report no. 2, Natal Regional Survey, University of Natal Press, 1960) found 38 per cent of the families to be joint. In a sample survey of 524 families living outside the Barracks, 22 per cent were joint. Whereas, according to Naidoo's estimate, suicide among Indians appears to be higher in the joint family than would be expected from their presence in the total population, according to Kuper it is proportionate to the distribution of the joint family in the total Indian population. Both estimates indicate one point at least: the joint family does not inhibit suicide as Durkheim's postulate suggests. A more recent study by P.N. Pillay and P.A. Ellison (Additional Report No. 6, Natal Regional Survey, University of Natal Press, 1960) found 25 per cent of the 835 sample households to be multiple. A sample survey of 1,788 households made between 1943 and 1944 in Durban indicated an average of 3.9 persons per household for Whites, 3.2 for Africans and 4.7 for Coloureds. These figures tend to confirm the predominance of nuclear families in these groups.

30 Estimated from the figures given by Kuper, op. cit., p. 106.
31 'The Durban Housing Survey', University of Natal Press, 1952, p. 85.
32 Kuper, op. cit., p. 107.
33 Durkheim, op. cit., p. 221.

CHAPTER 12 TEMPORAL FACTORS

1 Henrico A. Morselli, Suicide, in 'International Scientific Series', vol. XXXVI, New York, 1882.
2 John Rice Miner, Suicide and its relation to climatic and other factors, 'American Journal of Hygiene', no. 2, 1922.
3 Andrew F. Henry and James F. Short, 'Suicide and Homicide', Free Press, Chicago, 1954, p. 23.
4 He studied the situations in Paris, the French Departments and Prussian Provinces.
5 Emile Durkheim, 'Suicide. A Study in Sociology' Routledge & Kegan Paul, London, 1952, p. 117.
6 Romilly Fedden, 'Suicide. A Social and Historical Study', Peter Davies, London, 1938, pp. 337-8.
7 Durkheim, op. cit., p. 118.
8 Fedden, op. cit., p. 338.

9 Sunday sports meetings have been known to break out
   in violence because of the enthusiasm of Black
   audiences. Hungry for identification on a mass
   level, they become emotionally involved with the
   contending teams, and when confronted with the loss
   of the favoured one, let loose frustrations on the
   sports ground. When visiting teams of international repute appear against White South African
   teams, they become quickly identified with the
   visitors, using them as a lever for venting their
   racial antagonisms against local Whites. The
   anticipation of rowdyism at football matches is
   graphically confirmed in an article appearing in
   the Daily News (1 November 1963, reproduced from
   the Zulu in the Ilangalase Natal) – heading:
   'Perils of an African referee'; sub-heading:
   'Soccer will suffer if these assaults continue'.
   The article describes African referees as 'the most
   fleet-footed courageous South Africans', since they
   are continuously exposed to assault and are without
   police protection. The assault, the article states,
   is due partly to a tsotsi (socially delinquent)
   element and partly to 'the exuberance and colour
   which consciously and unconsciously are added to
   Black soccer by such team names as "The Young
   Rebels", "Braves United", and such sobriquets as
   "Hanger the Great", "Tereza Mau Mau", "Dr Lumumba",
   "Two to One"'. The article goes on to describe
   two matches which within two weeks had to be
   called off, because, after clashes between individual members of opposing teams, spectators entered
   the arena, 'fists flew, sjamboks cracked, knives
   were drawn'.

10 Of the total number of African suicides 44.1 per
   cent were committed by shack-dwellers and 11.6 per
   cent by men in barracks.

11 The largest percentages of suicides by African and
   Coloured women in the total number of cases were
   those of women described as 'living with men', 37
   per cent and 32.1 per cent respectively.

12 *Kipita* refers to the loose union between the sexes
   which has neither legal nor traditional sanction.

13 The only exception found was that of Fedden's
   reference to inconclusive Prussian statistics for
   1869 which showed a correspondence between the
   position of the moon and the incidence of suicide
   especially in the case of young men. Suicide was
   commoner in the first and last quarter of the moon
   (Fedden, op. cit., p. 337).

CHAPTER 13   METHODS ADOPTED IN COMMITTING SUICIDE

1   Emile Durkheim, 'Suicide. A Study in Sociology',
    Routledge & Kegan Paul, London, 1952, pp. 292-3.
2   Romilly Fedden, 'Suicide. A Social and Historical
    Study', Peter Davies, London, 1938, p. 345.
3   A.D. Frenay, 'The Suicide Problem in the United
    States', Richard G. Badger, Boston, 1927.
4   Paul Bohannan, 'African Homicide and Suicide', Prince-
    ton University Press, 1960.
5   Fedden, op. cit., p. 345.
6   Frenay, op. cit., p. 67.
7   Bohannan, op. cit.
8   Frenay, op. cit., p. 65.
9   The Inquest Court files have many deaths of African
    men particularly due to 'train accidents'. The
    evidence recorded is usually that of the engine
    driver and it is well-nigh impossible to know
    whether these are in fact accidents.
10 Bohannan, op. cit., p. 263.
11 Ibid.
12 The main Hindu sacrifice, or divine offering, usually
    of grains, fruits, sandalwood and clarified butter -
    ghee - made by Hindus through burning. It marks
    the central ritual of practically all important
    events in Hindu life - marriage, death, house-
    moving, etc.
13 Rabindranath Tagore expresses this sentiment in a
    short story written at the beginning of the century,
    on the suicide of a young wife who kills herself in
    remorse for her intended infidelity to her husband,
    and the realization that his death was occasioned
    by his discovery of this infidelity, in the state-
    ment: 'All were lost in admiration of the wifely
    loyalty she had shown in her sati, a loyalty rare
    indeed in these degenerate days' ('Great Stories
    by Nobel Prize Winners', ed. L. Hanalian and
    E. Volpe, Noonday Press Library, USA, 1970).

CHAPTER 14   THE PROBABLE FACTORS PRECIPITATING SUICIDE

1   Karl A. Menninger, 'Man Against Himself', Harcourt,
    Brace & World, New York, 1963, p. 5.
2   Paul Bohannan, 'African Homicide and Suicide',
    Princeton University Press, 1960, p. 26.

CHAPTER 15 THE PSYCHOLOGICAL AND EMOTIONAL STATES OF SUICIDE

1 Ruth Cavan, analysing 291 suicides in Chicago, estimated that 15 per cent of the male and 12.5 per cent of the female suicides were probably insane (Ruth Shonle Cavan, 'Suicide', University of Chicago Press, 1923, pp. 112–13).

CHAPTER 16 STRESS IN THE MARITAL AND FAMILY SITUATION

1 'Things are in my hand' is the idiom used by Hindustanis to denote 'I am in control'.
2 See table 18, p. 244.
3 Between 1963 and 1972 over 20 people detained under one law alone, the South African Security law, have died during detention. At least 50 people thus detained submitted sworn affidavits that they had been tortured under detention ('Pro veritate', 15 December 1972. P.O. Box 31135, Braamfontein).
4 Illegitimate African births in Durban: 1959, 64.86 per cent, 1960, 62.49 per cent of total births.
5 Literal translation, 'one who shows an ear', the implication probably being that they are eavesdropping outsiders.
6 The spirit of the worshipped deity is believed to possess selected worshippers and speak through them.
7 The factor of revenge is present in Durkheim's anomic suicide where the suicidal act is motivated by a desire to seek the group's rejection of the aggressor (M.D.W. Jeffreys, Samsonic suicide or suicide of revenge among Africans, 'Africana Studies', vol. XI, no. 3, 1952, pp. 118–22) defines Samsonic suicide as suicide in which the individual, unable to seek revenge in life, hopes to do so through supernatural powers in death.
8 These resemble Karl A. Menninger's account of the young boy who hanged himself in the barn a few hours after a scolding by his father for some minor dereliction ('Man Against Himself', Harcourt, Brace & World, New York, 1963, p. 3).

CHAPTER 18   SELECTED CASES IN GREATER DEPTH

1 Relationship without formal marriage.
2 Several cases have been brought before South African courts in recent years where employers have shot the visiting lovers of their domestics on sight, for trespassing.
3 South Africanism for vagina.
4 This case was reported in the 'Sunday Express', 20 July 1972.

CHAPTER 19   CASE STUDIES

1 Married Hindu women mark their brows with kunkun.
2 A gold disc given by the husband to the wife to signify that she is married.

CHAPTER 20   SUICIDE NOTES

1 Jerry Jacobs, A phenomenological study of suicide notes, 'Social Problems', vol. 15, no. 1, Summer 1967; Jacob Tuckman, Robert J. Kleiner and Martin Lovall, Emotional content of suicide notes, 'American Journal of Psychiatry', July 1959, p. 59.
2 Karl A. Menninger, 'Man Against Himself', Harcourt, Brace & World, New York, 1963, pp. 24-33.
3 Emile Durkheim, 'Suicide. A Study in Sociology', Routledge & Kegan Paul, London, 1952, pp. 284-7.
4 Menninger, op. cit., p. 29.
5 Durkheim, op. cit., pp. 284-5.
6 Menninger, op. cit., pp. 63-71.
7 Durkheim, op. cit., pp. 278-85.
8 Ibid., pp. 278-85.
9 Ibid., p. 283.
10 Menninger, op. cit., p. 80.
11 Jacobs, op. cit.
12 In the terminology of Jack Douglas.

CONCLUSION

1 Emile Durkheim, 'Suicide. A Study in Sociology', Routledge & Kegan Paul, London, 1952.
2 Ibid.

Index

Routledge Social Science Series

Routledge & Kegan Paul   London and Boston

68–74 Carter Lane   London EC4V 5EL

9 Park Street   Boston   Mass 02108

Contents

*Authors wishing to submit manuscripts for any series in
this catalogue should send them to the Social Science Editor,
Routledge & Kegan Paul Ltd, 68–74 Carter Lane,
London EC4V 5EL*

●*Books so marked are available in paperback
All books are in Metric Demy 8vo format (216 × 138mm approx.)*

For Product Safety Concerns and Information please contact our EU
representative GPSR@taylorandfrancis.com
Taylor & Francis Verlag GmbH, Kaufingerstraße 24, 80331 München, Germany